Commercialising Secur

C000118028

This book examines the political consequences of European security commercialisation through increased reliance on private military and security companies (PMSCs).

The role of commercial security in the domestic setting in Europe is widely acknowledged; after all, the biggest private security company globally – G4S Group – has its roots in Scandinavia. However, the use of commercial security contracting by European states for military purposes in international settings is mostly held to be marginal.

This book examines the implications of commercialisation for the peace and reconciliation strategies of European states, focusing specifically on European contracting in Afghanistan. Drawing upon examples from Scandinavia, Central Europe and Continental Europe, each chapter considers three key factors:

- the national contexts that give security contracting in Afghanistan its meaning;
- the national contracting practices;
- the political consequences for the operation in Afghanistan.

This book will be of much interest to students of critical security studies, global governance, peace and conflict studies, European politics and IR in general.

Anna Leander is Professor of International Political Sociology at the Department of Management, Politics and Philosophy of the Copenhagen Business School. Her research focuses on the development of sociological approaches in international relations and on the commercialisation of military practices.

PRIO New Security Studies

Series Editor: J. Peter Burgess, PRIO, Oslo

The aim of this book series is to gather state-of-the-art theoretical reflexion and empirical research into a core set of volumes that respond vigorously and dynamically to the new challenges to security scholarship.

Commercialising Security in Europe

Political consequences for peace operations

Edited by Anna Leander

LONDON AND NEW YORK

First published 2013
by Routledge
2 Park Square, Milton Park, Abingdon, Oxon, OX14 4RN

Simultaneously published in the USA and Canada
by Routledge
711 Third Avenue, New York, NY 10017

Routledge is an imprint of the Taylor & Francis Group, an informa business

British Library Cataloguing in Publication Data
A catalogue record for this book is available from the British Library

Library of Congress Cataloging-in-Publication Data
Commercialising security in Europe : political consequences for peace
operations / edited by Anna Leander.
p. cm.
Includes bibliographical references and index.
1. Private military companies--Political aspects--Europe. 2. Private security
services--Political aspects--Europe. 3. Contracting out--Political aspects--
Europe. 4. Peacekeeping forces--Europe. 5. Combined operations (Military
science)--Europe. 6. Europe--Military policy. 7. National security--Europe.
I. Leander, Anna.
UB149.C66 2013
355.3'5--dc23
2012034231

ISBN: 978-0-415-50988-6 (hbk)
ISBN: 978-0-415-50989-3 (pbk)
ISBN: 978-0-203-37534-1 (ebk)

Typeset in Baskerville
by Taylor & Francis Books

Printed and bound in Great Britain by MPG Printgroup

Contents

Figures and tables

Figure

Tables

Contributors

Joakim Berndtsson is an associate senior lecturer and researcher at the School of Global Studies, University of Gothenburg. His research examines the role and remit of private security actors in stable societies and armed conflicts. Recent work on security privatisation and the case of Sweden has been published in the *Millennium Journal of International Studies* and *International Political Sociology* (with Maria Stern). For more information, www.globalstudies.gu.se/kontakt/personal/berndtsson_j/ (accessed on 24 September 2012).

Beata Górka-Winter is a research fellow at the Polish Institute of International Affairs where she coordinates the programme in international security. Her research concentrates on different aspects of Polish security policy, including NATO, Common Security and Defence Policy of the European Union, missile defence, and Security Sector Reform. Her latest publications include *Afghanistan in Transition: Crafting a Strategy for Enduring Stability* (edited with Wiśniewski); 'From Followers to Leaders as "Coalition Servants": The Polish Engagement in Afghanistan' in Hynek and Morton (ed.), *Statebuilding in Afghanistan*; and 'Poland's participation in the ISAF: mission (not yet) accomplished', in *Yearbook of Polish Foreign Policy*.

Elke Krahmann is Professor of Security Studies at Brunel University, London. She has published widely on non-state actors in foreign and security policy making, including the proliferation of private military and security companies and the political, normative and practical implications of the commodification of security. Her latest publications include 'From "Mercenaries" to "Private Security Contractors": The (Re)Construction of Armed Security Providers in International Legal Discourses' (*Millennium*, 2012) and 'Beck and Beyond: Selling Security in the World Risk Society' (*Review of International Studies*, 2011). Her monograph *States, Citizens and the Privatization of Security* was published by Cambridge University Press in 2010.

Anna Leander is Professor MSO at the Department of Management, Politics and Philosophy of the Copenhagen Business School. Her research focuses on the development of sociological approaches in international relations and on the commercialisation of military practices. She has recently published 'The

Promises, Problems and Potentials of a Bourdieu Inspired Approach to International Relations' (*International Political Sociology*, 2011) and 'What Do Codes of Conduct Do? Hybrid Constitutionalization and Militarization in Military Markets' (*Global Constitutionalism*, 2012). She is associate editor of *Security Dialogue* and *International Political Sociology*. For more information and a list of publications see www.cbs.dk/staff/ale.

Marek Madej, PhD, born 1978, is Assistant Professor at the Institute of International Relations, University of Warsaw. In the years 2006–2010 he was a research fellow at the Polish Institute of International Affairs, programme on International Security. His research focuses on contemporary transatlantic relations, Polish security policy and non-traditional threats to state security. Author of two monographs and numerous articles published in Polish scientific journals and books (in Polish). Co-editor (with Beata Górka-Winter) of the report: NATO Members States and the New Strategic Concept: An Overview (*PISM*, Warsaw, 2010). For more information and the list of publication see: www.en.ism.uw.edu.pl (accessed 24 September 2012).

Thomas Mandrup holds a PhD in international relations, University of Copenhagen, an MSc in public administration and history, Roskilde University and an MA in area studies Africa, University of Copenhagen. He is currently an assistant professor at the Institute of Strategy, Royal Danish Defence College. From 2001–2006 he was a PhD candidate at the Institute of Political Science, University of Copenhagen and the Danish Institute of International Studies. Security governance in Africa is his primary area of research and he has published articles and book chapters on the securitisation process in South African foreign policy, sovereignty and the post-colonial state and privatisation of security in Africa.

Christian Olsson is associate professor in international relations at the *Université Libre de Bruxelles* (ULB) in Belgium. He received his PhD in political sciences from *Sciences Po Paris*. He is associate editor of the journal *Cultures & Conflicts* (http://conflits.revues.org/, accessed 26 September 2012). His research concerns amongst others the use of military force in the context of overseas military operations (Afghanistan and Iraq), political violence and security practices and international political sociology. Publications include: (with Bigo D. *et al.*) 'Security Practices' in R. Denemark (ed.) *International Studies Encyclopedia*. Blackwell Publishing, 2010. For more information and electronic versions of publications, see: http://repi.ulb.ac.be/fr/membres_olsson-christian.html (accessed 26 September 2012).

Liliana Pop is an independent researcher and writer based in London. She has a doctorate in politics from the University of Warwick and held academic posts at universities in Romania and the UK. She is the author of *Democratising capitalism? The political economy of post-communist transformations in Romania, 1989–2001* (Manchester University Press, 2006) and has published articles in peer-reviewed journals such as *Review of International Studies, Perspectives on European*

Politics and Societies, and *Economy and Society*. Liliana is currently working on a book exploring conceptions of honour and honourable behaviour in international politics.

Stefano Ruzza is Adjunct Professor of Strategic Studies at the University of Turin and Head of Research of the Torino World Affairs Institute (T.wai). His research interests focus on conflict transformation and on private military/security companies. He has recently published 'Guerre conto terzi: Aziende di sicurezza e privatizzazione della funzione militare' ('Fighting others' war: Security firms and military privatization' – *Il Mulino* 2011) and lectures regularly in advanced programmes of the Italian Army. Formerly a visiting scholar at Cornell, he is a member of the Italian Political Science Association (SISP) and of the editorial board of *WARning: Biannual Journal of International Studies*.

Christopher Spearin is Associate Professor in the Department of Defence Studies of the Royal Military College of Canada, located at the Canadian Forces College in Toronto, Ontario. His research concerns change in militaries, global security governance, non-state actors and conflict, mercenaries, the privatisation of security, piracy, and Canadian foreign and defence policy. For information on Dr Spearin's publications please see www.cfc.forces.gc.ca/136/297-eng.html (accessed 2 October 2012).

Maria Stern is Professor of Peace and Development Research at the School of Global Studies, University of Gothenburg. She is the guest co-editor of the Security-Development Nexus Revisited, *Security Dialogue* (2010), co-editor of *Feminist Methodologies for International Relations* (Cambridge University Press, 2006), the author of *Naming Security – Constructing Identity* (Manchester University Press, 2005) and numerous journal articles.

Marcin Terlikowski is an analyst at the Polish Institute of International Affairs. His area of research: European Union Common Security and Defence Policy (CSDP), European defence industry and defence equipment market, and privatisation of security. He is the author of various policy reports and academic papers on EU crisis management operations, European collaboration on defence capabilities, the use of private entities by contemporary militaries, and the Polish security policy. Since 2007 PhD student in Warsaw School of Economics, researching economic policy towards the European defence industry.

Krisztian Varga is an invited lecturer at the Institute of Political Sciences of the ELTE University Faculty of Law, Budapest. He is going to receive his doctoral degree (PhD) in 2013 at ELTE University. His research focuses on the consequences of military outsourcing to war and diplomacy. He is a member of editorial board of *Nation and Security – Security Policy Review* (a monthly peer-review journal in Hungarian).

Åse Gilje Østensen is a PhD candidate at the Department of Comparative Politics, University of Bergen. Her dissertation focuses on commercial military and security companies and ways that these companies influence policy making and policy execution in different contexts. She has published works on the United Nations' use of private military and security companies, as well as an article on the legitimisation of the industry. For details on the publications, see www.uib.no/personer/Ase.Ostensen#publikasjoner (accessed 21 September 2012).

Acknowledgements

This book is a collective work. Most of the contributors volunteered not only their expertise for its production. They made sure the book evolved through the two workshops held in the process of producing it and they had the patience to carry it through. The original framework and ambition as well as the conclusions have changed substantially as a consequence. I wish to thank them for their enthusiasm, engagement and endurance. All of this would not have been possible without the support of the Norwegian Ministry of Foreign Affairs and the Peace Research Institute in Oslo. For us two people have come to incarnate this support: Peter Burgess and Mareile Kaufmann. They have been indispensable for this project. Amongst other things, they helped us find John Carville who has had the unenviable task of trying to make our language readable. He did more than we could possibly have paid him for. Finally, I want to thank my two homes in Denmark: my department (Management, Politics and Philosophy) at CBS and my family on Gammel Kongevej for their patience with and support for my idiosyncratic work habits.

1 Introduction

Anna Leander

The UK and the US are well known to be commercialising security in their international military operations. Europe is not. The role of commercial security in the domestic setting in Europe is widely acknowledged. After all the biggest private security company globally – G4S Group – has its roots in Scandinavia. However, the use of commercial security contracting by European states for *military* purposes in *international* settings – such as Afghanistan, which this volume draws on for examples – is mostly held to be marginal. This is not surprising considering that most European states have regulations underscoring that they remain attached to strict state control over the use of force *internationally* and that when prompted, European ministers of foreign affairs, of defence, chiefs of staff and experts routinely respond that they do not rely on *military* contractors. However, in international operations the line between the military and the security contractor is most often blurred. Security/military contractors in international settings are therefore increasingly (including in this book) referred to as Private Military and Security Companies (PMSCs). By insisting that they do no *military* contracting while keeping silent about their *security* contracting, European public officials create an impression that the controversies surrounding PMSC contracting by the US and the UK are of little relevance to them. To the extent the PMSC contracting is discussed in Europe, it is therefore as a potential, future development. As its title indicates, this volume challenges this view.

European security commercialisation for military operations has gone further than assumed outside specialist circles. The resulting gap between perceptions (that security commercialisation is insignificant in military operations) and practices (of growing reliance on PMSCs) has made Europeans singularly ill-equipped to deal the resulting political and regulatory challenges. By misrecognising that they rely on PMSCs, Europeans miss an opportunity to ensure the accountability of contractors and those contracting them and more generally they evade their responsibilities for regulation (national and international). The ambition in this volume is to diminish misrecognition by insisting on the extent to which Europeans have commercialised security in relation to their military operations; that is by taking stock of what is *already* going on. The book does so by focusing on European contracting in Afghanistan and its political implications. The countries we look at are three Scandinavian, three Central European and three Continental European states. The chapters follow a common logic: they focus on the national contexts that give security contracting in Afghanistan its meaning, they look at national contracting practices and they discuss the political consequences for the operation in Afghanistan. The reminder of this introduction will justify and explain this focus and the logic of the chapters to follow.

Situating of the book

The steep increase in the reliance on PMSCs since the end of the Cold War has generated a multifaceted discussion about how and why this change has taken place as well as about what its consequences are. While the debate was initially driven largely by the practical, immediate and therefore technical/specific concerns that emerged as commercial actors began to figure centrally in military affairs, it is by now extensively covered in public debate and in the relevant academic disciplines, including economics, law, sociology, philosophy, political science and international relations/international political economy. The result is a cacophony of ideas and arguments (see Krahmann 2010a, Leander 2009b, Leander 2010a). This section sketches out how this book contributes to that cacophony. It does so by shedding light on the *political* consequences of commercialising security for the *international military operations* undertaken by *European* countries.

A book about the political consequences of commercialising security

Questions about politics are not the only ones posed when the consequences of the growing reliance on PMSCs is discussed. On the contrary, the rapidly expanding body of academic and para-academic research on security commercialisation through reliance on PMSCs has reserved a rather minor place for questions about politics. Possibly, because the research agenda has been driven by the practical concerns of armed forces, companies and their employees, governments and human rights lawyers, the discussion has revolved around the economic and regulatory issues of most immediate concern.

The centrality of *economic efficiency* in the debate about the consequences of increasing reliance on PMSCs is hardly surprising considering that promises of cost saving and efficiency were motivating and justifying commercialisation (Kaldor 1998, Markusen 2003). In the critical debate the urge to show that PMSCs are not cost effective but rather a source of squandering, corruption and waste is correspondingly omnipresent. In the formulation of two US government fraud experts it leads to the 'betrayal of our troops' (Rasor and Bauman 2007) and ultimately to the 'destruction' of the public good (Dickinson 2011). Inversely, the defenders of the growing reliance on PMSCs have a penchant for reiterating that quite to the contrary, the market is efficient, while public institutions are inefficient and wasteful (BENS 2001, Gansler 2010). This 'managerial' focus on cost-effectiveness makes the question of how to ensure a more effective administration and management of contractors the key issue in the debate about the consequences of commercialisation. 'Consequences' are in other words discussed mainly to gain insights about how to alter (or not) the management at some level and by some actors in ways that ensure economic efficiency. This leads straight to the second issue that has played a central role in the discussion: the issue of regulation.

Any suggestion for improving the administration and management of contracting practices involving PMSCs has regulatory implications, as does the commercialisation process itself. Therefore *regulatory issues* occupy a close second (if not shared first) place on the agenda regarding the consequences of security commercialisation. They are raised primarily to highlight questions of accountability and responsibility (e.g. Dickinson 2005, Leander 2010b). The concern in this debate is over whether or not there are regulatory systems capable of ensuring that contractors, the companies employing them and those who rely on their services (including states as well as individuals, companies and non-state organisations such as NGOs) can be asked to respect pertinent rules and can be taken to task if they do not. The regulatory discussion has been most visible when PMSCs have been involved in gross human rights violations (as TITAN and CACI were in Abu Ghraib or Blackwater was in the Nisour Square incident,[1] but it spans the full spectrum of regulatory issues emerging in relation to the growing reliance of PMSCs. This spectrum is fractured by the contradictory, overlapping and conflicting administrative, military, criminal, civic, commercial and international regulatory systems that have a bearing on contracting practices, not to mention the rapid development of soft forms of regulations including codes of conduct, various standards and best practice schemes (Teubner 2002, Leander 2009a, Leander 2012). The resulting regulatory complexity will no doubt continue to be a fertile ground for the politicians, lawyers and academics engaged in the 'mad scramble' to bring contractors to justice (Kierpaul 2008). However, from whatever perspective 'regulation' is approached, it produces a discussion of 'consequences' with distinctly legal overtones; consequences are about what (if any) legal innovations and reforms are necessary for regulation to be effective.

Even if economic and regulatory issues have dominated the discussion about the consequences of the increased PMSCs presence, a third issue keeps appearing in the debate and has increasingly come to occupy a space of its own: *politics*. It has sneaked in as a necessary real-world anchor in the other discussions. Participants in the debates about efficiency and regulation are acutely aware that proposing changes without reference to the political context is as useful as prescribing medicine that is either unaffordable or unavailable. Legal and economic arguments are therefore frequently couched in explicitly (and surprisingly strong) political terms (e.g. Minow 2003, Tiefer 2007, Martin 2007). In addition to this, politics has also become a focus in its own right. Scholars have placed it at the centre of their investigations, implicitly or explicitly treating politics as logically prior to managerial and regulatory issues. Peter Singer's (2003) discussion of the consequences of privatisation in five key areas has since been followed by numerous studies going into depth while looking at the consequence of privatisation for some specific area of politics such as sovereignty (Verkuil 2007, Leander 2009c), the state monopoly on the legitimate use of force (Leander 2006b), state control over the use of force (Avant 2005, Berndtsson 2009), democratic institutions (Krahmann 2010b) or the global governance of security (Abrahamsen and Williams 2010). This book builds on this growing body of literature focusing on political consequences. Its ambition is to deepen understanding of one specific political consequence of commercialisation: the consequence for the politics of international military operations (IMO).

A book about the politics of international military operations

This book is not the first to ask questions about the political implications of commercialisation through the increasing presence of PMSCs for international military operations (IMO) in the context of multilateral operations such as that in Afghanistan, which is the focus of this volume. The recurring proposals to solve the difficulties of finding adequate troops for multilateral missions by relying on market actors (Brooks 2000, Ghebali 2006) have generated considerable debate focused also on the political consequences of the growing reliance on PMSCs for IMO. The distinct contribution of this book is that it brings together three aspects of politics that are usually dealt with in separation when the consequences of PMSCs for the politics of IMO are discussed: the politics of formulating strategies for IMO, the politics of implementing IMO and the politics surrounding the imprint left by IMO. This move we would argue is not only desirable because it gives a more 'complete' or 'complex' picture of the political consequences for IMO, it is necessary because the politics at the three levels is intertwined as professional networks of practice span across the three levels. Hence, bringing them together is the prerequisite of a realistic account.

The idea that commercialisation through the increased presence of PMSCs has strong implications for the politics surrounding *the formulation* of IMO strategies has received considerable attention. One line of inquiry has been to look at the extent to which the reliance on PMSCs reshuffles policy priorities as companies engage in lobbying, agenda setting from within or reframe security understandings by their presence in the field (e.g. Leander 2005b). This in turn brings forth questions regarding the implications for the political democratic and social processes underlying foreign policy strategies (Krahmann 2010b, Leander 2007, Leander 2010b). IMO strategies have figured prominently in this discussion. It has been suggested that commercialisation skews priorities and hence tends to alter what kind of projects are pursued in multilateral operations, often in ways that bias them towards the priorities of security professionals generally and not only towards the PMSCs (Whyte 2007, Leander and van Munster 2007, Olsson 2007).

Analogous conclusions have been reached by rather different routes in the debate about the effect of commercialisation through the reliance on PMSCs on IMO as articulated when focus is placed on how these are *implemented* in practice. The emphasis in these studies has therefore been on how commercialisation alters the way IMO are implemented not so much by shifting formal authority over these strategies but by altering the form and fashion of their implementation; the how of implementing IMO (Singer 2007, Leander 2010a). From this perspective, the way contractors carry out a strategy becomes central, as demonstrated by their role in the occupation of Iraq (Isenberg 2008, Young Pelton 2006). Along these lines it can for example be expected that the focus on conventional, military values among contractors shapes how the IMO in which they are involved are carried out, even if these values can be expected to vary with e.g. the nationality of the contractors or the company culture in which they are embedded (Higate 2012). Analogously, the presence of contractors implies a change in the rules governing IMOs. De facto, the pivotal role of PMSCs in practice often gives these considerable sway over the rules governing IMO; the 'big boys rules' as Triple Canopy employees in Baghdad dubbed the self-made rules governing their activities (Fainaru 2008). By setting rules and fashioning processes, commercialisation demonstrably (re-)shapes the landscape of IMO and the links between actors on the ground where the intervention is taking place. PMSCs refashion the actions of other actors including of public armed forces (Singer 2007, McCallion 2005, Zamparelli 1999) and NGOs (Cockayne 2006, Spearin 2008). The extent to which PMSCs are reshaping the implementation of IMO is best visible in the surge in initiatives to replace the present muddle-through handling of PMSC, to a clearer regulatory framing; whether formal (as e.g. the Montreux Document, see Gomez del Prado 2010) or informal (as e.g. the development of codes of conduct by companies, organisations and governments, see Leander 2012).

Finally, the concern with whether or not the reliance of PMSCs is skewing politics towards the military concerns is reflected in the debate about how security commercialisation shapes the *imprint* of IMOs. Companies (and those advocating an extended role for PMSCs) have emphasised the potential of security commercialisation for displacing activities from the military to the commercial sector; hence easing the development of non-military political processes. Company advocates highlighting the 'local knowledge', 'gender sensitivity' (Schultz and Yeung 2008) and the integration of locals (Zarate 1998) point in this direction. The critique points the opposite way; insisting that on the contrary companies are reducing the space for the non-military within the IMO by, for example, increasing the resources (including arms and other equipment), status and money flowing into the military/security-related aspects of the IMO while diverting it from other aspects including the humanitarian ones (Francis 1999, Leander 2005a, Leander 2013).

This book *brings together these three aspects* of the discussions surrounding the political consequences of commercialisation through reliance on PMSCs. It does so because the political processes at the three levels are tightly linked. Indeed, the extent to which PMSCs formulate IMO strategies can only be captured if their weight in implementing the IMO and hence their imprint on the ground are kept in view. Similarly, the impact of PMSCs on the implementation of the IMO only becomes visible if the formulation and that imprint are taken into account. Finally, unless both national formulation and the implementation are taken into account, it is impossible to understand the imprint on the ground and the role of PMSCs in making it. In clear, looking at the three levels in combination is imperative for capturing the political implications of security commercialisation. By doing precisely this, the volume contributes to the debate about the political implications of PMSCs for IMO.

A book about European security commercialisation

Last but not least the discussion about PMSCs has so far taken place as if it was irrelevant to Europe beyond the UK. The single most striking characteristic of the debate regarding PMSCs in Europe is its paucity. No European country has had a significant public debate on the topic. There are comparatively few publications about Europe (exceptions include Krahmann 2010b, Buzatu 2008). Studies from other places rarely insist that the insights gained might be pertinent also for Europe. Research reports by para-public think tanks (some cited in the chapters below) and the occasional news story about a co-national somehow involved in the market sums up the extent of information in most of Europe. This volume contributes by breaking the silence surrounding Europe; by drawing a link between the PMSC discussions and Europe.

The limited discussion surrounding PMSCs in Europe is partly attributable to *the scarcity of information*. No European country publishes systematic, readily accessible data about contracting. Those interested therefore have to piece together partial, dispersed and heterogeneous pieces of information (as visible also in the chapters below). The absence of information is often taken as an indication that commercialisation is insignificant. However, as the US case shows there is no reason to believe that this is the case. The US provided data as a consequence of the debate about PMSCs not the other way around. When Singer began researching PMSCs in the US context he lamented that the ministry of defence could not provide even the most basic information on contractors (Singer 2001–2). A decade later the situation was much different, however the Government Accountability Office (GAO 2010) and the Commission on Wartime Contracting (CWC 2011) still complained that the information was patchy and insufficient. This book therefore departs from the rather reasonable assumption that the absence of information is not a sufficient reason for assuming that contracting is unimportant in Europe. On the contrary it strives to collate the information that is available.

The assumption that there is little to say about PMSC contracting in Europe is *sustained by European security experts and policy makers*. When pressured to answer questions about PMSCs in public, they resort to vague statements (of which there are many examples in the chapters below) underlining that they do not outsource military functions, carefully avoiding to say anything about what that means. They do not seem to find this inconsistent with the increasing (and publicly formulated) efforts to outsource non-core functions and develop various forms of public–private partnerships. The result is an ambiguity and duality running through most public policy in the area. The chapters that follow call it hypocrisy, discrepancy or inconsistency. By way of example, France has a restrictive law banning mercenarism, declares in multilateral contexts that it does not allow the use of contractors in military operations, and French policy makers routinely distance themselves from reliance on contractors (Assemblée Nationale 2003, FINABEL 2008). Yet, France also has a series of regulatory provisions that make it possible to include contractors inside the armed forces (Assemblée Nationale 2003) and (consequently) on both formal and informal accounts French companies are thriving, including through their work for the French state and French armed forces in the context of operations related to peace and reconciliation (Lobjois and Hugo 2009, Bigo 2004, Wither 2005, Wodarg 2008). This volume is indiscrete enough to pry into the obvious gap separating the principled declaration and the policy practice in Europe; a gap that is often matched by a gap between security experts and insiders from the broader public but perhaps also concerned policy makers. Focusing on Europe it is hence not only building a bridge to the discussions about PMSCs in the world at large but also a bridge between two separate European discussions: the insider/expert and the public/lay.

This book is, to sum up, situated in relation to a lively ongoing international debate about the consequences of security commercialisation to which it will add its own grain of salt. It does so by drawing on and developing the discussion about the *political* consequences of commercialising security with specific reference to consequences for *IMO* in the *European* context.

The framework of analysis

The framework of analysis used in this book derives from the outline of its empirical and theoretical aspirations. This section explains how. It clarifies the methodological foundations and coherence of the work that follows. It begins by outlining how and on the basis of what cases it will study the 'European contexts'. It proceeds to clarify how the commercialisation of security is analysed, insisting that the study includes both direct practices (outsourcing processes and integration of PMSCs inside the state) and indirect contracting (when PMSCs play a role because other actors central to the IMO contract them in). Finally, the section outlines how it will look at political consequences of commercialising security in the context of IMO by focusing on the formulation, implementation and imprint of the IMO.

Studying national contexts: lexica, practices and regulation

In the discussion, so far 'European' has been presented as something relatively coherent and unitary, the UK excluded. A specific European, statist and centralising understanding of the link between statehood and control over the legitimate use of force makes such a presentation warranted (e.g. Sofsky 1996, Badie and Birnbaum 1983). This is particularly true when 'European' is contrasted with some part of the rest of the world (as it will be in the concluding chapter). The US for example has a tradition of seeing citizen militias as useful counterweights to the strong centralised state (Deudney 1995) and many contemporary states rest on decentralised control over the use of force (e.g. Reno 1998, von Trotha 1997). However, as soon as we direct attention to the details of the 'European' the image fractures.

Each European country has a distinct national context that profoundly shapes both how contracting is handled in general and in the context of IMO. There are distinct '*national lexica*' (Leander and Joenniemi 2006) – tied to specific 'generative grammars' (Ruggie 1982) – that give meaning to the organisation of the use of force; they produce the connotations attached to various organisations of the use of force, including that by contractors in international contexts. This under-standing is reproduced in the *historical practices* of when, how and why to use force internationally and in the *regulatory frameworks* emerging in these practices. National contexts are thus defining for European security commercialisations and its consequences. The idea of 'civilian power' is as foundational for Germany as is the communist legacy for Romania. In this sense, national contexts (lexica, his-torical practice and regulation) constitute a necessary point of departure, for the chapters in this volume, for understanding the commercialisation of security (as indicated in the upper part of Figure 1.1). This said national contexts are

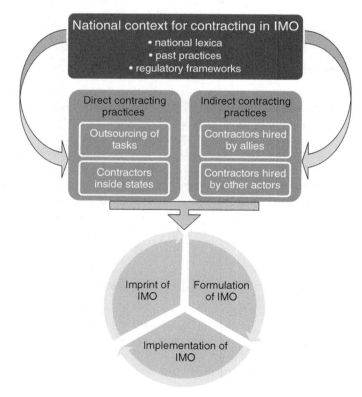

Figure 1.1 The political consequences of security commercialisation

obviously difficult to capture, compress and serve in neat standardised fashion. They are evolving and contested. As such they are difficult to pin down and pinning them down is a political act in its own right. It reinforces a specific understanding of the national context. Therefore, the authors in this volume have focused on different aspects of their national contexts; the aspects of the national context they consider most salient for their analysis. This should be seen as an inevitable correlate of the responsibility each one of them has had in making choices.

Insisting on the distinctiveness and diversity of national contexts opens the question of which countries to include in the study of Europe. This book focuses on *three core groups* with three countries in each. The first, the Scandinavians including Norway, Sweden and Denmark, are all marked by the strong imprint of the welfare state on the way that the relations between the armed forces and the state have been conceived (Ulriksen 2002, Matlary and Østerud 2001, Kronsell and Svedberg 2005, Leander 2006a, Sørensen 2000). The second group, the Central European countries, Poland, Hungary and Romania, are characterised by an uncertainty surrounding national sovereignty and boundaries and a recent history of moving from the Warsaw Pact membership to integration into NATO (Zaborowski and Longhurst 2007, Kuzniar 2001, Degratu 2005, Degratu 2003, Pascu 2008). The third group is the large Continental countries, Germany, France and Italy, whose national contexts bear the traces of the European world wars, global and colonial ambitions and also a concern with the common European security architecture (Longhurst 2004, Krahmann 2010b, Olsson 2009).

This selection of cases makes the book a significant contribution to current work on commercialising security in Europe. But *as any selection it also excludes*. In particular, it excludes both the Mediterranean countries (Portugal, Spain, Greece and Turkey), whose history has earned them a central place in discussions about military coups and authoritarian politics in the twentieth century, and the small European countries (the BENELUX and Switzerland). It also excludes by locating 'the context' at the national level hence excluding common institutions such as NATO, CSDP or the OSCE. These institutions play an obvious and crucial role in shaping European politics surrounding IMO as well as in shaping European approaches to contracting. For this study this is especially true of NATO since it deals with the IMO in Afghanistan. When we began to work on this project we thought these common institutions would be reflected in the national contexts. We did not realise the extent to which the common has become a context in its own right, to some extent replacing the national. Especially in Central Europe discussions about the formulation, implementation and imprint of the IMO in Afghanistan are left to NATO. Yet NATO debates are not reflected in the national ones; there is no national debate. The common has replaced the national. Of course the national contexts may well be reflected in the common debates but we do not explore it here. However, this book is intended to open (not conclude) a discussion about the political consequences of European security commercialisation. Hence if it triggers interest and research including on these missing dimensions, the book will have served its purpose.

Last but not least, what the 'national context' is varies depending on what IMO is considered. The chapters are therefore written with reference to political consequences of security commercialisation for the IMO *in Afghanistan*. IMOs vary considerably depending on the nature of the conflict, the actors (including the PMSCs) involved and the formal and informal delimitations of the ambitions of this involvement; viz. the difference between the UN-led primarily humanitarian mission in the DRC (MONUSCO) and the NATO-led primarily military mission in Afghanistan (ISAF). The national lexica, historical practices and regulatory settings relevant to any given IMO will vary correspondingly. To reduce the difficulty of selecting within national contexts, it is therefore useful to focus on one case. More than this it makes cross-cutting discussions easier. Situating the argument in one context makes the kinds of issues raised through the IMO, the actors involved and overarching rules and regulations similar. This makes it possible to compare how countries have reacted to similar challenges, pressures and debates both with regard to handling the reliance on PMSCs and with regard to the pressures on their IMO strategies. Afghanistan is the only place where this is possible as the countries studied are *all* involved.

Studying contracting practices: direct and indirect contracting

To understand the political consequences of security commercialisation in Europe it is obviously important not only to clarify how Europe is analysed but also how 'security commercialisation' is understood. The terms '*contracting*' and '*PMSC*' draw attention to the phenomena we are trying to capture. 'Contracting' captures the process of organising the military on the basis of contractual relations – as opposed to hierarchical orders or trust-based mutual agreements – which is at the heart of commercialisation. PMSC captures the related growing role of companies that often span the legal and formal distinction between the military (international/war) and security (national/policing). Private usefully indicates that the companies are for profit and operate on market terms even if private is – as the chapters below show – often a misnomer in the European countries since the companies tend to be partly or even fully publicly owned, and even when they are not they are so closely intertwined with the public that European contracting appears as a hybrid undertaking rather than as a 'public' contracting of 'private' firms.

The most straightforward way of capturing security commercialisation is to look at when countries are *directly contracting PMSCs*. Core state institutions including ministries, embassies, armed forces or public development agencies engage commercial companies for tasks that were previously undertaken by the military, including for example personal, convoy or infrastructure protection, collection and analysis of information about local developments or providing of logistics such as contracting or transportation. This contracting may take the form of classical outsourcing where the institutions contract an independent company. However, it may also take less conventional forms as for example when companies or individuals are contracted to work *within* the institution as when contractors become integrated as 'sponsored reserves' in the armed forces.

In addition to this, commercialisation may take place through what we have decided to term *indirect contracting* – that is forms of contracting where states rely on the contracting of PMSCs although they themselves undertake no direct contracting. In IMOs that have a multilateral character this kind of contracting is very significant. State institutions often share infrastructure, bases, logistics arrangements and operational responsibilities. Logically they therefore organise these in common. This means that if one of the allies contracts PMSCs, the others will rely on the services provided without necessarily having any direct contractual relation to the contractor. If the reliance is formal, it will involve some form of compensation to the state that is paying for the contract. But the reliance may also be informal and just de facto accepted. The PMSC contracting done by other actors – such as NGOs carrying out part of the public policy, companies involved in carrying out national policies – may result in a similar indirect reliance on PMSCs. Tasks that would otherwise have to be carried out by the national armed forces are carried out by contractors although there is no direct contractual link between the state and the company.

Analysing the politics of military operations: formulation, implementation, and imprint

Each chapter is geared to analyse the consequences of security commercialisation for the politics of IMO. The chapters follow the same pattern in discussing these implications. As summarised in the lower part of Figure 1.1, a core ambition is to keep focus on the link between the formulation, implementation and imprint of the policies to understand if politics are shifting and becoming skewed towards military/security issues as often suggested in the literature. We do this by focusing on two related kinds of shifts.

First, there may be a shift in the relative weight of actors and agendas *within the IMO*. Commercialisation has not only introduced a range of actors that previously had no place in IMO, it has also placed them in positions where they make core decisions pertaining to the IMO. In the process they displace other actors and their agendas. This entails a shift in who has what kind of say over the IMO with implications for the political values and objectives informing the IMO as well as for the input and accountability involved. The second is the shift in the weight of *the IMO in the context* of other types of operations and activities. The fact that commercialisation introduces a new range of actors may indeed also lead to an expansion of the IMO in society as it becomes a greater priority, more resources are devoted to it and its agenda comes to shape other agendas. PMSCs work as a troop multiplier as their advocates often underscore. If this multiplication is simply expanding the weight of the IMO the expansion scenario is indeed likely. The chapters analyse the extent to which this kind of shift is resulting from European security commercialisations in Afghanistan.

The book outline

As the framework of analysis shows, the chapter covers considerable empirical and theoretical terrain. They do this following a similar organisational logic (the one outlined in Figure 1.1). Each chapter provides key indications about the (1) national context; it outlines (2) the direct and indirect practices of commercialisation and it analyses (3) the politics of IMO (formulation, implementation and coordination). The practices of commercialisation and the implications are illustrated primarily with reference to Afghanistan. The chapters place varying emphasis on these three core building blocks and their subparts reflecting both the contextual diversity and the expertise and preferences of their authors. Similarly, while most chapters discuss national context, contracting practices and impact in that order, two chapters are otherwise structured. The chapters can and should therefore be read both as contributions to this collective project and as individual statements about the significance of security commercialisation for the politics of IMO. The overall impression is that security commercialisation in Europe is diverse. Even though we decided to present the contributions in groupings that should bring out some of the similarities, the varieties within each grouping are striking.

Starting with the Scandinavian countries, Østensen begins the volume by arguing that Norwegian security commercialisation is marked by the concern to 'keep up appearances' in the face of the inconsistencies between declared policies rejecting the use of PMSCs and practices relying on them. The result is a reactive inconsistent approach to contracting that affects the capacity to pursue a coherent strategy in Afghanistan. Mandrup shows that in Denmark, the situation is rather different. Commercialisation and contracting is generally – except when the use of 'lethal force' is involved – approached in a *how* not *if* manner. The regulation and policy is consequently following suit and allowing for a relative consistency. However, the public is unaware of this with obvious consequences for accountability and input in the formulation of the IMO and hence for the imprint left. The grouping is concluded by Berndtsson and Stern. They show that Sweden manages to circumvent both the need to 'keep up appearances' and to acknowledge the 'how' question about security commercialisation by treating it as involving 'public servants from the private sector'. Sweden even grants diplomatic status to the employees of the company coordinating security at the embassy in Kabul. This makes it possible to gloss over the de-facto shifts in the politics surrounding the IMO.

The Central European countries are similarly diverse. Terlikowski, Madej and Gorka-Winter suggest that Poland has a mainly indirect and ad-hoc approach to the politics of contracting in Afghanistan. Its approach to IMO is to rely heavily on the lead nation, including with regards to the contracting of PMSCs, while its approach to contracting is highly restrictive. The consequence is that concrete issues arsing from contracting are dealt with in an ad-hoc technocratic manner and that Poland can behave as if contracting was of limited significance for its operations in Afghanistan. Inversely in Hungary, Varga shows a reflected change of approach to security commercialisation, which has moved 'from outsourcing to in-sourcing' in order to favour national companies in contracting under control of the state. Both this move and the indirect contracting dealt with as a technicality continue to be treated as unrelated to the politics of the IMO in Afghanistan. Pop concludes the section along analogous lines, arguing that in Romania the politics of the IMO are understood to be a matter of state-led 'high politics' largely unrelated to the 'low politics' of indirect and direct contracting on which Romania relies. However, by contrast to the chapters on Poland and Hungary, Pop insists that this leads to a misrecognition of the role of low politics in shaping high politics and, by the same token, of Romania's responsibility for the IMO and contracting within it.

Finally, the chapters about Continental European countries also highlight variation. For France, Olsson suggests (along lines similar to Pop) that the core concern has been to 'make ends' meet both economically and by joining the microcosm of PMSCs and the large-scale public security contracting. In spite of this publicly vented concern, security commercialisation and (even more so) its political implications remain sensitive, contested and difficult to debate in public. The processes, institutions and regulations surrounding commercialisation are correspondingly 'heterogeneous'. The picture Krahmann paints of Germany is one of a more clear-cut 'revision' of the conventional 'civilian power' approach to the military and related suspicion of commercial security especially in international operations. However, it is an expert and elite driven revision. The reluctance to publicly acknowledge this revision has made Germany 'miss the opportunity' to develop adequate regulation and accountability and hence to control the impact on the ground in Afghanistan. Ruzza concludes the grouping, arguing that Italy is characterised by extensive security commercialisation with far-reaching implications for the Italian approach to the IMO in Afghanistan. However, the changes have gone 'under the radar', possibly because Italians prefer 'selling stocks' to keeping them and consider discretion as the best marketing.

The conclusion reverses the focus; instead of highlighting European diversity it draws attention to the commonalities. It insists on three overarching commonalities: first, European national contexts are marked by a sharp division between a wider public unaware of security commercialisation and security experts that understate or obfuscate it, reinforcing the widespread misrecognition of security commercialisation in the process. Second, European states share a predilection for indirect and/or hybrid contracting forms. Since these are inherently opaque, contracting remains badly understood, poorly regulated and the prevailing misrecognition is reinforced. Finally, as a consequence Europeans are ill-equipped to understand, let alone control or harness to their advantage, the impact of commercial security on the formulation, implementation and imprint of their IMO. To make these shared features stand out, the conclusion contextualises the European experience with that of the US. The contrast could not be more striking: the US publicly debates and informs about its commercialisation, which tends to take more straightforward forms, and is consequently more adequately understood, regulated and drawn upon to further the national priorities in the context of the IMO in Afghanistan.

Note

1 In Abu Ghraib prisoner abuse scandal the companies Titan and CACI were involved
in interrogations and in the Nisour Square (Baghdad), Blackwater employees escorting
state department officials shot 17 civilians on 16 September 2007.

References

Abrahamsen, Rita and Michael C. Williams. 2010. *Security Beyond the State: Private Security in International Politics*. Cambridge: Cambridge University Press.
Assemblée Nationale, France. 2003. 'Loi n° 2003-2340 du 14 avril 2003 relatif à la répression de l'activité de mercenaire', Paris: Assemblée Nationale.
Avant, Deborah. 2005. *The Market for Force: The Consequences of Privatizing Security*. Cambridge: Cambridge University Press.
Badie, Bertrand and Pierre Birnbaum. 1983. *The Sociology of the State*. Chicago: University of Chicago Press.
BENS, Business Executive for National Security. (2001) 'Tail to Tooth Commisson: Report', available at: www.bens.org/page.aspx?pid=465 (accessed 2 August 2012).
Berndtsson, Joakim. 2009. *The Privatization of Security and State Control of Force: Changes, Challenges and the Case of Iraq*. Göteborg: Univerity of Gothenburg.
Bigo, Didier. 2004. 'Les entreprises para-privés de coercition: de nouveaux mercenaires?', *Cultures & Conflits* (été): 1–3.
Brooks, Doug. 2000. 'Write a Cheque, End a War: Using Private Military Companies to End African Conflicts', *Conflict Trends* (1): 33–35.
Buzatu, Anne-Marie. 2008. *European Practices of Regulation of PMSCs and Recommendations for Regulation of PMSCs through International Legal Instruments*. Geneva: The Centre for the Democratic Control of Armed Forces.
Cockayne, James. 2006. 'Commercial Security in the Humanitarian Space', *International Peace Academy*, available at: http://web.gc.cuny.edu/dept/rbins/IUCSHA/fellows/Cockayne-paper-final.pdf (accessed 2 August 2012).
Commission on Wartime Contrating in Iraq and Afghanistan (CWC). 2011. *Final Report: A Decade's Lessons on Contingency Contracting*. Washington, DC: Congress.
Degratu, Claudiu. 2003. 'The Security Sector in Romania', in Philipp Fluri and Garmisch Velizar Shalamanov, eds, *Security Sector Reform, Does It Work? Problems of Civil–Military and Inter-Agency cooperation in the Security Sector*. Washington, DC: DCAF & George C. Marshall Association, pp. 115–32.
——— 2005. 'Romania's Participation in the Fight Against International Terrorism: Implications for Civil-Military Relations and the Security Sector Reform', in Philipp Fluri, E. Gustenau and Plamen Pantev, eds, London: Institute for Security and International Studies, pp. 189–96.
Deudney, Daniel H. 1995. 'The Philadelphia System: Sovereignty, Arms Control and Balance of Power in the American States – Union, circa 1787-1861', *International Organization* 49: 191–228.
Dickinson, Laura. 2005. 'Accountability of State and Non-State Actors for Human Rights Abuses in the "War on Terror"', *Tulsa Journal of Comparative and International Law* 12: 53–60.
——— 2011. *Outsourcing War and Peace: How Privatizing Foreign Affairs Threatens Core Public Values and What We Can Do About It*. New Haven, CT: Yale University Press.

Fainaru, Steve. 2008. *Big Boy Rules: In the Company of America's Mercenaries Fighting in Iraq.* Cambridge: Da Capo Press.

FINABEL (Organisation promoting the interoperability of armed forces in the EU). 2008. *Possibilities and Limitations of the Operational Co-operation with Private 'Military' Companies.* Report: A.24.R.

Francis, David J. 1999. 'Mercenary Intervention in Sierra Leone: Providing National Security or International Exploitation?', *Third World Quarterly* 20 (2): 319–38.

Gansler, Jacques. 2010. 'The Global War on Contractors Must Stop', *ExecutiveBiz*, 15 January.

GAO. 2010. *Continued Actions Needed by DOD to Improve and Institutionalize Contractor Support in Contingency Operations*, www.gao.gov/products/GAO-10-551T (accessed 7 October 2012).

Ghebali, Victor-Yves. 2006. 'The United Nations and the Dilemma of Outsourcing Peacekeeping Operations', in Alan Bryden and Marina Caparini, eds, *Private Actors and Security Governance*. Zürich: LIT Verlag, pp. 213–30.

Gomez del Prado, Jose L. 2010. 'A pyrrhic victory at the United Nations over the 21st century's "privateer industry"?', edited by UN Working Group on Mercenaries, www.rightrespect.org/2010/10/14/a-pyrric-victory-at-the-united-nations-over-the-21st-centurys-%C2%A8privateer-industry%E2%80%9D/ (accessed 7 October 2012).

Higate, Paul. 2012. '"Cowboys and Professionals": The Politics of Identity Work in the Private and Military Security Company', *Millennium* 40 (2): 321–41.

Isenberg, David. 2008. *Shadow Force: Private Security Contractors in Iraq*. New York: Praeger.

Kaldor, Mary. 1998. 'Introduction', in Mary Kaldor and Basker Vashee, eds, *Restructuring the Global Military Sector: New Wars*. London: Pinter, pp. 3–33.

Kierpaul, Ian. 2008. 'The Rush to Bring Private Military Contractors to Justice: The Mad Scramble of Congress, Lawyers, and Law Students after Abu Ghraib', *The University of Toledo Law Review* 39 (2): 407–35.

Krahmann, Elke. 2010a. 'Private Actors and Security', in Robert Denmark, ed., *International Studies Encyclopedia*. Oxford: Blackwells.

—— 2010b. *States, Citizens and the Privatization of Security*. Cambridge: Cambridge University Press.

Kronsell, Annica and Erica Svedberg. 2005. 'The Swedish Military Manpower Policies and Their Gender Implications', in Pertti Joenniemi, ed., *The Ideational Power of Conscription*. London: Ashgate.

Kuzniar, R., ed. 2001. *Poland's Security Policy 1989-2000*. Warsaw: Scholar Publishing House.

Leander, Anna. 2005a. 'The Market for Force and Public Security: The Destabilizing Consequences of Private Military Companies', *Journal of Peace Research* 42 (5): 605–22.

—— 2005b. 'The Power to Construct International Security: On the Significance of Private Military Companies', *Millennium* 33 (3): 803–26.

—— 2006a. 'Enduring Conscription: Vagueness and *Värnplikt* in Sweden', in Pertti Joenniemi, ed., *The Changing Face of European Conscription*. London: Ashgate, pp. 112–30.

—— 2006b. *Eroding State Authority? Private Military Companies and the Legitimate Use of Force.* Rome: Centro Militare di Studi Strategici.

—— 2007. 'Regulating the Role of PMCs in Shaping Security and Politics', in Simon Chesterman and Chia Lehnardt, eds, *From Mercenaries to Markets: The Rise and Regulation of Private Military Companies*. Oxford: Oxford University Press, pp. 49–64.

—— 2009a. 'New Roles for External Actors? Disagreements about International Regulation of Private Armies', in Karin Aggestam and Annika Björkdal, eds, *War and Peace in Transition: Changing Roles for External Actors*. Lund: Nordic Academic Press, pp. 32–52.

——— 2009b. 'The Privatization of Security', in Myriam Dunn Cavelty and Victor Mauer, eds, *The Routledge Handbook of Security Studies*. London and New York: Routledge, pp. 200–10.

——— 2009c. 'Securing Sovereignty by Governing Security through Markets', in Rebbecca Adler-Nissen and Thomas Gammeltoft-Hansen, eds, *Sovereignty Games: Instrumentalising State Sovereignty in Europe and Beyond*. London: Palgrave, pp. 151–70.

——— 2010a. 'Commercial Security Practices', in Peter J. Burgess, ed., *Handbook of New Security Studies*. London and New York: Routledge, pp. 208–16.

——— 2010b. 'The Paradoxical Impunity of Private Military Companies: Authority and the Limits to Legal Accountability', *Security Dialogue* 41 (5): 467–90.

——— 2012. 'What Do Codes of Conduct Do? Hybrid Constitutionalization and Militarization in Military Markets', *Global Constitutionalism* 1 (1): 91–119.

——— 2013. 'Markets Matter: The Frail Constitution of Political Being and the Marketing of Commercial Security', in Jef Huysmans and Xavier Guillaume, eds, *Security and Citizenship: The Constitution of Political Being*. London and New York: Routledge.

Leander, Anna and Pertti Joenniemi. 2006. 'In Conclusion: National Lexica of Conscription', in Pertti Joenniemi, ed., *The Changing Face of European Conscription*. London: Ashgate, pp. 151–62.

Leander, Anna and Rens van Munster. 2007. 'Private Security Contractors in Darfur: Reflecting and Reinforcing Neo-Liberal Governmentality', *International Relations* 21 (2): 201–16.

Lobjois, Philippe and Franck Hugo. 2009. *Mercenaires de la République: 15 ans de guerres secrètes: Birmanie, ex-Yougoslavie, Comores, Zaïre, Congo, Côte d'Ivoire, Irak*. Paris: Nouveau Monde Editions.

Longhurst, Kerry. 2004. *Germany and the Use of Force: The Evolution of German Security Policy, 1990–2003*. Manchester: Manchester University Press.

Markusen, Ann R. 2003. 'The Case Against Privatizing National Security', *Governance: An International Journal of Policy, Administration, and Institutions* 16 (4): 471–501.

Martin, Jennifer S. 2007. 'Contracting for Wartime Actors: The Limits of the Contract Paradigm', *New England Journal of International and Comparative Law* 14 (Fall): 11–33.

Matlary, Janne Haaland and Øyvind Østerud, eds. 2001. *Mot et avnasjonalisert forsvar?* Oslo: Akstrakt Forlag.

McCallion, Kristen. 2005. 'War For Sale! Battlefield Contractors in Latin America & the "Corporatization" of America's War on Drugs', *The University of Miami Inter-American Law Review* 36 (Spring): 317–53.

Minow, Martha. 2003. 'Public and Private Partnerships: Accounting for the New Religion', *Harvard Law Review* 116 (March): 1229–70.

Olsson, Christian. 2007. 'The Politics of the Apolitical, PMCs, humanitarians and the quest for (anti-)politics in post-intervention environments', *Journal of International Relations and Development* 10 (4): 332–61.

——— 2009. *Conquérir les coeurs et les esprits? Usages et enjeux de legitimation locale de la force dans les missions de pacification extérieures (Bosnie, Kosovo, Afghanistan, Irak; 1996–2006)*. Paris: Thèse soutenue à l'IEP de Paris.

Pascu, Ioan Mircea. 2008. *Bătălia pentru NATO (The Battle over NATO)*. Bucharest: Tritonic.

Rasor, Dina and Robert Bauman. 2007. *Betraying Our Troops: The Destructive Results of Privatizing War*. New York: Palgrave.

Reno, William. 1998. *Warlord Politics and African States*. Boulder, CO and London: Lynne Rienner.

Ruggie, John. 1982. 'International Regime, Transactions, and Change: Embedded Liberalism in the Postwar Economic Order', *International Organization* 36 (2): 379–415.

Schultz, Sabrina and Christina Yeung. 2008. *Private Military and Security Companies and Gender (Tool 10)*, Geneva: DCAF with OSCE/ODIHR, UN-INSTRAW, www.dcaf.ch/Publications/Private-Military-and-Security-Companies-and-Gender-Tool-10 (accessed 7 October 2012).

Singer, Peter W. 2001–2. 'Corporate Warriors: The Rise of the Privatized Military Industry and Its Ramifications for International Security', *International Security* 26 (3): 186–220.

—— 2003. *Corporate Warriors. The Rise of the Privatized Military Industry*. Ithaca, NY and London: Cornell University Press.

—— 2007. 'Can't Win with 'Em, Can't Go to War without 'Em: Private Military Contractors and Counterinsurgency', *Foreign Policy at Brookings. Policy Papers* (4).

Sofsky, Wolfgang. 1996. *Traktat über die Gewalt*. Frankfurt: Fischer.

Sørensen, Henning. 2000. 'Conscription in Scandinavia During the Last Quarter Century: Developments and Arguments', *Armed Forces and Society* 26 (2): 313–34.

Spearin, Christopher. 2008. 'Private, Armed and Humanitarian? States, NGOs, International Private Security Companies and Shifting Humanitarianism', *Security Dialogue* 39 (4): 363–82.

Teubner, Gunther. 2002. 'Hybrid Laws: Constitutionalizing Private Governance Networks', in Robert Kagan and Kenneth Winston, eds, *Legality and Community*. Berkley, CA: Berkely Public Policy Press, pp. 311–31.

Tiefer, Charles. 2007. 'The Iraq Debacle: The Rise and Fall of Procurement-Aided Unilateralism as a Paradigm of Foreign War', *University of Pennsylvania Journal of International Economic Law* 29 (Fall): 1–56.

Ulriksen, Ståle. 2002. *Den Norske Forsvartradisjonen: Militærmakt eller Folkeforsvar*. Oslo: Pax Forlag.

Verkuil, Paul. 2007. *Outsourcing Sovereignty: Why Privatization of Government Functions Threatens Democracy and What We Can Do about It*. Cambridge: Cambridge University Press.

von Trotha, Trutz, ed. 1997. *Soziologie der Gewalt*. Wiesbaden: Westdeutscher Verlag.

Whyte, Dave. 2007. 'The Crimes of Neo-Liberal Rule in Occupied Iraq', *British Journal of Criminology* 47 (2): 177–95.

Wither, James K. 2005. 'European Security and Private Military Companies', *The Quarterly Journal* (Summer): 107–26.

Wodarg, Wolfgang. 2008. *Private military and security firms and the erosion of the state monopoly on the use of force*. Strasbourg: Parliamentary Assembly, Political Affairs Committee.

Young Pelton, Robert. 2006. *Licensed to Kill: Hired Guns in the War on Terror*. New York: Crown Publishers.

Zaborowski, M. and Kerry Longhurst. 2007. *The New Atlanticist. Poland's Foreign and Security Policy Priorities*. London: Blackwell (Chatamhouse Papers).

Zamparelli, Colonel Steven J. 1999. 'Competitive sourcing and privatization: Contractors on the battlefield', *Air Force Journal of Logistics* XXIII (3): 1–17.

Zarate, Juan Carlos. 1998. 'The Emergence of a New Dog of War: Private International Security Companies, International Law and the New World Disorder', *Stanford Journal of International Law* 34 (1): 75–162.

2 Norway

Keeping up appearances

Åse Gilje Østensen

Introduction

In terms of strategies for peace and the choice of partners for peace and reconciliation activities, Norway's international operations have until now been more closely associated with the 'human security civil society complex' than with the 'strategic commercial complex'. In other words, Norwegian operations have usually teamed up with NGOs and civil society organisations in pursuit of a human security agenda, rather than cooperating with the commercial sector and following a narrower and more strategic understanding of national security (Bolton 2010). In an environment such as Afghanistan, however, the distinctions between the two 'complexes' appear to have become less than crystal clear, and Norwegian military, development and diplomatic actors have also resorted to the use of commercial private security in their efforts to comply with Norway's development and security agendas in the country.

This chapter takes a closer look at Norwegian policies and practices related to the use of private military and security companies (PMSCs), and seeks to analyse the implications that these might have for Norway's engagement in Afghanistan. The chapter begins by taking a step back in order to identify some of the national traditions and rationales that may contribute to explaining the development of the particular Norwegian approach to PMSCs. It then addresses the nature of Norway's approach towards PMSCs in terms of both policy and practice, before discussing some implications of this approach for the country's peace and reconciliation efforts in Afghanistan. The chapter argues that an inconsistency has emerged between Norway's formal policies and its actual practices in relation to PMSCs. Norwegian practices appear inconsistent not only with the country's official policies but also more generally with the foreign political image the country is seeking to promote. More importantly, these practices have consequences for the implementation of Norway's peace and reconciliation efforts in Afghanistan.

The Norwegian context

As the chapters in this volume show, the inclination to use commercial solutions as components of civil or military contributions to international engagements varies across European countries. In the end, pragmatism may be decisive. However, in most cases, it seems that national legacies or rationales also have consequences for the articulation of the relationship between the state, the citizen and the armed forces in particular countries. These legacies in turn have a bearing upon norms and practices for civil–military relations and the role of non-state actors in security governance. In the case of Norway, there appears to exist a national inclination that largely speaks *against* the outsourcing of security and that contextualises the policy approach to PMSCs in relation to international operations.[1] The following sections will elaborate on some of the factors which contribute to this particular inclination.

Norwegian self-images and motivation

Norway has projected an image of itself as a 'peace nation' more or less since it achieved independence in 1905, and the country's role as 'benefactor, mediator and moralist' has been increasingly advocated and articulated since the end of the Cold War (Lange *et al.* 2009: 21–22). A central component of this self-conceptualisation has been the idea that Norway not only is unusually concerned with peace and development, but also is particularly well suited for assuming a central role in peace and reconciliation efforts, particularly in terms of mediation or diplomacy (Skånland 2010: 39).

In recent years, leading politicians have focused more on what has been termed the 'policy of engagement' rather than on peace mediation *per se*. This shift implied promoting a representation of Norway not only as a peace facilitator but also as a particularly generous aid donor and advocate of human security (Leira *et al.* 2007: 16).

Despite efforts to create a self-image based on benevolent international engagement, however, Norway is not portrayed as exclusively altruistic. More recent governments have made it increasingly clear that Norwegian foreign policy also seeks to achieve a functional balance between self-interest and global engagement, where the latter is instrumental for the pursuit of the former. In fact, national security considerations remain a strong motivating factor for Norway's global engagement (Ministry of Foreign Affairs 2011). While, on the one hand, peace activism and policies that promote global development are intended to create a positive image of Norway abroad, they also often create commercial opportunities for Norwegian industry and, importantly, access to international decision-making processes. This combination of idealism and *realpolitik* is also reflected in Norway's strong support of the UN.[2] A strategy of UN alignment not only favours the image of Norway as a peace nation, but also promotes vital global governance arrangements that are crucial to Norway's existence (Ministry of Foreign Affairs 2008: 98). In fact, as it is a small state with vast natural resources, Norway's interests depend on the maintenance of a world order founded upon international principles of justice. By institutionalising international justice in security policy, a strong UN thus serves the particular interests of

Norway (Leira *et al.* 2007: 21). The current Red–Green coalition government, now in its second term, has particularly stressed the continued promotion of the UN, but defence–alliance considerations have meant that Norway's policy of engagement has since 1995 increasingly been spelt out in terms of participation in international operations led by NATO rather than the UN. NATO operations in turn have led the Norwegian Armed Forces (NAF) to assume a more central role within the engagement approach, a development that has entailed both practical and conceptual consequences for the NAF. The humanitarian profile that traditionally characterised Norway's military contributions to UN operations has thus gradually assumed a more military character and function (Haaland 2007: 497).

The evolving role of the Norwegian Armed Forces

While most of NATO's other member states initiated processes to adapt their defence structures, doctrines and operational concepts to the changing international security environment during the 1990s, the restructuring and modernisation of the Norwegian defence system was somewhat slower to materialise. According to Græger (2011), the slow pace of change was largely due to three factors. The particular nation-building role played by the Norwegian defence system made it resistant to change. At the same time, the weight of the organisation (stemming from its extensive geographical presence and deeply rooted patterns of practice) worked to counteract reform. Finally, the fact that defence policy in Norway is intertwined with other domestic policy areas, such as settlement and employment issues, has complicated the process of change in the defence political domain. Consequently, it was not until 2001 that political agreement emerged concerning the restructuring and modernisation of the NAF. At the same time, in contrast to the slow-moving nature of political change, since the 1990s there has been a tendency for the NAF to adapt to new realities related to international operations more quickly than the political establishment (Græger 2006; Ulriksen 2007). In other words, practical experiences in international operations and the need to adapt to coalitional or allied force structures often compelled parts of the NAF to reform somewhat ahead of political initiatives.

Political and operational developments were also accompanied by certain cultural changes. While conscription will 'remain the backbone of the Defence' (Ministry of Defence 2003: 75), it now serves largely as a way of providing a recruitment base for soldiers who receive more specialised training and who can be signed up for international operations. Participation and training for expeditionary missions, however, implies changes to the traditional model of the soldier.[3] The conventional characterisation of the ideal Norwegian soldier saw the soldier as a patriot citizen who could be mobilised in the event of territorial invasion, an image that contrasts with the ideals of professional soldiery or rigid military training. Consequently, within Norway's military establishment there has been considerable scepticism towards soldiery as a profession, and professional soldiers have frequently even been compared to mercenaries (Ulriksen 2002: 211–212, 263). Nonetheless, the Afghanistan engagement in particular not only meant that soldiers would need to undergo specialised training and increased professionalisation, but also contributed to the return of something that has been characterised as a 'warrior culture' within the deployed divisions (Matlary 2009: 93, 100). These shifts, along with the overall nature of the Afghanistan mission, have led to schisms with the peace image and to a tendency to discursively translate the use of military power into an engagement for peace (Matlary 2009: 109).

As part of the need to reform the NAF, public–private partnerships (PPPs) in the defence sector have been encouraged since 2001. Again, however, the idea came late, and the implementation process has been slow and limited. A common concern related to PPPs is that becoming dependent on private partners could limit the general preparedness of the forces (Solstrand 2005: 145). The National Security Authority has also identified other objections of a more principled nature, which often relate to a weakening of the state's monopoly on legitimate use of force, as well as concerns related to profit-oriented motivation and information security (NoNSA 2005).

In general then, despite some recent changes, Norway's military culture has generally been disinclined to embrace private military actors. However, considering that organisational learning often has taken place in international missions, a greater tolerance for PMSCs may be emerging within deployed divisions, especially in terms of support services that allow military personnel to focus on tasks closer to the military core.

Civil society

The 'Norwegian model' has been the designation used to refer to the particularly close collaboration between Norway's Ministry of Foreign Affairs and humanitarian NGOs. This cooperation has been described as a 'marriage of convenience' in which all parties gain: the state gains NGO expertise, political legitimacy, public trust, contacts and implementation capacity, while, for NGOs, close state cooperation often means secure state funding (Lange *et al.* 2009: 11–12). However, there have been concerns that the close relationship may lead NGOs to function as vehicles for Norwegian development policy (Tvedt 2009).

The rhetoric of the Norwegian model and its concomitant conception of 'civil society' has not normally embraced for-profit actors (Tvedt 2009: 114), and most of the commercial sector does not enjoy the inclusion within foreign policy that is often enjoyed by NGOs. At the same time, major corporations that operate abroad are expected at least to some extent to reflect Norway's foreign policy profile. Hveem *et al.* (2000) contend that Norwegian companies are in fact given a role to play within Norwegian foreign policy, as the Norwegian authorities have clearly expressed expectations that companies that establish themselves abroad contribute to promoting human rights and environmental issues in line with government policies. The Norwegian national image is also reflected in the management of the public investment fund that manages Norway's oil revenues, the Government Pension Fund Global. This fund is overseen by a specially appointed council whose task it is to evaluate investments according to established ethical guidelines (Ministry of Finance 2011). The main driving force for the council's investment-screening procedures and its decisions to exclude companies that fail to live up to required standards appears to be the avoidance of complicity in ethically unsound activity, rather than any attempt to ensure that these companies redirect their course of action and raise ethical standards (Chesterman 2008: 588–589, Ministry of Finance 2003: Section 2.2). A somewhat similar logic appears to lie behind much Norwegian policy regarding PMSCs, my concern in the next section.

The Norwegian policy approach to PMSCs

In response to increasing media focus on both national private guard services and international PMSCs, in 2009 Norway made explicit legal reference to PMSCs by amending its existing legislation on guard services, the Security Guard Services Act. The amended law applies to all Norwegian companies regardless of whether they are operating domestically or abroad (Standing Committee on Justice 2008: 10).

The amended law contains an additional statement of purpose that clearly addresses PMSCs: the purpose of this law is stated as being

> to hinder security guard services that on account of their military or other security-related character do not correspond with ordinary guarding activities and would otherwise be in contravention of guarding activity as correspondent with this law, or which are otherwise illegal or in contravention of international law.
>
> (Ministry of Justice and the Police 2009: Section 1d)[4]

The 2009 amendment to the Security Guard Services Act thus expressed a clear denunciation of PMSCs and received broad political support. The only political party that supported a more lax approach to PMSCs was the right-wing Progress Party, which in its 2009–13 action programme proposed that Norway should rely on PMSCs for force protection and NGO security in international operations (Progress Party 2008: 37), a suggestion that was promptly dismissed by the Norwegian chief of defence, Sverre Diesen. An incident from 2009 that received considerable media coverage, in which two Norwegians connected to a Norwegian PMSC were arrested and subsequently convicted of charges of murder and espionage in the Democratic Republic of the Congo, appeared to confirm the importance of the legal amendments. Congolese accusations of Norwegian state complicity resulted in intense diplomatic efforts and also appeared much to the disgrace of the Norwegian foreign political self-image, which increased the incentives to prevent similar embarrassments from occurring again.

Despite its clear intent, the amended law on security guarding does contain significant ambiguities – for example, in relation to the types of services that it actually bans. While the text makes clear that personnel from Norwegian companies are prohibited from carrying arms,[5] the formulation lacks specificity, referring only vaguely to services of a 'military or other security-related character'. A government white paper declared that one of the objectives of the amendment was to avoid a situation in which 'security companies that carry out regular guarding services in Norway also offer services that contravene national or international regulations abroad. This often concerns tasks that resemble military activities' (Ministry of Justice and the Police 2008–09: 46).[6] The concept 'military activities' is not further defined, however, and the formulation of the objective gives considerable room for interpretation. Furthermore, these imprecise formulations also create ambiguities regarding the legality of some of the international security conglomerates that are already operating within Norway's domestic market. For example, the leading provider of private security services in Norway, G4S, also sells force protection and personal security detail services in war zones such as Afghanistan and Iraq, and thus appears to operate in contravention of the stated objectives of the law.[7] While the ambition of the law is evidently to restrict Norwegian companies from selling armed services abroad and to prevent the formation of a PMSC industry in Norway, the text is insufficiently clear in terms of distinguishing between legal and illegal activity. Nonetheless, the banning of armed activity has effectively prohibited Norwegian companies from offering some of the more common PMSC services abroad. This in turn has led some Norwegian companies to re-register in other countries.[8] The manager of one Norwegian PMSC registered in the UK claimed to know of about a dozen Norwegians who run PMSCs abroad, including some that operate in Iraq. While registered abroad, some of these nonetheless operate out of Norway and hire Norwegian operators who smuggle their weapons in and out of the country.[9]

Recently, the Norwegian Ministry of Defence has also suggested legal restrictions regarding what additional occupational activities defence personnel are allowed to undertake while employed by the NAF. Thus far, no formal regulations exist to prevent NAF employees from taking on additional work in the security sector (Ministry of Defence 2011). The initiative seems mainly to have been spurred by specific events that have received negative media attention – particularly an incident in 2009 in which at least two members of the Norwegian special forces were involved in a private initiative to 'extract' two children from Morocco (Ministry of Defence 2011). The suggested changes, which are yet to be endorsed, indicate that on the political level there are perceptions of a need to increasingly control NAF personnel's side activities. The proposed changes would mean that NAF personnel would need to apply for approval before taking on any extra activities of a 'military character', paid or otherwise and regardless of whether such activities are carried out privately or as a matter of commercial enterprise (Ministry of Defence 2011: 19–20).[10] Assignments of a 'security-like' character, including those for the PMSC industry, are explicitly mentioned as requiring an application. The apparently low tolerance for such activities would suggest that few such applications are approved. This is confirmed by an NAF employee with experience as a PMSC contractor in Iraq, who contends that these days the message from the NAF is clear: 'Once the step over to the PMSC industry is made, there is no way back'.[11] Nonetheless, the main rationale behind restrictions on the involvement of defence personnel with the PMSC sector seems not to be to tighten control over Norwegian defence capacities and activities abroad, but rather to secure societal trust in the NAF and 'out of consideration for the reputation and credibility of the defence sector' (Ministry of Defence 2011: 8, 13).

Somewhat curiously, in the midst of these restrictive developments, a legal amendment that goes in the opposite direction has recently been approved. Even though the Act relating to guard services explicitly exempts guarding activity on ships or ports covered by the International Ship and Port Facility Security (ISPS) Code, in July 2011 an amendment to the Ship Safety and Security Act was implemented. This explicitly allows Norwegian ships to use armed guards in order to prevent or deter pirate attacks.[12] Moreover, the regulation of such activities is lax at best, sacrificing proper oversight and control in deference to the shipping companies' need for speedy and uncomplicated access to armed guards. Companies are not required to go through an application procedure, though they do have limited reporting obligations designed to supply the authorities with oversight over the use of armed guards onboard Norwegian vessels. The legal environment concerning PMSCs is thus somewhat incoherent: while Norwegian companies may sell armed maritime security services, they are simultaneously restricted from the land-based segment of the armed security service sector. Consequently, since July 2011, a range of maritime PMSCs have been registered in Norway, many of which aim to attract former Norwegian law enforcement and military personnel in order to offer armed security service.[13] Officers from the Home Guard have in particular been inclined to accept work within the emerging maritime PMSC sector, as they are not formally employed by the NAF except on the few days a year in which they take part in exercises (Brox 2012).

In terms of initiatives to establish international regulation of PMSCs, Norway has generally maintained a remarkably low profile. Unlike Denmark and Sweden, Norway has even declined to sign the 'Montreux Document', an international endeavour designed to remind states of their already existing international legal obligations in relation to the use of PMSCs in the context of armed conflict. The Norwegian Ministry of Defence has recommended to the Ministry of Foreign Affairs that Norway endorse the Montreux Document,[14] but five years after the document's release no political decision has been taken on the matter. The mere signing of a reminder of international humanitarian law should be rather uncontroversial for Norway. However, the document also identifies some 'good practices' concerning relations between PMSCs and customer states, states on whose territory PMSCs operate, and states that house PMSCs, and it thus places certain commitments on states in terms of maintaining more conscientious relations with the PMSC industry. Norway's failure to sign the Montreux Document may thus indicate a hesitation to directly confront the issue of PMSCs, which itself may stem from perceptions that state regulation of PMSCs implies a degree of endorsement of such companies.

Norway is, however, a signatory to the 'Voluntary Principles on Security and Human Rights', which sets out a self-regulatory framework for companies within the extractive and energy sectors who, in their dealings with security forces, are obligated to ensure 'respect for human rights and fundamental freedoms'.[15] By supporting this initiative, Norway has condoned the hiring of armed security by businesses provided 'human rights and fundamental freedoms' are not violated in the process. However, as with the stance concerning the armed guarding of ISPS ships, this approach delegates the responsibility for practising responsible PMSC deployment entirely to the commercial clients themselves. In sum, then, Norway's approach to PMSCs is strict with respect to the domestic arena, but on the international level the country adopts a hands-off approach that does little to further functional control over PMSCs or to establish transnational regulatory measures.

The Norwegian approach to PMSCs in Afghanistan in practice

Since 2005, Norway has been the lead nation in the Provincial Reconstruction Team (PRT) in Meymaneh, in Faryab province, northwestern Afghanistan,[16] and has deployed on average about 500 soldiers to Afghanistan (the majority of which have been stationed at the PRT).[17] Unlike most other commanders-in-chief of national ISAF contingencies, since 2008 the Norwegian military commander has had no role in aid-implementation projects, which means that no 'hearts and minds' funds are available to the military. Aid and development funds are instead coordinated by the Norwegian embassy in Kabul, which channels more than €85 million a year (across a five-year period) through a variety of other actors, NGOs and UN organisations (Ministry of Foreign Affairs *et al.* 2009: 3). While this arrangement is reflective of the principled Norwegian political stand on civil–military relations, which emphasises that there should be no functional overlap between civilian and military activities, it has also been criticised for leading to fragmented activities and thus failing to constitute a 'comprehensive approach' (Harpviken 2011: 15). Due to the particular division of labour of the Norwegian contribution, the Norwegian military, Norway's diplomatic efforts and Norwegian NGOs[18] can all be considered integral to the national peace and reconciliation effort in Afghanistan (although, as will be discussed below, the various actors do vary in terms of their approach to PMSCs).

The Norwegian military outsourcing in Afghanistan

While Norwegian Foreign Minister Jonas Gahr Støre contends that the Norwegian Armed Forces do not use private security companies in Afghanistan (Ministry of Foreign Affairs 2010), back-end support services have been to a large extent outsourced. The Norwegian contingency to the International Security Assistance Force (ISAF), for example, relies on the French multinational Sodexo for most support functions (see also the chapter by Olsson in this volume). The company is also responsible for the procurement and subcontracting of services that Sodexo itself cannot supply, meaning that it functions as a one-stop solution that acquires the services needed to support the day-to-day running of the contingency (provisions, canteens, construction, sanitary services, laundry, etc.). The Sodexo contract is part of a common NATO procurement brokered through the NATO Maintenance and Supply Agency (NAMSA).

All combat-related tasks and the handling of prisoners more clearly pertain to the core functions of the NAF, and are hence not to be purchased in the commercial market (Norwegian Defence Staff 2007: 46). Combatant functions are further defined as functions that under the terms of international humanitarian law can be performed only by persons who can rightfully participate in hostilities without criminal liability (Ministry of Defence 2004: 15). This policy is not particularly surprising, as none of the allied forces would a priori concede that civilians are being hired with the intention that they will perform combatant tasks. Dilemmas more often surface when PMSCs are hired for more peripheral tasks, but then face situations that lead them into combat or near-combat situations because of the need to defend legitimate or illegitimate targets. To help avoid such dilemmas, Colonel Peter Lindqvist of the Norwegian Ministry of Defence contends that the category of non-outsourceable tasks should also include force protection – that is, camp guards, bodyguard details, convoy protection and call-out driving services (Leer-Salvesen 2008). Civilian personnel performing these tasks may be forced to defend installations, personnel, materials or legitimate military targets from attack (albeit without qualifying for prisoner-of-war status if they are taken prisoner). While the NAF generally do not buy force protection and security services from PMSCs, they have in the past bought *training* for these types of tasks. The Norwegian company Ronin Consulting,[19] for example, supplied force-protection training to soldiers in preparation for deployment to Afghanistan from 2001 until 2008, when the contract was abruptly terminated following massive media attention. Norway's Chief of Defence Sverre Diesen claimed that, upon learning of the contract, he ordered its immediate termination, however no operational rationale was given for this decision. This case thus exposed a dissension between the political level and the operational level in terms of attitudes towards using commercial ex-military expertise. What seemed to have worked well for almost seven years and was well accepted at the operational level was unacceptable at the political level.

Among legal experts, there has been some dissention as to whether civilian contractors may become legitimate targets if they are transporting weapons or ammunition directly to parties to a conflict (Hemmer 2008). Notwithstanding legal ambiguities, air transport and delivery of war machinery, tanks, ammunition, etc., to the Norwegian forces in Afghanistan are still carried out by unarmed civilian transport companies (Parliamentary Commissioner for the Armed Forces 2010). Norway is a member of the Strategic Airlift Interim Solution (SALIS), which charters strategic airlift services on behalf of a range of NATO countries. The aircrafts used, which are procured by NAMSA, are operated by civilian staff. However, by joining the multinational Strategic Airlift Capability, a multilateral arrangement to acquire, manage, support and operate three C-17 strategic transport aircrafts (operated by military personnel), Norway has reduced its need for civilian flights in recent years.[20] Nonetheless, in asymmetric warfare, where the laws of war are to a large extent either unknown or simply ignored by adversaries, the use of civilians for weapons transport and heavy lift may not rid the Norwegian military of the dilemma involved in possibly turning civilians into targets.

Coordination, cooperation or indirect use?

Though they may not be directly procuring security services from PMSCs, close cooperation with other force contributors in international missions such as those in Afghanistan and Iraq has compelled the Norwegian forces to relate to PMSCs that form part of the operational structures of allied nations. This interaction may at times amount to mere coordination and coexistence; at other times, to direct cooperation in order to solve a common task. In Afghanistan, close cooperation with and reliance on PMSC services seems rather unavoidable. This is especially the case when coordinating with US forces, which use PMSCs as an integrated part of their response (see, for example, Commission on Wartime Contracting in Iraq and Afghanistan 2011: 13).

A specific example of a planned operational cooperation between Norwegian forces and a US PMSC occurred in relation to the management of the personal security of Afghan President Hamid Karzai. From 2002 to 2005, DynCorp held a US Department of State Worldwide Personal Protective Services (WPPS) contract through the US Diplomatic Security Service, which included close protection duties for Karzai. As part of the Karzai security plan, Norwegian forces were to assist DynCorp personnel in the event of an evacuation by road. Norwegian forces and DynCorp personnel accordingly examined, coordinated and practised the execution of the plan in close cooperation (Svendsen 2008: 34). Norwegian forces have also cooperated with DynCorp in a structured manner in the police training programme managed by the company. Police mentoring is a central task in the Norwegian effort, and since the US' administrative structure does not allow for a federal police force to be seconded directly to international missions, the State Department relies entirely on private companies to supply the training (see, for example, Inspectors General *et al.* 2006).

More informal cooperation with PMSCs is also frequent. Sometimes this has involved taking advantage of 'safe havens' established by a PMSC or allied force personnel in the field. According to Svendsen (2008: 35), there has developed an unwritten gentleman's agreement that these secure zones, often camps or their perimeters, can be exploited by national force units as a way of reducing the need to perform additional safeguarding. This hospitality often also seems to work the other way around, and PMSCs are frequently granted access to camp facilities and security on the basis of connections and personal favours.[21] However, several sources claim that some of the minor Norwegian PMSC ventures operating in Iraq also lack the personal connections and contacts necessary to secure full access to camp facilities and are thus frequently only granted outer-perimeter security in military camps. For similar reasons, these companies often also lack the ability to attract support from fellow PMSCs or military contingencies in the event of attacks or emergencies.[22] Sometimes, more *ad hoc* type cooperation occurs simply as a result of shared operating environments or shared enemies. For example, contractors were given shelter in the Norwegian camp in Meymaneh in 2011 owing to fears that riots would break out in the city. At one stage, contractors were also hosted in the camp awaiting the establishment of their own premises.[23]

While informal cooperative practices have developed in the field between units, Norway's Ministry of Defence recently attempted to restrict cooperation between PMSC personnel and NAF employees at the individual level. According to a discussion paper from the Ministry of Defence (2011: 8), 'any contact with private security companies beyond the purely social shall take place through the unit, or with the approval of the unit'. In practice, however, this restriction may not be complied with, or even known. According to one NAF employee, the main rule of thumb seems to be that anyone with an ISAF accreditation and security clearance will be treated as an official ISAF member, notwithstanding their public or private affiliation.[24] Informally, PMSC contractors are often treated as coalition members in a broad sense (Svendsen 2008). Thus, while the Norwegian Ministry of Defence (2011) recently emphasised that NAF employees shall not *single-handedly* under any circumstances assist or contribute to the efforts of private security companies seeking to carry out their missions in the service of their customers, such activities nevertheless seem to take place on a collective level by way of coordination and cooperation with PMSCs.

Civilian state actors' use of PMSCs

Protection of diplomatic personnel and property is in principle the responsibility of a host state, but embassies and consulates located in weak states or in zones of conflict often rely upon security services from the private market. Norway aspires to keep a light footprint in terms of embassy security, and as far as possible restricts the use of armed guards. However, while keeping an unarmed appearance, most security companies in dangerous locations also offer 'panic button services', which bring armed guards to the scene within minutes. In zones of conflict and in countries with high crime rates, PMSCs are likely to be preferred, as they also offer close protection, risk assessments and emergency planning, and tend to be more advanced in their security approach than security and watchmen companies.

In the Afghan context, efforts to reform the Afghan National Police (ANP) have yielded disappointing results, and many still see the police force as part of the security problem rather than part of its solution (Wilder 2007: xii). Consequently, the ANP is rarely entrusted with sole responsibility for international property or personnel. Accordingly, all or most foreign embassies in Kabul are protected by private security companies (Van Praet 2010). The outer perimeter of the Norwegian embassy is guarded by ten Afghan police officers, but the Norwegian Ministry of Foreign Affairs has also hired the well-known PMSCs Saladin Security (Gjerstad 2009: 28), ArmorGroup and Page Protective Services for inner-perimeter and staff security. While this is not a matter that has been subject to public discussion, the arrangements are largely confirmed by the Ministry of Foreign Affairs (2010).

The NGO approach to PMSCs

Norwegian NGOs play a considerable role in the Norwegian development effort in Afghanistan. While they have needed to relate to the ISAF operation to ensure that they are informed of ongoing military operations in their operating areas, they have strived to not coordinate with ISAF and have made an effort not to be associated with any ISAF contingency.[25] Supporting this disassociation, the Ministry of Foreign Affairs is one of the main funders of the Afghanistan NGO Safety Office, an independent organisation tasked with providing security analysis and advice for NGOs conducting operations in the country. While information and advice is crucial to NGO security, the relatively high threat of violence against aid workers may mean that NGOs in some instances require safeguarding services from the private market. Former Foreign Minister Jonas Gahr Støre has insisted that Norwegian NGOs only use PMSCs for security purposes to a small extent (Ministry of Foreign Affairs 2010), but no directives or guidelines for such contracting have been provided by the Norwegian Agency for Development Cooperation (NORAD), which grants a large part of the funding for Norwegian NGO activities in Afghanistan. Consequently, it is entirely up to each implementing NGO to decide whether to interact with or deploy commercial security companies.[26]

Like most NGOs in general, the Norwegian NGOs that are present in Afghanistan maintain a sceptical attitude towards association with PMSCs. At the same time, maintaining an operational presence does seem to necessitate certain compromises. Norwegian Church Aid (NCA), for example, works mainly through local implementing partner organisations and thus may not have the same needs as, for example, the Norwegian Refugee Council (NRC), which sustains an operational presence. However, NCA does not interfere with its partner organisations' decisions regarding whether or not to use PMSCs.[27] The Refugee Council, on the other hand, claims not to use PMSCs in Afghanistan because it does not regard PMSCs as representing a viable solution to the insecurity faced by the organisation (owing mainly to the fact that PMSCs are often seen as military targets and hence may draw fire onto the organisation). Instead of relying upon PMSCs, then, the NRC relies mainly on locally acquired security information and local guards who are hired individually to perform static security. The organisation has a no-weapons policy, but will nonetheless (in certain environments) deploy armed escorts. In these cases, guards are generally hired individually, and the NRC provides for the safe handling of weapons training and devises the guidelines for the use of weaponry, while admitting that maintaining clear guidelines is 'very challenging for these personnel'.[28] Beyond March 2012, however, NGOs face less freedom of choice in terms of security arrangements in Afghanistan. Through Presidential Decree 62, President Karzai has signalled that in the future private security actors will be replaced by the Afghan Public Protection Force (APPF), which is to take over the contracts previously held by private companies. A state-owned company organised under the Ministry of the Interior, the APPF is composed of quickly trained and lightly armed gunmen, many of them transferred from private companies.[29] Consultancy services can still be performed by foreign companies who obtain a license to operate as 'risk management companies'. Questions have been raised however as to whether the APPF will be able to fulfil the security needs of international reconstruction and development clients.

The 'pragmatic' Norwegian approach to PMSCs in Afghanistan is also illustrated by the fact that Norway has financed the use of PMSCs through its implementing partners in the past. In 2009 and 2010, the United Nations Office for Project Services procured security services to be used in Afghanistan from a UK company that was financed by (among others) the Norwegian government (UNOPS 2010). Similarly, Norway has also funded security details supplied to the United Nations Development Programme in Iraq in the past (UNOPS 2010). While hiring private security in such cases is the decision of the implementing partner, Norway is funding the service and as such effectively consents to the practice.

Implications

With respect to land-based PMSC services, Norway combines a rather strict domestic approach with what can be described as a hands-off approach internationally. The transnational PMSC industry and the dilemmas associated with it apparently constitute a delicate and complex political matter that Norway has so far not been willing to engage with internationally. Nonetheless, the fact that Norwegian peace and reconciliation actors directly or indirectly rely on PMSC services may have consequences for the formulation, implementation and coordination of Norwegian policies and procedures in peace and reconciliation efforts.

Formulation

The practice of directly hiring PMSCs to supply security for diplomatic personnel in Afghanistan clearly breaks with Norwegian norms, as most clearly expressed in the Act relating to guarding services. That law prohibits Norwegian companies from selling armed services abroad, services that the Norwegian ministries themselves instead buy from foreign companies abroad. Accordingly, the practice of what can be interpreted as double standards in terms of diplomatic security may represent a hollowing out of the law and give the impression that it is essentially unworkable in practice. It may also, somewhat condescendingly, signal that the standards or considerations applied to the home environment are dissimilar to those applied abroad. The practices established by Norway's foreign ministry may also set an example for other actors involved in the Norwegian peace and reconciliation effort. In fact, one NGO representative contends that the organisation concerned had sought security consultation from a PMSC after having been recommended to do so by the Norwegian embassy in the country.[30] Although many NGOs see PMSCs as a suboptimal solution for tackling their security issues, the importance of maintaining a clear detachment from military forces may in the end lead PMSCs to be preferred in violent environments. Also, the fact that several UN humanitarian agencies routinely use PMSCs for a variety of security services may also serve as an example to Norwegian NGOs (Østensen 2011). While past changes to the Norwegian policy approach to PMSCs seem to have been driven by particular events in a largely reactive manner, the power of example may also lead policymakers in Norway to look to the experiences and policies of neighbouring countries. The Swedish solution – where one Swedish private company has been integrated into the structure of the country's foreign ministry and delivers security services in a hybrid arrangement – is likely to be of interest to the Norwegian foreign ministry.[31] While such approaches are certainly less eye-catching than contracting with US or UK PMSCs, they may, as the Swedish chapter shows, pose their own challenges in terms of private authority influencing the formulation of policies from within.

Military integration into multinational force structures implies adjustments not only to accelerating technological and doctrinal developments, but also to those actors and practices that international partners rely on. Interoperability and cooperation may thus imply introduction to a civil–military division of labour to which Norwegian forces are unaccustomed, as well as the development of new practices and, according to Haaland (2007: 505), less political control over Norway's armed forces. In general, procedures concerning interaction with PMSCs and their personnel appear to be acquired through a 'learning by doing' approach. This, in turn, may foster new and informal practices that initially go unregulated, and that may or may not be legitimised reactively by amendments to regulations. Frequent interaction and cooperation with PMSCs may accordingly amount to yet another field where personnel deployed in international operations gain experience that may later have consequences for the political approach. Decision makers thus face the challenge of devising carefully considered policies and regulation that preferably precede and guide actual practices. Policies that are too restrictive, however, may prove to be impracticable in the field, which may in turn foster disregard for the political leadership. Accordingly, if policies are to be acted upon, it is important that they also reflect realities on the ground. In terms of PMSCs, a challenge for the Norwegian military leadership is thus to ensure that Norway's armed forces are able to liaise with other forces' contractors yet still have guidelines for how the civil–military division is best maintained.

The formulation of Norwegian peace and reconciliation strategies may also be influenced in direct ways by PMSCs when these are granted status as integrated and authoritative elements in allied nations' contingencies or, in the case of the Norwegian foreign ministry and NGOs, as security consultancy experts. In fact, the NGO community, while relying to a small degree on international PMSCs for armed security services, contends that the complexity of the operating environments and the multiple risks that its members face do compel them to consider more advanced advisory security services supplied by PMSCs. In the case of the NRC, the more relevant services would include information gathering and analysis,[32] while NCA for its part has felt the need for assistance in building a crisis-management capability for kidnap and ransom situations.[33] While most NGOs wish to rely primarily upon local acceptance in order to operate safely, and tend to maintain a rather independent security strategy, leaving services such as information gathering and consulting to PMSCs grants these actors political influence over how the operational environment should be understood, what constitutes threats and which solutions are necessary in order to counter them. As most PMSCs rely on former military personnel, they may project a largely militarised understanding of security and insecurity, which may have an impact upon NGO security planning and crisis management. This, in turn, may influence the criteria for when, how and where to operate in the field, and have consequences for the overall formulation of strategies. However, it should also be noted that relying on local security is not necessarily a way to avoid all these concerns; to the contrary, local security contracting may bring its very own set of dilemmas.[34]

Implementation and coordination

The discrepancy between policy and practices, combined with the reactive formulation of policies, appears to generate an environment where Norwegian state actors involved in peace and reconciliation must rely either on their own best judgements or on the example set by partners to guide their interaction with PMSC personnel. In the case of the military, this may lead to *ad hoc* arrangements concerning how NAF divisions interact and relate to PMSCs in the field. Improvised collaboration with PMSCs generally poses particular challenges regarding unclear command-and-control arrangements, determining who's who in the operating environment, avoiding friendly fire, etc. A Norwegian patrol learned some of these lessons the hard way when it failed to identify Jonathan 'Jack' Idema as a wanted civilian bounty hunter and assisted him in a Kabul house search that led him to take civilian prisoners (NRK 2005). A related problem stems from the fact that PMSC personnel at times have been unpopular among local populations owing to the use of aggressive tactics and disregard for local conditions. In Afghanistan, association with these actors may impair the ability of Norwegian forces to gain trust and support in local communities, which in turn are imperative for mission success.

Differentiation between the different actors present in Afghanistan is also a more general problem. In recent years, there has been a blurring of the distinction between warlord militias and local private security companies in Afghanistan, where the former have tried to blend into the latter category. This intensifies the 'fog of war' and, for NGOs relying on local security agents, vetting and due diligence become more crucial than ever. These challenges are, however, also felt by customers of the more established PMSCs. Working on contracts with the UN and US governmental departments, ArmorGroup, a company that used to protect the Norwegian embassy, has in the past mistakenly relied on personnel who have had warlord and Taliban associations (Committee on Armed Services 2010). These experiences demonstrate the importance of having clear routines in order to safeguard against PMSC partners having unwanted or unknown affiliations, which in turn can have an impact upon the overall international effort.

Similarly, the practice of outsourcing logistics and support functions to a company that in turn relies on a plethora of subcontracts needs close monitoring. Most convoys transporting food and equipment within or into Afghanistan need security measures. This suggests that the Norwegian forces most likely also pay for armed security as part of their contracts with Sodexo and the Afghan contractor that supplies domestic transport. The Supreme Group, a food and fuel supplier serving the US Department of State, the UK Ministry of Defence, ISAF, NATO and UN clients, and which until 2009 served the Norwegian camp in Mazar-e-Sharif, uses Compass Integrated Security Solutions for convoy security, a company that has been reported to have a host of problems related to its local personnel. Some of the problems include guards failing to show up, engaging in criminal activity or corrupt practices, reporting fake ambushes in order to sell ammunition and fuel, etc. (Committee on Armed Services 2010: 71–73). The NAF should thus increase the level of control they exercise over the subcontracting practices of their prime contractors in order to prevent the establishment of rent-seeking practices and corruption, which eventually will work against the implementation of the Norwegian peace and reconciliation efforts.

Lax Norwegian regulations regarding the commercial use of PMSCs, as embodied in both the Ship Safety and Security Act and the Voluntary Principles, inevitably allow for a great deal of self-governance on the part of commercial companies concerning their deployment of armed actors. By way of implication or association, the security practices of Norwegian commercial companies may also influence the operating environment of peace and reconciliation actors. Extensive security measures may cause risk to be transferred upon other actors, which in turn may be forced to increase their own protective measures. They may also contribute to an influx of armed elements to the operating environment, complicating peace and reconciliation efforts.

Conclusions

Private military and security companies do not officially form part of the Norwegian approach to peace and reconciliation. Nonetheless, international collaboration, along with challenging realities on the ground, has led military actors to cooperate with allied contractors and to indirectly rely on private security actors through subcontracting arrangements. The Norwegian Embassy, for its part, has become a considerable customer of PMSC services, while the NGOs that regularly partner with the Norwegian foreign ministry tend to be more reluctant to use international commercial security. The use of PMSCs by governmental agencies and partners not only counteracts the rationale embedded in domestic law, but also appears disjointed from more fundamental national norms and military traditions. While the Norwegian approach succeeds to a degree in avoiding the establishment of a 'Norwegian PMSC industry', it does little or nothing to facilitate functional control of former Norwegian defence capacities operating globally. The Norwegian approach thus appears motivated more by a desire to avoid complicity or maintain deniability than by solidarity and problem-solving incentives. The lack of Norwegian engagement in international regulative initiatives, combined with *ad hoc* practices, suggests that Norway has yet to adopt a coherent approach to PMSCs on the international level. In fact, political controversy, alliance concerns and a lack of readily available quick fixes may contribute to explaining why the tendency for key allies to increasingly use contractors for military support is yet to be reflected in Norwegian defence policy debates. Such negligence may – as this chapter has discussed – have practical and policy implications that may complicate Norwegian efforts for peace and reconciliation in Afghanistan.

Nonetheless, the exceptionality of the Norwegian approach should not be overstated. National strategies of avoidance and non-policy are not uncommon in the realms of private security and military contracting, as illustrated by other contributions to this volume. In fact, strategies of avoidance may represent the more common approach in Europe. Such policies may be adopted owing to the absence of an alternative strategy, or intentionally chosen in order to avoid drawing attention to inconsistent rhetoric and action. In the case of Norway, the approach chosen is in fact very similar to the one so far most commonly encountered within the UN system (see Østensen 2011), and this harmony of approach may in fact be interpreted as a justification of the Norwegian policy.

Finally, Norway's engagement in Afghanistan has *de facto* changed the Norwegian approach to peace and reconciliation in a way that has put the traditional 'peace nation' image under pressure. In the future, a credible concern with international solidarity arguably requires acknowledgement of new issue areas of relevance to peace and security, such as private security and military contracting and its implications. Furthermore, policies of engagement should reflect that the challenges related to the proliferation of private military and security companies require open debate, and that dealing with these challenges requires maintaining a global perspective, as opposed to a perspective concerned primarily with national political appearances.

Notes

1 This account does not aspire to be exhaustive, but rather seeks to touch upon some of the more central factors.
2 Norway is the seventh-largest financial contributor to the world organisation; see www.norway.org/aboutnorway/government-and-policy/peace/un/ (accessed 21 February 2012).
3 For an analysis of the cultural transformation, see Haaland (2010).
4 Author's translation from Norwegian. The amendment entered into force on 1 April 2011.
5 In a domestic context this would be natural, as Norwegian police officers generally operate unarmed.
6 Author's translation from Norwegian.
7 See, for example, Parliamentary Proposition 49, which states: 'It is a known fact that companies with roots in Norway have performed guarding services abroad, including in situations of armed conflict. As long as this is done in accordance with valid

regulations, it is not a problem in this context. There are, however, clearly "grey areas" and the potentials for control are limited' (Ministry of Justice and the Police 2008–09: 46). This leeway may be designed to accommodate companies like G4S, in which Norway has also invested through the Government Pension Fund Global (Hagen 2008).

8 Among companies that flagged out were Omega Group (now Espen Lee Security) and Special Intervention Group (now morphed into iKey Solutions).

9 Interview, anonymous Norwegian PMSC company manager, Bergen, August 2011.

10 What qualifies as 'military activity' is not stated explicitly, but some activities that may need approval are listed. These include a broad range of the more common PMSC services (see Ministry of Defence 2011: 19–21).

11 Telephone interview, anonymous former PMSC employees/current NAF employee, August 2011.

12 Norway is a member of the European Economic Area and as such subject to EU regulation, which takes precedence over Norwegian law.

13 Examples of newly established companies include Navigare, Polar Security International and Njord Security AS.

14 Email correspondence, Lt Col. Joar Holen Sveen, Ministry of Defence, August 2011.

15 See www.voluntaryprinciples.org/participants/ (accessed 3 January 2010).

16 Supporting nations are Latvia, the former Yugoslav Republic of Macedonia and the US.

17 Not counting the deployment of around 150 special forces personnel between April 2008 and October 2009 (Harpviken 2011: 8).

18 Specific reference will be made to two of the most important government implementing partners in Afghanistan: Norwegian Church Aid and the Norwegian Refugee Council.

19 Ronin Consulting changed its name in 2011 to Security Partner. Its main service categories include business intelligence, security consultancy and anti-piracy services.

20 Telephone and email communication, Tord Hjalmar Lien, NAMSA Coordinator, Norwegian Armed Forces, August 2011. Transport within the borders of Afghanistan – that is, the transport of bulk goods – is supplied by one local contractor and the subcontractors that it hires at any one time.

21 Interview, anonymous Norwegian PMSC company manager, Bergen, August 2011.

22 These often minor companies frequently carry out subcontracted convoy security work for other security ventures. Interview, anonymous Norwegian PMSC company manager, Bergen, August 2011.

23 Interview, anonymous NAF employee, Oslo, July 2011.

24 Interview, anonymous NAF employee, Oslo, July 2011.

25 Telephone interview, Glenn Pettersen, Global Security manager, Norwegian Refugee Council, 5 August 2011.

26 Telephone conversation, Gunvor Skancke, Assistant Director, Civil Society Department, NORAD, 7 June 2011.

27 Interview, Bjørg Mide, Senior Security Advisor, Norwegian Church Aid, Oslo, 15 June 2011.

28 Telephone interview, Glenn Pettersen, Global Security Manager, Norwegian Refugee Council, 5 August 2011.

29 See www.appf.gov.af/ (accessed 24 September 2012).

30 Interview, anonymous NGO employee, Oslo, July 2011.

31 See the chapter on Sweden in this volume.

32 Telephone interview, Glenn Pettersen, Global Security manager, Norwegian Refugee Council, 5 August 2011.

33 Interview, Bjørg Mide, Senior Security Advisor, Norwegian Church Aid, Oslo, 15 June 2011.

34 Using local gunmen or security companies may have consequences for local power structures, disturb disarmament, demobilisation and reintegration processes, fuel money into an existing conflict, divert personnel from the state security apparatus to the private market, etc.

36   Åse Gilje Østensen

References

Bolton, Matthew. 2010. *Foreign Aid and Landmine Clearance: Governance, Politics and Security in Afghanistan, Bosnia and Sudan*. London: I.B. Tauris.

Brox, Johan. 2012. 'Krigar I Privat Tjeneste' [Fighting in Private Service], *Klassekampen*, 3 March.

Chesterman, Simon. 2008. 'The Turn to Ethics: Disinvestment from Multinational Corporations for Human Rights Violations – The Case of Norway's Sovereign Wealth Fund', New York University Law and Legal Theory Working Papers no. 84, available at http://lsr.nellco.org/nyu_plltwp/84/ (accessed 6 February 2012).

Commission on Wartime Contracting in Iraq and Afghanistan. 2011. 'At What Risk? Correcting Over-Reliance on Contractors in Contingency Operations', available at www.wartimecontracting.gov/docs/CWC_InterimReport2-lowres.pdf (accessed 6 February 2012).

Committee on Armed Services. 2010. 'Inquiry into the Role and Oversight of Private Security Contractors in Afghanistan', Washington, DC: Committee on Armed Services, US Senate.

Gjerstad, Tore. 2009. 'Bak Kabuls murer', *Dagbladet*, 1 August.

Græger, Nina. 2006. *Norsk forsvarsdiskurs 1990–2005: Internasjonaliseringen av forsvaret*, doctoral thesis. Oslo: University of Oslo.

——2011. '"Home and Away"? Internationalism and Territory in the Post-1990 Norwegian Defence Discourse', *Cooperation and Conflict* 46(1): 3–20.

Haaland, Torunn Laugen. 2007. 'Participation in Peace Support Operations for Small Countries: The Case of Norway', *International Peacekeeping* 14(4): 493–509.

——2010. 'Still Homeland Defenders at Heart? Norwegian Military Culture in International Deployments', *International Peacekeeping* 17(4): 539–53.

Hagen, Erik. 2008. 'Sikkerhetsvakter ber om Oljefond-hjelp', available at: www.framtiden.no/200806054442/aktuelt/etiske-investeringer/sikkerhetsvakter-ber-om-oljefond-hjelp.html (accessed 5 March 2012).

Harpviken, Kristian Berg. 2011. 'A Peace Nation Takes Up Arms: The Norwegian Engagement in Afghanistan', PRIO Paper. Oslo: PRIO.

Hemmer, Jarl Eirik. 2008. 'Humanitærrettslige aspekter ved kommersielle aktørers deltakelse i militære operasjoner', *Pro Patria* 4: 40–2.

Hveem, Helge, Per Heum and Audun Ruud. 2000. 'Globaliseringen og norske selskapers etableringer i utlandet. Virkninger på maktfordelingen i Norge', *Makt-og demokratiutredningens rapportserie* 23. Oslo: Makt-og demokratiutredningen 1998–2003.

Inspectors General, US Department of State and US Department of Defense. 2006. *Interagency Assessment of Afghanistan Police Training and Readiness*. Washington, DC, November.

Lange, Even, Helge Pharo and Øyvind Østerud. 2009. 'Utenrikspolitikken etter den kalde krigen', in Even Lange, Helge Pharo and Øyvind Østerud, eds, *Vendepunkter i Norsk Utenrikspolitikk. Nye Internasjonale Vilkår etter Den Kalde Krigen*. Oslo: Unipub Forlag, pp. 7–26.

Leer-Salvesen, Tarjei. 2008. 'Åpner for bruk av private', *NRK*, 17 November, available at www.nrk.no/programmer/tv/brennpunkt/1.6309901 (accessed 3 June 2011).

Leira, Halvard, Axel Borchgrevink, Nina Græger, Arne Melcior, Eli Stamnes and Indra Øverland. 2007. 'Norske Selvbilder Og Norsk Utenrikspolitikk', Oslo: Norsk Utenrikspolitisk Institutt (NUPI).

Matlary, Janne Haaland. 2009. 'Kriger i kamuflasje? Profesjonen og politikken', in Håkan Edström, Nils Terje Lunde and Janne Haaland Matlary, eds, *Krigerkultur i en Fredsnasjon*. Oslo: Abstrakt Forlag, pp. 92–130.

Ministry of Defence. 2003. 'Den videre moderniseringen av Forsvaret i perioden 2005–2008. St.prp. nr 42' [Government Proposal: Future Modernisation of the Norwegian Armed Forces 2003–2004], Oslo.

——2004. 'Konsept for Offentlig Privat Partnerskap (OPP) i Forsvarssektoren' [Concept for Public–Private Partnerships in the Defence Sector], Oslo, 24 February.

——2011. 'Høringsnotat om endringer i lov om personell i Forsvaret (lov 2. juli 2004 nr. 59)' [Discussion document on changes to the defence personnel law], Oslo, 15 April.

Ministry of Finance. 2003. 'Report from the Graver Committee', available at www.regjeringen.no/en/dep/fin/tema/statens_pensjonsfond/ansvarlige-investeringer/grave-rutvalget/Report-on-ethical-guidelines.html?id=420232 (accessed 11 July 2003).

——2011. 'The Government Pension Fund', available at www.regjeringen.no/en/dep/fin/Selected-topics/the-government-pension-fund.html?id=1441 (accessed 5 May 2011).

Ministry of Foreign Affairs. 2008. *Interesser, Ansvar og Muligheter. Hovedlinjer i norsk utenrikspolitikk 2008–2009* [Report to the Storting: Interests, Responsibility and Possibilities: Main Features of Norwegian Foreign Policy 2008–2009], Stortingsmelding 15, Oslo.

——2010. 'Svar på spørsmål om private sikkerhetsselskaper i Afghanistan' [Written Question from Member of Parliament to the Minister of Foreign Affairs], Spørjetimespørsmål og svar, 10 November, available at www.regjeringen.no/mobil/nn/dep/ud/Aktuelt/Svar-til-Stortinget/Sporjetimesporsmal-og-svar/2010/afghanistan_selskaper.html?id=623424 (accessed 24 May 2011).

——2011. 'Norway's Policy of Engagement', available at www.regjeringen.no/nb/dep/ud/tema/fred_og_forsoning/norway_engagement.html?id=587985 (accessed 21 August 2011).

Ministry of Foreign Affairs, Ministry of Defence and Ministry of Finance. 2009. 'Strategi for helhetlig norsk sivil og militær innsats i Faryab-provinsen i Afghanistan' [A Strategy for Comprehensive Norwegian Civilian and Military Efforts in Faryab Province, Afghanistan], available at www.regjeringen.no/en/dep/ud/Whats-new/news/2009/faryab_strategy.html?id=566387 (accessed 12 December 2011).

Ministry of Justice and the Police. 2008–09. *Om lov om endringer i lov vaktvirksomhet.* Ot. prp. nr. 49 [Proposal from the government for the enactment of the bill relating to security guard services], available at: www.regjeringen.no/nb/dep/jd/dok/regpubl/otprp/2008–2009/otprp-nr-49-2008-2009-.html?id=551457 (accessed 20 March 2012).

——2009. *Lov om Vaktvirksomhet* [Guarding Services Act], available at www.lovdata.no/all/nl-20010105-001.html (accessed 12 June 2011).

Norwegian Broadcasting Corporation (NRK). 2005. 'Norske soldater hjalp torturist', available at www.nrk.no/nyheter/1.515590 (accessed 19 May 2011).

Norwegian Defence Staff. 2007. *Norwegian Armed Forces Joint Operational Doctrine.* Oslo: Norwegian Defence Staff.

Norwegian National Security Authority (NoNSA). 2005. 'Markedsøkonomi og sikkerhet i forsvarssektoren', NSM temahefte 2/2005. Kolsås: NoNSA.

Østensen, Åse Gilje. 2011. 'UN Use of Private Military and Security Companies: Practices and Policies', Geneva: Geneva Centre for the Democratic Control of Armed Forces.

Parliamentary Commissioner for the Armed Forces. 2010. *Nemdas befaring i Afghanistan 2010*, available at www.ombudsmann.no/befaring-i-afghanistan-2010 (accessed 3 October 2011).

Progress Party. 2008. *Fremskrittspartiet prinsipper 2009–2013* [Principles of the Progress Party], available at www.frp.no/no/Vi_mener/Prinsipprogram_2009–2013/ (accessed 17 September 2011).

Skånland, Øystein Haga. 2010. '"Norway Is a Peace Nation": A Discourse Analytic Reading of the Norwegian Peace Engagement', *Cooperation and Conflict* 45(1): 34–54.

Solstrand, Rangvald H. 2005. 'Offentlig–Privat Partnerskap i det nye forsvaret', in Janne Haaland Matlary and Øyvind Østerud, eds, *Mot et Avnasjonalisert Forsvar?* Oslo: Abstrakt Forlag, pp. 107–62.

Standing Committee on Justice. 2008. 'Innstilling til Odelstinget fra Justiskomiteen. Ort. prp. nr. 49 (2008–2009)', Innst. O. nr 116 [Recommendations to the Odelsting].

Svendsen, Jahn Arvid. 2008. 'Det Norske Forsvaret Internasjonale Operasjoner: Utfordringer i Møte med Private Militære Aktører', Masters degree dissertation. Oslo: Norwegian Defence University College.

Tvedt, Terje. 2009. *Utviklingshjelp, Utenrikspolitikk og Makt: Den Norske Modellen*. Oslo: Gyldendal Akademisk.

Ulriksen, Ståle. 2002. *Den Norske Forsvarstradisjonen: Militærmakt eller Folkeforsvar?* Oslo: Pax Forlag.

——2007. 'Brytningstid: Paradigmeskiftet i det Norske Forsvar (2001–2005)', in Bertel Heurlin, ed., *Nationen eller Verden? De Nordiske Landes Forsvar i Dag*. Copenhagen: Jurist-og Økonomforbundets Forlag, pp. 143–81.

United Nations Office for Project Services (UNOPS). 2010. 'Project Data', available at www.unops.org/english/whatwedo/Pages/ProjectData.aspx (accessed 3 October 2010).

Van Praet, Nicolas. 2010. 'Garda Scrabbels To Stay in Afghanistan', *Financial Post*, 25 August.

Wilder, Andrew. 2007. 'Cops or Robbers? The Struggle To Reform the Afghan National Police', Issue Paper Series. Kabul: Afghanistan Research and Evaluation Unit.

3 Denmark

How not *if* to outsource military services

Thomas Mandrup

> The Danish Armed Forces are in need of soldiers. For that reason it is natural to consider whether or not the Defence can make better use of the existing soldiers by making other actors do the jobs that don't necessarily have to be done by soldiers.
> (Henriksen 2008: 2)

Throughout history, the issue of private contractors and private military and security companies (PMSCs) has both inspired novelists and triggered strong emotions. That this is still the case is shown by the recent example of Ken Loach's 2011 film *Route Irish*. In this context, the contemporary Danish case is interesting, in that little debate has been raised concerning Denmark's use of private security contractors, and because PMSCs have mainly been used in limited non-lethal support functions. When in 2008 the former Danish chief of defence argued that the Danish Armed Forces were looking at increasing the number of tasks to be subcontracted to private contractors, it was for the reasons mentioned by Henriksen above, and it signalled a drastic change from what previously had been the practice within the Danish Defence. However, the announcement created only a limited public debate. In a report published in 2008, the recommendations of the Danish Institute for Military Studies concerned not whether but rather to what extent the Danish Armed Forces should make use of PMSCs (Henriksen 2008). The argument basically was that a number of national and international developments – including increased subcontracting of security tasks to private contractors at the international level, the growing number of international operations, shortages of qualified personnel, lower birth rates, the nature of international operations, budgetary shortages and cutbacks necessitating less expensive solutions, casualty sensitivity, etc. – had led to an increase in the role of and requirement for private actors. Denmark has increasingly been involved in expeditionary international operations and currently has 720 soldiers deployed in Afghanistan as part of the combined Danish effort.[1] Since 2008, debate on the issue in Denmark has barely moved forward, and a 2011 report from a Danish think-tank concluded that there was no question as to whether Denmark's defence forces should subcontract tasks to private actors. Rather, the question was how to regulate such activities, and how to secure oversight and unity of control (Moesgaard and Heiselberg 2011). Much of the commercialization of security in the Danish context has happened indirectly and as part of a slow sliding process, which explains why discussions of privatization have turned not on the question of 'if', but rather of 'how' and to what extent. Accordingly, despite the lack of debate and the associated lack of knowledge of the extent of privatization of security-related tasks in Denmark, commercial actors and mechanisms are today a common phenomenon in Denmark – and their involvement was expanded even further in 2012, when the responsibility for all maintenance, cleaning and cafeteria services at Danish military installations was privatized. This chapter will try to map out the nature and extent of the use of private contractors by the Danish Armed Forces both in general and with particular reference to the ongoing war in Afghanistan.

The state–private distinction

Since the late 1970s, privatization, subcontracting and outsourcing have gained momentum and been seen as a way for governments to increase efficiency and service delivery to their citizens, while at the same time saving resources. The mantra seems to have been why let the government do something that the private sector can do better. Such a tendency has been visible in all sectors of government, where tasks previously carried out by public employees are now performed by private contractors – for example, cleaning, maintenance and cafeteria services. As Abrahamsen and Williams (2011: 60) argue, this has resulted in a move away from the state-centred, vertical and hierarchical systems of service provision, to a more horizontally and complex system with many actors. In short, the state is moving away from doing the actual rowing and is now focusing simply on steering the ship.

Following Pierre Bourdieu's (1999) definition of the state, the central question in relation to the growth of private security at the end of the twentieth century is not whether the state is gaining or losing sovereignty owing to the increased number of private actors, but how the state's role and relationship to other actors in the field of power is shifting – and how this is reconfiguring the power of the state itself (Abrahamsen and Williams 2011: 9). However, it is essential to keep Patricia Owens' (2010) point in mind that there is no such thing as public and private security, but only violence that is made public or private – the argument being that the distinction between what is considered public and private is a construct of time and not given by nature (Colás and Mabee 2010: 9). This is also very much related to the Bourdieu-inspired argument that the boundaries between private and public actors coexist within historically shifting boundaries (Abrahamsen and Williams 2011: 111) – the point being that the relationship between public and private is not necessarily that of two opposites, but that the two often should be seen as integrated parts, where the latter is integrated as part of the state's provision of security to its citizens, which takes on different forms and historical expressions.

Another central element to this is the change, or at least perception of change, that has taken place in war and warfare since the end of the twentieth century – often referred to under the rubric of the 'new wars' (Münkler 2005; Kaldor 2007; Wulf 2005; Jung 2003; Fleming 2009). Since the end of the Cold War, different coalitions of states have engaged themselves in wars of this type as well as a range of interventions all over the world, in multidimensional military operations that have placed severe strains on their armed forces and created a growing role for contractors. As a result, the concept of what being a soldier is all about is changing. Modern-day soldiering involves much more than just being a war fighter, and the soldier operating in conflict in the early part of the twenty-first century needs to be able to perform several roles at the same time. As Wulf (2005: 1) argues, this change should be seen as partly stemming from the principle of the 'responsibility to protect' (R2P), which was introduced by the UN member states in 2001, and from the concept of nation building, which requires that military forces are capable of operating within the framework of 'coalitions of the willing' as part of an intervention force, while also functioning as a stabilization force in the next phase of a operation as part of a subsequent nation-building project. Consequently, armies of the early twenty-first century need to be flexible in order to meet the demands and expectations made of them. This has to be combined with the increased costs of modern hi-tech weapons systems and shrinking defence budgets. Adjusting to the demands of the new multifaceted and often expeditionary missions can be very expensive, and growing public–private partnership offers an apparently more affordable way to increase flexibility and response-preparedness. At the end of the twentieth century, the increasing number of military operations directed against what Western military analysts have described as asymmetric opponents has put modern armies under strain, with their being increasingly involved in what Wulf (2005) terms stability operations within police-type operations, something for which the armed forces are in general not trained. Faced with the reality of the wars in Afghanistan and Iraq, the US and the UK transformed their armed forces to improve their ability to respond to the challenges posed by operational realities on the ground (Foley *et al.* 2011). The transformation of their defence forces was based on the lessons learned during the operations in those countries. Learning from conflict is not a new phenomenon, as the writings of, say, T. H. Lawrence, David Galula and André Beaufre show. But what has shaped the current posture of the Danish Defence?

The Danish context: privatization in the Danish Armed Forces

To enable us to better understand the strategic and military culture that shapes today's Danish Armed Forces and their attitude towards the contracting of security- and military-related tasks, this section will create a framework for exploring the current roles and concepts of Denmark's defence forces in peace and reconciliation strategies within international operations. This section will therefore initially present a brief picture of the armed forces' historical and constitutional role in Denmark. The focus will be on the transformation of the armed forces, especially after the end of the Cold War, and will end with a look at Danish perceptions of Denmark's international role and how those influence the role of contractors in Danish peace and reconciliation operations.

The Danish Defence Law and the constitutional role

The Danish Defence Law (DDL) of 2001 stipulates that the purpose of the Danish Armed Forces is to contribute to the promotion of peace and security. This is to be done by pre-empting conflict and war, protecting Danish sovereignty, and by promoting peaceful development with respect for international human rights (Ministry of Defence 2001). The DDL also stresses the importance of NATO membership for Danish defence policy. The armed forces need to be organized in ways that permit them to fulfil the tasks assigned to them within the overall NATO strategy. The Danish Defence furthermore needs to have capabilities within all three branches of the armed forces in order to be able to protect Denmark's national sovereignty. In 2006, the DDL was amended, with the changes placing emphasis on the ability of the defence forces to engage in confidence-building and stability-type international operations both within and outside the NATO alliance and its geographical area of operation. The framework described in the DDL is permeated by the republican state tradition according to which defence and lethal security provision are things that should be controlled by the state. However, the increased number of international deployments, as mentioned above, has placed republican ideals of the state being the sole provider of lethal security under pressure.

The NATO membership

Since 1948, Denmark's membership of NATO has been of considerable importance for defence and security issues. The fact that Denmark, along with Norway, opted for NATO membership – rather than non-alignment like Sweden – has had an instrumental effect not only on Denmark's strategic outlook and its perception of its own international role, but also on the structuring of its armed forces. Until the 1990s, Denmark to a large extent 'piggy-backed' on its larger alliance partners and had a relatively small defence force. During the 1980s, it was renowned for its so-called footnote policies, which made Denmark a 'reluctant' member of the alliance. The end of the Cold War changed all that, however, and Denmark has since been increasingly involved in NATO's international operations. Among the reasons for this – in addition to the DDL provision about promoting international peace and stability and human rights – was the fact that Danish decision makers opted for NATO-led operations in a shift away from the large UN-mission prioritization that had dominated until the mid-1990s, and with which the Danish Armed Forces had had bad experiences going back to the operations in the Balkans. Another reason was the fact that Denmark had a number of opt-outs from its EU membership, including one in relation to defence cooperation that excluded it from participating in EU military missions.

The end of the Cold War also meant a significant change in the organization of Denmark's armed forces, since their role also changed. The 2001/06 DDL emphasizes the shift to an international expeditionary role. This has had a dramatic effect on the structure of the Danish Defence. Before the end of the Cold War, Denmark's armed forces had been structured around the capacity to stave off the threats posed by the neighbouring Warsaw Pact countries and therefore had a relatively large armoured capacity, air-defence systems and near-coast maritime capabilities. The organizational structure was based around a relatively small permanent force, with a large mobilization capability based on conscription. As a result of the most recent reforms, the Danish Defence is now increasingly professionalized and expeditionary, while the territorial defence role has been scaled down. However, though the conscription system has been reformed, it has been retained for political and recruitment purposes, and Danish politicians have so far refrained from basing the country's armed forces exclusively on professional soldiers.

The Danish navy has been transformed into an expeditionary force with blue-water capacity, something it did not have during the Cold War years. This means that the number of ships has decreased, but the ships themselves have become bigger and have an increased span of operation. This change was based on lessons learned from the 1990s, when the navy was sent into operations in the Persian Gulf and the Mediterranean, while the need for close-water protection was reduced significantly. The transformation means that Denmark now has ships in international operations such as NATO's anti-piracy operation off the coast of the Horn of Africa, and can provide strategic sealift capability for NATO.

The Danish army has also had to adapt to the new types of operations, and especially the increased number of international deployments. The lessons learned from the operations in Balkans in the 1990s meant that the army had to change its structure, training and modus operandi. During the Cold War, the army had been structured around a large mobilization force, with a relatively large armoured capacity. The army, the main recipient of conscripted soldiers within the Danish Armed Forces, altered its training format, reduced the time of military service to three months, and focused on using this as a means of preparing and recruiting soldiers for international operations. In terms of organization, international operations placed a heavy burden on Denmark's army, which had to alter its inventory to improve its ability to conduct the types of operation that it was being expected by the politicians to carry out and to replace its equipment more frequently than it had budgeted for. The Danish army is today a more professional, mobile, and flexible force than it was at the end of the Cold War. Its focus is on the ability to conduct complex, counterinsurgency operations as part of so-called nation-building projects. Until the end of the Cold War, the army's international operational experience stemmed from Chapter VI UN operations like the one in Cyprus.

The end of the Cold War also constituted a challenge for Denmark's air force, which for a large part also had been focused on territorial-defence capabilities. It had relatively large fighter-wing and ground-to-air-missile capabilities, which were of little or no use in the operations the air force was now being asked to undertake. Air-defence systems such as the HAWK battery were scrapped, and the number of jet fighters was reduced. One of the challenges facing the Danish Air Force has been the need for strategic lift capability, as this was previously very limited.

The problem for the Danish Defence has been the existence of a discrepancy between the current level of activities, force structure, and tasks undertaken by the armed forces, on the one hand, and the available budget, on the other. The budget is to be cut from €3.12 billion in 2011 to €2.76 billion by 2015 (Ministry of Defence 2012). This mismatch is therefore going to become even bigger in the coming years and could open for a new market for private contractors. Another element in the Danish Defence's transformation has been an increased professionalization of the armed forces, which – as Krahmann argues elsewhere in this volume in relation to Germany – has also led to an increase in the use of contractors through privatizations and outsourcing.

Privatization within the armed forces

Internally within the Danish Defence, the 2008 decision to increasingly look into contracting was merely seen as an integrated element in a process that was already under way. Since the 1980s, the Danish Defence had increasingly subcontracted private actors to take care of a whole string of what might be considered softer tasks, such as logistics and support functions. The reality in Danish international operations is that a large portion of such softer tasks are today conducted by commercial actors. Transport to and from Afghanistan is carried out by commercial airlines; the camps are run and serviced by private contractors; and some protection tasks have been subcontracted to a PMSC that is responsible for the protection of civilian development workers, etc. The argumentation used by the Danish Ministry of Defence has predominantly been of both a practical and an economic nature, involving claims, for instance, that private actors would be less expensive than their military counterparts, that privatization would release military resources for the hard military tasks, and that it was impossible to act differently owing to the requirements of the alliance with larger partners like the US and the UK. The process has therefore been driven both by the neoliberal privatization tendencies that have affected the entire public sector and by the heavy burden put on the armed forces owing to the war efforts in both Iraq and Afghanistan. The Danish Ministry of Defence (2011) estimates that the operations in Afghanistan cost the armed forces an estimated €152,311 million per year. In addition to this, the global financial crisis has resulted in proposed and actual budget cuts that have meant that Denmark and the other NATO members are looking for alternative ways of organizing the future defence forces, including burden- and capability-sharing and the use of public–private partnerships. In this way, commercialization of security in NATO also affects Denmark, as also illustrated by the debate on capability sharing and smart defence. The Danish Defence is already using a wide range of private contractors for a wide range of

Table 3.1 Danish defence expenditure for private contractors used in international operations 2003–07 (in € million)

Task	2003	2004	2005	2006	2007
Transport	7.58	6.84	8.51	15.92	20.99
Food services	1.80	2.68	3.75	3.69	2.16
Construction	0.0	0.91	0.11	0.32	0.20
Maintenance	1.04	0.14	0.24	0.59	0.55
Other	1.76	0.28	0.37	0.85	1.23
Total	12.26	10.85	12.98	20.99	25.14

Source: Rigsrevisionen (2008)

different tasks. In 2008, the Auditor of the State Accounts conducted a study of the use of private contractors, which showed that Denmark was following an international trend in terms of subcontracting an increasing number of tasks to private actors, with the money spent on contractors increasing from €12.26 million in 2003 to €25.21million in 2007 – an increase of more than 100 per cent (Rigsrevisionen 2008).

What is noticeable in the statistics is that the increase is almost exclusively tied to increased costs of transport to the wars in Iraq and Afghanistan. As noted in the report, 83.5 per cent of the expenses used on private contracts in 2007 went on transport (Rigsrevisionen 2008: 3). However, this shows that Denmark has been more reluctant to use private contractors for lethal tasks, and has more or less exclusively used contractors for logistical tasks conducted in support of its military efforts. In 2008, G4S was hired to protect Danish development officers working in Helmand province in Afghanistan. Yet, transport remains the area where the most tasks have been subcontracted to private contractors. Here, two major strategic transport projects stand out: the so-called Sea and Air Ark projects. These were established in an attempt to cover Danish – and NATO – shortfalls within the area of strategic transport by sea and air, constituting important elements in the new expeditionary role played by the Danish Armed Forces. The contracting of private companies to perform these tasks was also seen as a way of generating income, thereby reducing the costs involved in maintaining a strategic transport capability.

The contract with DFDS – the Sea Ark Project

> The ARK project aims to avoid the overheating of the charter rates on the spot market in times of crises through bilateral Technical Arrangements, thereby offering ARK ships to NATO and allied nations at cost-price. ... The ARK project has served as a kick starter for the project and will hopefully function as a showcase for other nations to copy.
>
> (Royal Danish Navy 2011)

In 2002, the Danish Armed Forces signed a strategic transport agreement with the Danish shipping line DFDS, in an arrangement known as the Ark Project.[2]

This was the result of the signing of a statement of intent at the NATO summit in Prague earlier that year, regarding access to future sealift capabilities for the alliance. The aim of the Ark Project was – and still is – to establish a strategic sealift capability that would be permanently available to NATO members, coalition partners, and NGOs. The Danish Defence Commission concluded in 2008 that the Ark Project was a direct result of the increased Danish involvement in international operations in, for instance, Afghanistan and Iraq, which called for expanded transport capabilities (Forsvarskommisionen 2008). The strategic transport capability was seen by the Commission as an essential part of the transformation of Denmark's defence forces into a deployable and expeditionary unit.

The Ark Project's primary task has been to provide a strategic sealift capability for NATO's Response Force, the aim being to ensure that such a capacity was always available to the alliance and its member states. The Ark Project has furthermore been included in the UN's Military and Civilian Defence Assets (MCDA) database as a potential Danish contribution (Forsvarskommisionen 2008: 131). For the Danish Defence, it was therefore seen as part of the efforts to enable Denmark to contribute to international operations undertaken primarily by NATO, but also by other organizations such as the UN and the African Union.

The Ark Project – in detail

The Ark Project was launched in 2003, and the Danish Defence in the first phase charted two so-called roll-on/roll-off ships on a full-time basis. This model ensured that Denmark could provide the NATO alliance with affordable sealift capacity, circumventing the price-inflated commercial market in times of crisis. Surplus capacity was to be sold on the commercial shipping market. The exact figures are unavailable owing to commercial confidentiality clauses, but the Danish Defence claims that the model has been a success and generated an income. The project has come to function as a 'parastatal' shipping line based on a public–private partnership, in many ways functioning in 'direct' competition with the private shipping industry. The charter agreement with DFDS means that the ships are manned and run by the shipping company. However, DFDS also has the responsibility for selling surplus capacity on the private shipping market. This means that the company has to sell a capacity on the private market for which it already has received a full-time charter payment, and in competition with its own ships, while there are no contractual terms to ensure that DFDS does not prioritize its own ships first. The Danish Defence argues that so far this has not been a problem. In November 2006, the Ark Project was expanded via a partnership with Germany's armed forces from two to four vessels – among other things to accommodate Germany's needs for strategic sealift facilities. The project is today controlled and run by a joint German–Danish Administration Board, with income and costs shared by the two nations (Royal Danish Navy 2011). A whole range of NATO partners have made use of the Ark Project's services, which they hire on a commercial basis, and the roll-on/roll-off capability has been committed to NATO until the year 2021.

One of the arguments for this public–private model was that it would make it possible to avoid the inflated prices that defence forces often experience during time of crisis and in emergencies. In one sense, the question of commercialization is in this case turned upside down, with a parastatal/public company moving into the field of private contractors – in direct competition with them. However, another element is that the defence forces are increasingly entering into partnerships with private companies through the signing of long-term joint-venture framework contracts – in the case of the Ark Project for five to ten years. This could be a model for future cooperation between private industry and the Danish Defence. The arms industry in general is looking for ways of securing public funding in an increasingly more competitive arms market. By signing long-term contracts with government institutions like the Danish Defence, corporations secure long-term income. This type of private–public relationship is an example of what was described above, where the state and the private sector should not be seen as two opposites, but where the latter is something that is an integrated part of the state's service delivery. The commercial security sector, including the arms industry, is increasingly looking for ways of expanding its share of the defence budget. One way of doing this involves the signing of long-term lease agreements with the defence forces – for instance, for transport ships, trucks, or even fighter planes. This makes it possible for the armed forces to transfer responsibility for maintenance away from themselves and over to the private sector. The idea is that the armed forces would be guaranteed functioning military equipment at all times, without having to establish a large support structure. The relative success of the Sea Ark project has meant that the Danish Defence has sought to apply the same model to other capabilities in an attempt to reduce transport costs for international operations and as a way of filling out NATO capability shortfalls, creating a useful niche role for Denmark within the alliance.

The Air Ark Project

Where the Sea Ark project in many ways has been successful, the Danish Air Force's attempt to apply the public–private charter model to air transport has been less so. From 2004, Denmark signed up for the so-called NATO Prague Capability Commitments (PCC), which in addition to a naval component also includes an airlift capability dimension. Initially, Denmark took part in the joint NATO Strategic Airlift Capability Project (SAC), but withdrew from this project in December 2007.[3] Denmark then opted for a public–private charter model using civilian aircraft (Forsvarsudvalget 2008). In 2008, a proposal was tabled in the Parliamentary Defence Committee for a civilian lease that was estimated to cost €22.17 million per year from 2009 to 2012 – a total of €88.67 million. The Ministry of Defence argued that this would turn out to be a less-expensive solution for the armed forces, which had suffered from increasing costs for strategic airlifts, especially within the context of the operations in Afghanistan.

The cost of civilian charters decreased from €8.34 million in the first six months of 2010 to €3.64 million in the first half of 2011. However, the full-time

Table 3.2 Cost of commercial strategic transport in Denmark 2005–08

Year	Cost in € million of chartered commercial strategic transport
2005	13.97
2006	18.40
2007	20.55
2008	28.21

Source: Forsvarsudvalget (2008)

charter agreement – the Air Ark project – was in effect at a cost of €22.17 million per year. The total cost of private charters therefore seems to be at least €28.94 million for the financial year 2011, and even more for 2010.

The contract

The Danish Parliament had agreed to the proposals from the Ministry of Defence for the creation of the Air Ark project by a large majority. A consortium consisting of Adagold Aviation and Inversija Ltd. won the tender, while the broker service was given to Avico, a British-based company.[4] Denmark signed a full-time charter on what is known as a 'wet lease' agreement for two IL-76 transport aircraft and one Boeing 337 passenger jet.[5] At the time of the signing of the agreement, it was estimated that the excess capacity for the aircraft of some 3,500–4,000 flying hours per year would be relatively easy to sell to other members of the NATO alliance, because the two IL-76s were the only ones of their kind within the alliance. And, it was estimated that if the armed forces managed to sell just 50 per cent of this excess capacity, this would save the Danish Defence hundreds of millions of US dollars over the four-year period in question (Finance Committee 2008–09).[6] However, the Air Ark project has proven problematic, and among other things the choice of partners led to questions, criticism and ultimately a lawsuit.

What has the net result been – a question of delivery and resources

The PMSC industry in general has been criticized over many different issues in connection with its increased role and involvement in the international operations in, for instance, Iraq, but especially in relation to Afghanistan. These problems are related to issues regarding regulation (or otherwise) of PMSC activities, the legality of their operations, the de facto impunity of contractors, the discipline and nature of their employees, etc. Many of these issues were raised when Adagold was awarded the contract following a competition that included Danish airline Cimber Sterling. The Danish company accused the Adagold bid of being flawed in several ways that would ultimately jeopardize the safety of Danish military personnel. According to Cimber, Adagold and its Latvian partner had been involved in illegal activities in Africa and the transport of prisoners for the

CIA. Furthermore, it was argued that since the pilots used by Adagold were not Danish nationals, they could not get a Danish security clearance, which would constitute a security risk. Finally, it was claimed that since the Adagold bid came from a relatively small contactor, there was a greater risk of economic vulnerability that would leave it unable to fulfil the contract (Public Tender Complaints Office 2009). All these claims were rejected by both the Defence Command and the Adagold consortium, and to a certain extent it seems that Cimber was seeking to use all means available to secure for itself a very lucrative contract. However, the contract with Adagold has turned out be problematic for a number of other reasons. The two IL-76 planes were civilian chartered planes and operated under civilian air-traffic regulations, and they were not exempted from this despite the fact that they were used for military transports. This meant that when the European Aviation Safety Agency conducted an inspection in late 2009, its inspectors found several breaches of security and retracted the air-worthiness certificate, which created much debate and critique in Denmark. Much of the critique can to a certain extent be linked back to the agenda pushed by Cimber, which lobbied heavily in parliament to secure political support.

It is difficult to estimate how successful this particular public–private arrangement has been in terms of costs and earnings, etc. The main reason for this is that the arrangement is covered by a commercial confidentiality clause, which makes it more or less impossible to access the relevant data. The Ministry of Defence argues that the lease process has had some initial problems, but is now working well. The Defence Command has taken a more critical view on the matter, arguing that it has turned out to be difficult to sell the excess flight capacity on the private spot market. As noted above, it was suggested in a reply to the Parliamentary Finance Committee that the Danish Defence would easily be able to sell at least 50 per cent of the flight capacity on the private market or to NATO partners, saving a figure of hundreds of millions of euros over a four-year period (Finance Committee 2008–09). This turned out to be far from the case, and in 2010 only 100 hours were sold to NATO partners – while the Defence Command had expected to sell at least between 1,500 and 2,000 per year (Kristensen 2011). Part of the reason for this has been that it proved impossible to charter a civilian aircraft without protection to several of Denmark's closest allies, including the Netherlands and the UK. Unlike Denmark, these countries do not permit such flights into Afghanistan. The choice of broker also turned out to be problematic, since the cooperation between Adagold and Avico proved difficult, which hindered efforts to sell the excess capacity on the private spot market. Prices for airlift capacity have furthermore decreased, making the existing contract more expensive than it was initially thought would be the case. In late 2011, the Defence Command began an evaluation of the Air Ark project in order to decide on its future. It is expected that the total costs for a new contract will go down, and that the demands for usability to partners will increase. An important element in this calculation is that Denmark expects to have withdrawn its troops from Afghanistan by 2014, which will reduce the need for and thereby the costs of strategic airlifts significantly.

The Danish strategy for Afghanistan

On the website of the Danish Ministry of Foreign Affairs (2011), it is stated that the main objective of the Danish engagement in Afghanistan is help secure national, regional and international security by ensuring that the country does not once more become a safe haven for terrorism. In addition, the Danish engagement should support the creation of a stable and self-sustaining Afghanistan, based on international human rights principles. The main argument for Danish involvement in the multinational international operation has from the beginning been the need to combat threats to national security from international terrorism. In the summer of 2008, the Danish government launched its strategy for Afghanistan for 2008–12, which was estimated would cost a total of €137 million per year (Udenrigsministeriet 2011). The ambition of the strategy was to help reach the five stages of achievement highlighted by NATO and announced in 2003, which would ideally create a basis upon which it would be possible to withdraw international military combat forces from Afghanistan, leaving the responsibility for security to the national security forces. The objective of the Danish strategy was closely tied to the increased focus within the NATO alliance on stability and crisis-management type operations.[7] The main ambition was to extend and increase the Afghan government's authority to the whole of the country as a means of neutralizing the Taliban. As a follow-up to the strategy, in February 2011 the Danish government launched a joint foreign and defence ministry plan, the Helmand Plan 2011–12, which would continue along the lines set out in the previous strategy but sought to incorporate the goal, decided at the political level, that Denmark would withdraw the last of its combat troops by 2014 (Forsvarsministeriet 2011). In the new plan, the focus was on scaling down combat operations, while scaling up efforts to enable the Afghan security forces to take over responsibility for the provision of security – for example, via capacity-building operations and training. This of course put pressure on the Danish Armed Forces, because these types of operations require a much more comprehensive and multifaceted approach than narrow military operations. Both the NATO alliance and its individual member states in general have been slow in reforming and adjusting to the new operational circumstances. The private sector has been a useful tool in this regard, in the sense that it can provide specialized functions and services as integrated elements of the combined effort. However, the use of PMSCs has generally been on the initiative of individual states, primarily the US and the UK, while the other smaller members have predominantly 'privatized indirectly' via their partnerships with the bigger partners. The smaller members buy services from the bigger members of the alliance, services that in many cases have been subcontracted to PMSCs. In the case of Denmark, this means that in the joint bases in Afghanistan – for instance, Camp Bastian – the UK is running the camp, while Denmark pays rent to the UK for its use of the facilities. This means that it is not Denmark that has contracted a PMSC for camp facilities, but Britain. However, in the case of softer tasks, the Danish foreign ministry is making use of a number of NGO and private companies to conduct development and reconstruction tasks. The Danish Demining Group, a subsidiary of the Danish Refugee Council, is working on a large contract to clear the countryside of mines and unexploded ordnance – which is technically a military task (Forsvarsministeriet 2011).[8] However, the Ministry of Foreign Affairs has subcontracted the responsibility for security at the Danish Embassy to a private contractor, a task that was previously managed by Danish special forces and national intelligence services. The use of private security consultants by the Ministry of Foreign Affairs is widespread and has been criticized as an expensive and unnecessary use of resources, since the same services can be provided by the intelligence services. The private sector, however, offers the advantage that service providers need only be paid for the duration of their contracts, which means that public institutions do not have to create a permanent capacity – which may ultimately turn out to be more expensive. Furthermore, aid workers often prefer to receive security from private contractors rather than uniformed military units, which they believe attract unwanted attention.

In the political debate over the Afghanistan mission, the focus was upon reducing the military effort while at the same time increasing the civilian reconstruction and development activities. Consequently, the mission resulted in a number of new tasks for the Danish Armed Forces, shifting from predominantly regular war fighting against a so-called asymmetrical enemy to a focus on increased stability operations and a scaled reduction and handing over of responsibility for security to local security forces. The decision to withdraw the Danish forces by 2014 has increased the urgency of the effective transfer of security, and therefore the need for training missions to prepare local forces for this task.

Danish reliance on PMSCs: the case of Afghanistan

As shown above, Denmark is using contractors to handle a number of the logistical tasks related to the Danish Defence's increased expeditionary role. However, in the Afghan theatre the picture is more mixed. In Denmark's Afghanistan strategy for 2008–12, the main objectives for the Danish involvement were stated as being increasing the capacity of the Afghan security forces, state building, expanding access to education, and the development and enhancement of economic growth in Afghanistan's formal economic sectors (Ministry of Defence 2008). Within the strategy, it was stressed that the Danish engagement would be based on a joint effort between various government departments – comprehensiveness being the keyword and overarching principle. The aim was to increase the national capacity within Afghanistan to enable a scaling down of the Danish effort. Consequently, the Danish military contingent, as part of Task Force Helmand, has a large area of responsibility and a diverse portfolio of tasks that it has to undertake. To reduce the number of these tasks, it was decided that security provision for Provincial Reconstruction Team (PRT) Lashkar Gah[9] should as far as possible be subcontracted. Accordingly, in late 2008, the Danish Ministry of Defence announced that it had signed a contract with UK-based PMSC Armor Group International (AGI)[10] to handle the protection of the

Danish civilian development and reconstruction workers in Afghanistan (Rottbøll 2008). The role of PRT Lashkar Gah is seen as being of vital importance, since the activities of the civilian advisers sent out by Denmark's Ministry of Foreign Affairs are seen as key to the success of the reconstruction of Afghan society. AGI was given the responsibility for facilitating this by providing necessary protection for the civilian advisers, enabling freedom of movement for the civilian experts (Ministry of Defence 2008).

By doing this, the Danish government moved in the same direction as a whole range of other Western governments active in the Afghan theatre. Søren Gade, Denmark's minister of defence at the time, described the development as an unproblematic way of relieving the regular army of some of its tasks, enabling it to focus on the military tasks at hand. The Danish Armed Forces would use the same contractor as their UK allies, and British judicial experts would make sure that the private contractors did not operate in ways that would contravene either Danish interests or international law. That said, G4S has worked for the Danish government since 2008, and so far the service record of the company and its employees has been unproblematic, and the contract between the Danish Ministry of Foreign Affairs and the British Foreign and Commonwealth Office was rene-gotiated and extended in late 2011. However, the Danish case has also shown that arguments advanced in favour of the private sector often fail to take into account the total costs of a private contract. When, for instance, the Ministry of Foreign Affairs signs a contract with NIRAS for development tasks in Afghanistan, the costs of security and protection are not paid for out of the foreign ministry's budget, but are covered by the Ministry of Defence. This was stated clearly in Parliamentary Decision B24 from December 2008, which argued that the costs for the provision of security should be covered by the special Section 12 account in the Ministry of Defence (Parliament 2008). This means that the Danish foreign ministry negotiates a contract with the UK Foreign and Commonwealth Office, which has a contract with G4S, and then passes the costs of that contract onto the Danish defence ministry. Denmark is therefore buying this service via the UK, which acts as a go-between, and this also means that it is Britain that has the responsibility for oversight over G4S. The costs of the contract are not publicly accessible, because the agreements are protected by a commercial-confidentiality clause, something that is very common in the PMSC industry (Greyling 2010). However, the contract is based on a flat rate based on the number of individuals, housing units, office facilities, etc., that need protection, and is paid on a monthly basis.

Yet, the subcontracting of potentially lethal security tasks should also be understood as part of an international tendency, in which defence forces around the globe – in different forms and for different reasons – are increasingly sub-contracting tasks to private contractors. These private actors have become increasingly important in the different phases of international operations, both as integrated parts of stabilization operations and in the reconstruction efforts that follow. The International Stability Operations Association (ISOA) – the US-based PMSC industry trade organization – argues that this public–private partnership has reached a level where modern militaries can no longer function without private contractors. Nevertheless, such arrangements are also an expensive solution, one that the British newspaper *The Times* in 2008 estimated costs US $1 million per aid worker in Afghanistan owing to the security problems faced in that country (Evan 2008). Whether US $1 million is a large figure depends on the way this is measured, because the figure needs to be compared to the costs of regular army units providing the same service. The perception within the Danish Ministry of Defence was that it was actually less expensive to buy the protection service from G4S than to have to establish and maintain the appropriate capacity within the Danish Defence itself. The increased focus within Denmark's Afghanistan strategy on reconstruction, training, capacity building, and transfer of responsibility to local security institutions and authorities has resulted in a number of new tasks, such as training missions (especially for the Afghan police) and development projects (Ministry of Defence 2008). Denmark's foreign and defence ministries are currently starting to look into what is going to happen when the 2012 strategy for Afghanistan comes to an end. Currently, most of the Danish military efforts are concentrated in and around the town of Gharesk, while the development projects have a wider geographical span. However, the Danish military effort is in the process of being transformed and will eventually be phased out by 2014, which means that future activities might be more spread out geographically than they are today. One of the challenges with this is how to secure and protect an increasing number of development workers geographically spread out over a larger operational area. One of the options examined might be to subcontract responsibility to PMSCs, as the US State Department is doing in Iraq, though of course on a smaller scale.

Conclusion

In the introduction to this article, it was argued that the use of private contractors by the Danish Defence was by many considered not a question of 'if' but rather one of 'to what extent'. This was based on the underlying neoliberal assumption that private contractors should be a less expensive and more flexible option than the armed forces themselves. The Danish Armed Forces are faced with increasingly complex and expensive expeditionary operations – and from 2013 shrinking budgets. The need to reform the Danish Defence is therefore pressing if it is to meet the challenges envisioned by politicians, who continue to suggest that it will be possible to maintain an efficient and effective defence force while using fewer resources than is the case today.

This chapter has shown that there is widespread use of private contractors within the Danish Defence, though primarily in support functions and for softer tasks. The one exception is the contract with G4S in Afghanistan, which in reality is not a Danish contract since it concerns a service being bought from the British partner. This also points to an important finding, which is that when Denmark uses private contractors as part of its military involvement on the ground in Afghanistan, it is primarily in an indirect form – that is, it involves the purchase of a given service from one of the larger alliance partners. This is the case in relation to camp facilities and support, camp protection, protection of development workers in the field, etc. All tasks that have a more military nature, including training missions, are performed by the forces of the Danish Defence themselves. That said, this study has also shown that when it comes to softer tasks, such as logistics and transport, the Danish Defence has integrated private contractors and thereby boosted its own capacity in an attempt to meet the challenges posed by international operations. As argued by Abrahamsen and Williams (2011), private contractors are not something that is viewed as being outside the state and solely in the private sphere, but something that is integrated into the state's attempts to produce the needed capabilities to tackle the challenges at hand. This has happened within a special Danish model, whereby the state – i.e. the Danish Armed Forces – in principle moves into the private market and competes with private industry by selling its excess capacity on the private market. The public sphere is therefore expanding into the private sphere via public–private partnership. In theory, this model should allow the forces of the Danish Defence to possess capabilities that would otherwise lie outside the range of their ordinary and shrinking budgets. The public–private partnership is also valuable in that it enables Denmark to provide its NATO partners with a strategic transport capability, something that is much needed within the alliance. However, the public–private partnership model has had mixed results. While the Sea Ark Project has turned out to be a success, building on a functioning bi-national partnership between Denmark, Germany, and the DFDS shipping line, the Air Ark project has been problematic and has failed to deliver what was predicted by the Danish Defence to the Danish Parliament's financial oversight committee in 2008.

The Sea Ark Project has been a success in the sense that it provides the Danish Defence forces with a strategic sealift capability, not just for national use but also – more importantly – for use within NATO. Through this capability, Denmark fills a critical NATO shortfall, something that is of great practical and political value to Denmark – that is, Denmark provides something that its alliance members need. Problems related to the Sea Ark Project are linked to the contract between the armed forces and the shipping line, where the latter has a dual function in terms of both providing the full-time charter while also being responsible for selling excess capability on the private spot market for shipping. Given that the shipping industry has been hard hit by the global financial crisis, this seems to be a potentially dangerous construction filled with conflicting interests. The Air Ark Project has been problematic in a number of ways. Planes have been grounded for various periods of time, while the contractors have been unable to live up to the initial contractual agreement that they should be able to transport equipment and passengers at the same time. Furthermore, owing to the levels of noise and pollution caused by the planes, they are allowed to land at only a very limited number of airfields in Europe, which of course devalues their usefulness. Combined with the fact that the chartered aircrafts do not have self-protection, which means that a number of partners have been unwilling or unable to use the flights for transport to Afghanistan, this means that the Danish Defence has been unable to sell its excess capability either to NATO partners or on the private spot market. The Danish Parliament's financial oversight committee was promised that this model would make it possible to save resources through the sale of excess capacity, which has turned out not to be the case. Part of the problem is that the market for the Air Ark has been much smaller than that for the Sea Ark. Denmark also opted for a national model without international partners, instead of a partnership with one or more international partners. The experience from the Air Ark Project shows that it has so far not been possible to find a public–private partnership model for strategic airlift capacity that can fulfil the criteria mentioned above. Another lesson from the Air Ark Project is that the choice of partners is critical. The experiences from the two cases show that it cannot be assumed that subcontracting to private contractors necessarily saves money, because if the armed forces fail to sell excess capability they will be stuck with a full-time capability for which they have no use. This might indicate that small countries like Denmark should not enter into public–private partnerships by themselves, but should seek rather to share a capability and thereby reduce the risks of financial losses.

Notes

1 In addition to its military contribution, in 2011 Denmark contributed 20 police officers.
2 Interestingly enough, only one shipping line bid on the navy's tender.
3 In the SAC project, member countries buy a share of flying time in three military aircraft. However, the Danish Ministry of Defence concluded that the SAC provided a service that was too expensive per flying hour and too advanced in terms of the capabilities needed by the Danish Defence.
4 The four-year airlift contract was estimated as having a value of around €93.12 million, while the broker contract had a value of around €2.43 million EUR (Public Tenders Complaint Office 2009).
5 Since the initial signing of the contract, Adagold has signed a contract with a company called Maximus, increasing the number of available planes to five. This makes service delivery more secure in the event that one plane is grounded.
6 Furthermore, the full-time charter meant that Adagold would be responsible for maintenance, pilots, etc., relieving the Danish Defence of those responsibilities.
7 At the Lisbon NATO summit in 2010, it was decided that NATO needed a new strategy and future focus should be on collective defence, cooperative security and conflict management. The three priorities were also the central point of the new NATO strategic concept, which was made public in 2011.
8 In 2010, the budget for development aid to Afghanistan was €53.79 million, of which €5.86 million was allocated via NGOs (Udenrigsministeriet 2011).
9 PRT Laskhar Gah is a joint UK, Danish, and Estonian development team responsible for different types of capacity building at the regional and local levels.
10 In March 2008, ArmorGroup was bought by the British–Danish international security giant G4S for £43 million. The earnings of PMSCs in general had been negatively influenced by the decline of the Iraqi market for private security.

References

Abrahamsen, Rita and Williams, Michael C. 2011. *Security Beyond the State: Private Security in International Politics*. Cambridge: Cambridge University Press.

Bourdieu, Pierre. 1999. 'Rethinking the State: Genesis and Structure of the Bureaucratic Field', in Georg Steinmetz, ed., *State/Culture: Stateformation after the Cultural Turn*. Ithaca, NY and London: Cornell University Press, pp. 53–76.

Colás, Alejandro and Mabee, Bryan. 2010. *Mercenaries, Pirates, Bandits and Empires: Private Violence in the Historical Context*. London: Hurst & Company.

Defence Commission (Forsvarskommisionen). 2008. *Forsvarskommisionen af 2008 beretning*. Copenhagen: Ministry of Defence.

Defence Committee (Forsvarsudvalget). 2008. *FOU alm. del – Bilag 96 – Offentlig*, J.nr.: 4.kt. 2008/006075. Copenhagen: Parliament.

Evan, Michael. 2008. 'Analysis: growing threat to foreign aid staff'. *The Times*, 20 October.

Finance Committee (Finansudvalget). 2008–09. *Endeligt svar på § 12 spørgsmål 3', Aktstk. 117*. Copenhagen: Parliament.

Fleming, Colin M. 2009. 'New or Old Wars? Debating a Clusewitzian Future'. *The Journal of Strategic Studies* 32(2), April: 213–241.

Foley, Robert T., Griffin, Stuart and McCartny, Helen. 2011. '"Transformation in contact": learning the lessons of modern war'. *International Affairs* 87(2), March: 253–270.

Greyling, Chris. 2010. *President, Pan-African Security Association*. 7 December. Cape Town: T. Mandrup, Interviewer.

Henriksen, Anders. 2008. *Principper for pragmatisme: Perspektiver for forsvarets brug af Private Militære Firmaer*. København: Dansk Institut for Militære Studier.

Jung, Dietrich (eds). 2003. *Shadow Globalization, Ethinic Conflict and New Wars: A political Economy of Intra-state war*. London and New York: Routledge.

Kaldor, Mary. 2007. *New and Old Wars*. Stanford, CA: Stanford University Press.

Kristensen, Henrik. 2011. *Major*, Danish Defence Command. 5 October. Copenhagen: T. Mandrup, Interviewer.

Ministry of Defence (Forsvarsministeriet). 2001. *Lov om forsvarets formål, opgaver og organisation m.v.*, LOV nr 122. 27 February. Copenhagen: Ministry of Defence.

—— 2006. *Lov om ændring af lov om forsvarets formål, opgaver*, LOV nr 568. 9 June. Copenhagen.

—— 2008. *Afghanistanstrategien 2008–2012*. Copenhagen: Ministry of Defence.

—— 2011. *Helmand-Planen 2011–2012*. Copenhagen: Ministry of Defence.

—— 2011. *Notat – Udviklingen i Forsvarsbudgettet i Danmark. Faktaark 2020*. Copenhagen: Ministry of Defence.

—— 2012. *Defence Expenditure*. Version of 26 January, available at www.fmn.dk/eng/all-about/Pages/Defenceexpenditure.aspx (accessed 28 January 2012).

Ministry of Foreign Affairs. 2011. 'Den Danske Indsats i Afghanistan', version of 25 March, available at www.afghanistan.um.dk/da/menu/IndsatsenIAfghanistan/ (accessed 1 February 2012).

Ministry of Foreign Affairs (Udenrigsministeriet). 2011. *Fordeling af Danmarks Genopbygnings-bistand til Afghanistan i 2010*. Version of January 2012, available at www.afghanistan.um. dk/da/menu/Medier/TalOgGrafik/ (accessed 28 January 2012).

Moesgaard, Christa and Heiselberg, Stine. 2011. 'Private Military Companies in Counter-Insurgency Operations', DIIS Policy Brief. Copenhagen: DIIS.

Münkler, Herfried. 2005. *The New Wars*. Cambridge: Polity.

Office of the Auditor General (Rigsrevisionen). 2008. *Notat til Statsrevisorerne om forsvarets brug af private aktører i internationale operationer*. København: Rigsrevisionen.

Owen, Patricia. 2010. 'Distinctions, Distinctions. "Public" and "Private" Force?' in Alex Colás and Brian Mabee, eds., *Mercenaries, Pirates, Bandits and Empires: Private violence in the Historical Context*, London: Hurst & Company, pp. 15-32.

Parliament (Folketinget). 2008. 'Forslag til folketingsbeslutning om styrkelse af det danske bidrag til den internationale sikkerhedsstyrke', B 24. December. Copenhagen: Parliament.

Public Tender Complaints Office (Klagenævnet for Udbud). 2009. *Cimber Air A/S mod Forsvarskommandoen*, J.nr. 2009-0018467. 7 May. Copenhagen: Public Tender Complaints Office.

Rottbøll, Emil. 2008. 'Danske lejesoldater', *Dagbladet Information*, 14 November.

Royal Danish Navy (SOK). 2011. 'Ark', version of 25 May, available at http://forsvaret. dk/SOK/eng/International/ARK/Pages/default.aspx (accessed 25 May 2011).

Wulf, Herbert. 2005. *Internationalizing and Privatizing War and Peace*. New York: Palgrave Macmillan.

4 Sweden

Public servants from the private sector

Joakim Berndtsson and Maria Stern

Introduction

Sweden's participation in the international operations in Afghanistan conveys the image of Sweden as a key European actor that takes responsibility for global security and development. On the government website for the Swedish mission in Afghanistan, the nature, aim and challenges of the operations are described as follows:

> Sweden's involvement in Afghanistan is based on a holistic approach. In order to promote stability and long-term development, the four dimensions of Sweden's involvement – civilian, military, development assistance and diplomatic – collaborate closely. Sweden's involvement ... is aimed at supporting and strengthening Afghan capacity in all areas of society so that the Afghan people can gradually take over responsibility for their continued development themselves. The challenges in Afghanistan are considerable in all parts of society. Security is problematic, poverty is widespread, and there are major flaws in the country's governance. It is important that the concerted international efforts are as comprehensive and well coordinated as possible.
>
> (Sweden in Afghanistan n.d.)[1]

Importantly, Sweden's engagement in Afghanistan must be seen in relation to a global discursive and policy shift that emphasizes the intimate connections between security and development. Sweden's current security and development policies reflect a move away from its traditional 'neutrality policy' towards a 'solidarity policy', and away from sectored thinking and acting. Instead of the latter, Sweden has embraced the idea of the so-called security–development nexus and the related 'holistic' ('whole of government' or 'comprehensive') approaches (Sida 2010a). According to this rationale, peace, security, development and good governance are best promoted through coordination and cooperation between civilian and military actors.

Sweden's military contribution to the International Security Assistance Force (ISAF) – about 650 troops – forms only one out of four 'cooperating parts' of the

Swedish efforts in Afghanistan; the other three consist of diplomatic, development and other civilian efforts that seek to 'strengthen Afghanistan's ability to create stability, security, democracy and human rights' (Sweden in Afghanistan n.d.). These efforts occur under the auspices of several different state institutions, including the Ministry of Justice, the Swedish Armed Forces (SAF), Sida (Swedish International Development Cooperation Agency), the National Contingencies Agency and the National Police Board. In addition, Swedish engagement in Afghanistan involves, and to some extent is made possible by, the contracting of private military and security companies (PMSCs).

Sweden's operations in Afghanistan have come under public scrutiny in sporadic flurries, most prominently when Swedish soldiers and officers have lost their lives and the public is reminded that Sweden, with its long history of non-alliance in peacetime and neutrality in war, is militarily engaged in a conflict zone (see Petersson 2011). Yet, despite the complex and deeply political nature of the concerted international engagement, the level of ongoing public debate about the instantiation, continuation or remit of the Swedish peace operations in Afghanistan, including the increasing reliance on PMSCs by Swedish agencies, has been relatively low. Indeed, the use of PMSCs has largely remained under the radar of the Swedish public, while the issue has only rarely figured as a subject of debate among people working in agencies that contract PMSCs.

Nonetheless, the reliance on commercial security within the different Swedish missions (diplomatic, aid and military), as well as by the various NGOs and semi-public bodies that work in conjunction with, or even under contract to, Swedish state institutions, has become integral to the different operations and to Sweden's presence in Afghanistan. Indeed, Swedish security–development efforts depend upon a hybrid mix of public–private actors for their security provision. Yet, the Swedish use of PMSCs is still relatively unknown and rarely debated. This chapter offers an initial mapping of the contracting of private security in the service of Swedish state authorities in the international operations in Afghanistan. It does so in order to set the stage for future research on the political consequences of the contracting of security in the international operations. The chapter aims to invite further inquiry into how the use of PMSCs informs both the parameters for and the impact upon the stated aims of the Swedish presence in Afghanistan. In addition, it contributes to an understanding of how the contracting of security in foreign operations reconfigures authority over security decisions. Ultimately, the chapter also invites wider questions about the changing politico-ethical landscape of security governance, and invites a rethinking of the ways in which we conceive of the security–development nexus.

The analysis is based on official documentation of contracts and contracting processes, as well as interviews with key actors at the Swedish Ministry for Foreign Affairs and Sida regarding the use of PMSCs, along with interviews and informal conversations with representatives of PMSCs (Vesper Group), NGOs and development-cooperation consultants, and the Swedish Armed Forces. It is also based on an analysis of relevant policy texts and contracts between state agencies and PMSCs, since some – but certainly not all – of the information on security contracts is legally accessible to the public.

The chapter proceeds as follows. First, we provide an overview of the national context within which the contracting of security takes place, including discussions of national identity, the security–development nexus as a basis for Swedish policy and the security sector in Sweden. We then explore the contracting practices of Swedish state authorities and organizations in relation to Afghanistan. Here, we also discuss how the question of regulation has been handled within the Swedish government, as well as the silences that surround commercial contracting. We conclude with a discussion of the impact of security contracting on foreign operations in Afghanistan, focusing on the coordination, formulation and implementation of these strategies.

The national context

Understanding Swedish engagement in Afghanistan requires a degree of familiarity with some of the dominant logics, ideologies and histories of Swedish national identity and Swedish foreign, military and development efforts, as well as commercial security contracting. To be clear: by speaking of 'Swedishness' and 'identity', we do not claim that there is a national identity or culture that awaits description and can be seen as a fixed explanatory factor. Instead, we understand identity as a relational, multiple and open-ended process of becoming that is fiercely contested and that is not *a priori* to its evocations or performances (Hall 1996). That said, we can discern several historically embedded discourses/practices of what it means to be Swedish that inform Sweden's activities in Afghanistan.

National identity / national culture

The policy of neutrality (first coined in the 1830s) was the cornerstone of Sweden's foreign engagement for the greater part of the last two centuries. Sweden's neutrality policy during the Cold War was formulated as 'non-alliance in peace-time aiming towards neutrality in war based on a strong defense' (Jervas 1986: 44). It thus implied only military, not economic or ideological neutrality. During the 1960s, this policy increasingly became an 'activity doctrine' that outlined 'the right and duty of a neutral state to be active internationally' (Andrén 1971: 67). Sweden's neutrality implied an international obligation as well as a national and regional obligation.

While the policy has been quite flexible throughout history, allowing for different security and foreign policy stances, it has nonetheless been an important identity marker for Sweden, both 'at home' and in the world (Andrén 1996; Eliæson 2002; Petersson and Kronvall 2005). Importantly, Sweden's identity as 'neutral' involved a commitment to its long history of peace and its role as an important international actor in terms of promoting peace, development and social justice. This latter aspect of Sweden's identity can arguably be traced to the emergence in late nineteenth-century Sweden of strong civil society movements, including the free churches movement, the women's movements and, most importantly, the labour movement, with its ideals of internationalist socialism (Lindqvist 1982: 79; Bergman 2007; Østensen, this volume). After the end of the Cold War, Sweden gradually abandoned its neutrality policy. Sweden joined NATO's Partnership for Peace in 1994, the EU in 1995 and shouldered the leadership of the latter's Nordic Battle Group. Nonetheless, the idea of Swedishness as entrenched in Swedish neutrality informs current policies and the public's reactions to Swedish foreign involvement. The dual character of Swedish neutrality – with the country's strong tradition of peace and its rejection of direct military engagement in warfare and military alliances, on the one hand, and its moral duty to the international community, on the other – can be traced in Sweden's security–development efforts in Afghanistan. For instance, according to the Swedish government's policy, the engagement in Afghanistan is the 'prime example of Sweden's solidarity and engagement in situations of international crisis' (Ministry for Foreign Affairs 2010: 3).

Furthermore, the centrality of Swedish neutrality within discourses of Swedish identity following the end of the Cold War has arguably gradually given way, in part, to the framing of Sweden as the ultimate 'gender equal state' in the mid-1990s (Towns 2002: 164). Sweden's particular success in achieving and working towards gender equality (which is well recognized internationally) has been, and continues to be, promoted as an important aspect of the Swedish contribution to bettering social justice worldwide. Thus, 'the gender equality identity was incorporated into previous Swedish representations of the Self as a "model" state with "moral obligations" to the international community' (Towns 2002: 162). A government communication on gender-equality policy, for instance, states that 'in Sweden, we have come far by international comparison; in fact, we have come the farthest in the world. We gladly share our experiences, we readily export our Swedish model for gender equality' (government communication on gender-equality policy, cited in Towns 2002: 163).

This focus on Sweden as 'leading the way' and 'enlightening' less equal states (and peoples) in relation to gender equality clearly informs the country's policies and practices in Afghanistan. Indeed, gender equality and the end to the oppression of Afghani women and girls are vital cornerstones of Swedish efforts (and prominent in public information about the 'reasons for' Swedish involvement), garnering support across political divides for continued Swedish presence and peace and reconciliation efforts in Afghanistan. As Sweden's former Minister of Defence Sten Tolgfors (2009) explained in an article in *Dagens Nyheter*:

> Today, Afghanistan is a country where two million girls go to school. But, schools are still being burned, while schoolgirls are being threatened and are targets for attack from the opposing forces. Recently, acid was sprayed on a group of schoolgirls.

The liberation of Afghani girls and women from a repressive regime is a prime goal of peace and reconciliation efforts and has served as a legitimating reason for

the continued international presence in Afghanistan. This is particularly important for Sweden, given its international reputation and its investment in its identity as
a model of gender equality.

A third aspect that warrants a brief explanation is Sweden as a flat-hierarchical,
strongly democratic state that encourages and promotes active civil society
engagement in all areas of society, including its international commitment.
Indeed, as is also the case with Norway, an important aspect of 'Swedishness' can
be seen in a widespread state-sanctioned encouragement for citizens to actively
engage in civil society (see Østensen, this volume). In this sense, the 'strong' and
'settled' state (Loader and Walker 2007: 23) gains part of its legitimacy through
activating the population in its own governing through citizens' participation in
nongovernmental organizations and movements. This practice plays out in the
ways in which development assistance and international solidarity movements
function. For instance, Sweden has a policy whereby those NGOs that are included in Sida's partnership agreements pay only 10 per cent of the total cost of
their development assistance; the remaining 90 per cent is covered by Sida. This
makes it possible for many NGOs, such as the Swedish Afghanistan Committee,
to flourish. Attention to the central importance of civil society in terms of how it
functions – in part – *inside* the Swedish state allows for a better understanding of
both the makeup of international operations and the context of the use of private
security contracting in these efforts.

Security–development in Afghanistan

Following the shift towards more deliberate and novel forms of meshing that which
has traditionally been 'security' work with 'development' work both globally and in
Afghanistan more specifically, Sweden has adopted a stance that explicitly enga-
ges in security–development work as interconnected. This calls for new forms of
intervention:

> Security and development are interdependent and success in these areas is
> often connected. Sweden's involvement in Afghanistan includes political and
> diplomatic efforts, military operations – both operational and capacity-
> building – policing and other civilian operations, as well as development
> efforts of various kinds.
>
> (Sweden in Afghanistan n.d.)

On its website for Sweden's engagement in Afghanistan, the government states:

> We have a humanitarian responsibility to contribute to the stabilisation and
> democratisation of Afghanistan, create respect for human dignity and human
> rights and help rebuild the country. Afghanistan's population has been sorely
> tested by war, oppression and poverty and the Swedish assessment is that the
> situation would worsen considerably were it not for the presence of the
> international community … It is also in Sweden's national interest that

Afghanistan, and the region as a whole, remains secure and stable. It is an important part of the fight against international terrorism … A strong UN and a strong EU fosters our security. By helping to prevent and manage international conflicts we are also safeguarding Sweden's security.

(Sweden in Afghanistan n.d.)

Sweden's activities, designed to comprise a 'comprehensive approach' to peacebuilding, reconstruction and reconciliation, thus involve a blurring of boundaries between the provision of security and the enabling of responsible development. Furthermore, coordination and cooperation occur not only between the distinct realms of type of effort, but also in terms of a hybrid mix of public and private security–development provision. In the framing of the Swedish missions, the goals of promoting security and development are clearly intertwined not only in terms of being mutually constitutive in a general sense insofar as development and security for the Afghani people are mutually interdependent, but also in terms of how security for one referent object (Sweden) depends upon the development of another (Afghanistan) (see Stern and Öjendal 2010).

Simply put, according to the Swedish government, development and peace-building must be secured (through military means, including the responsibiliza-tion and capacity building of the Afghan National Army and the Afghan National Police). Furthermore, in order for peacebuilding and development to occur, a base level of security must be achieved both for the people living and working in Afghanistan and for the functioning of the country's fledgling democratic pro-cesses and infrastructure. Additionally, creating security infrastructures, enabling development, and 'responsibilizing' both the government and the civilian popu-lation in Afghanistan also promises security for Sweden, the EU, Western democracies and their ways of life (including – and symbolized by – gender equality), as well as the globe more generally.

In light of this, innovative solutions for security provision – in all of its different guises – are called for. As highlighted above, one of the most prevalent (and iro-nically also one of the most veiled) solutions to the many challenges of security provision is the contracting of commercial security. Swedish security–development actors employ PMSCs in order to fulfil their mission of fostering peace and reconstruction in Afghanistan. Yet, before we probe these practices further, it will be instructive to take a brief look at the Swedish security sector.

The Swedish security sector

Commercial security actors abound in Sweden, yet only rarely do they form the subject of political debate. While state agencies have certainly employed private security companies in the past, the scope of security contracting in Sweden is now unprecedented, mirroring global trends.

Historically, the private security sector in Sweden has existed since the early twentieth century, when the first companies were created (Munck *et al.* 2005). In recent decades, the domestic security sector in Sweden has seen substantial growth. The estimated turnover for companies in this business sector (investigation and security services) tripled between 1990 and 2008, and the number of companies increased from around 100 in 1980 to 788 in 2009 (Statistics Sweden/SCB n.d.; Munck *et al.* 2005: 17). The market, which is tightly regulated, is dominated by the two global giants: Securitas, which has about 9,000 employees in Sweden, followed by G4S, which has about 4,000 employees (Sweguard 2011). In total, there are about 20,000 security guards in Sweden, roughly matching the number (20,292 in 2010) of police officers (Sweguard 2011; Polisen 2010).

In addition to conventional security companies, Sweden also has a fairly large defence industry, dominated by companies such as SAAB, Hägglunds and Bofors (the latter two are part of BAE Systems). In a list of global arms-producing companies for 2009, SAAB ranked number 31 (SIPRI 2009). Technology companies (e.g. Niscayah or Ericsson) work closely with both private security companies and public bodies, including the police, emergency services and the military, to provide security technology, expertise and sometimes risk-management solutions. Additionally, the Swedish Defence Material Administration (FMV) – an independent civil authority – provides both the Swedish Armed Forces and the civil security sector with procurement, materiel, systems and technology aimed at increasing 'the safety and security of Swedish society' (FMV n.d.).

When it comes to PMSCs providing services in high-risk or conflict areas, there are not more than a handful of Swedish companies in total (Bergman 2010). Even so, Swedish PMSCs such as Scandinavian Risk Solutions (SRS) and Vesper Group have prospered in the past few years, securing contracts with both public and private clients in unstable regions. As we shall see below, Vesper Group in particular plays an important part in securing Swedish diplomatic and development-cooperation activities in Afghanistan. Just as in the case of the domestic market for security services, the contracting of PMSCs by Swedish state agencies has only sporadically caused debate. Yet, there have been some interesting exceptions to the silence that generally surrounds private security in Sweden.

In Sweden, as in other settings, domestic debate centres around the remit of commercial security actors in the light of the sovereign state's role as guarantor of security as a public good, along with the state's monopoly over the use of force. In response to the criticism levelled at the security industry, a number of laws have been passed since the 1950s to strengthen state control. Also, in 1964, a hybrid solution was developed: a state-owned security company (Sw. *Allmänna Bevakningsaktiebolaget*, ABAB) was created, partly because the government considered it problematic that private companies contracted to protect certain objects were given access to sensitive locations and information (Swedish Government 1964; 1978: 90–91). In addition, a law was passed (the so-called monopoly law) that made ABAB the only legal provider of protective services at locations such as foreign embassies and defence installations. Partly as a result of complaints by Securitas that the monopoly law created unfair competition within the Swedish security market, the law that gave ABAB its special status was eventually revoked in 1991, and in 1992 the company was privatized and eventually became part of

Falck Sweden, which is now part of G4S (Munck *et al.* 2005: 18–24; Swedish Government 1990–91).

However, the idea of allowing private companies to provide services did not appeal to everyone. For instance, the military supreme commander argued forcefully in favour of keeping ABAB's special status in order to retain full public insight into the company's activities and prevent the spreading of classified information to private (possibly non-Swedish) companies (Swedish Government 1990–91). Protests such as this attest to the highly charged politics of where/when/how one draws lines of distinction between the public and the private spheres. Underlying such protest is the view that only security actors deemed appropriate by, and under the direct rule of, the sovereign state are qualified to gain access to information that might affect national security. According to this logic, the risk that foreign security companies might obtain sensitive national security information undermines critical sovereign power. While the supreme commander's arguments were taken seriously by the government, Securitas' complaints about unfair competition ultimately prevailed and helped put an end to ABAB's 25-year monopoly.

As the revoking of the monopoly law and the subsequent increase in security contracting clearly demonstrate, the general trend has been towards more security contracting, not less. Thus, Sweden can be said to follow a pattern similar to that of several other European countries, although, within the Scandinavian context, it has perhaps gone a bit further in its security contracting practices than its closest neighbours (see the chapters on Norway and Denmark in this volume). Indeed, as will be shown below, the contracting of PMSCs is now key to securing the Swedish efforts in Afghanistan.

PMSCs and the Swedish missions in Afghanistan

Given its identity as a strong democratic 'model' state, why did Sweden choose to contract for security in its missions in Afghanistan? One reason was that Sweden aimed to maintain a diplomatic presence in the country, yet could not find a feasible state-based solution to meet the perceived need for enhanced protection. Also, because many other states within ISAF were using PMSCs for similar tasks, the final decision to hire public servants from the private sector became partly a matter of following suite.[2] Surprisingly, given the sensitive and precarious nature of the theatre of operation, officials from Sweden's foreign ministry stated that the hiring of a security company was seen as unproblematic within the ministry. As many of the private security personnel are former police or military officers, the ministry's Security Secretariat in Stockholm implied that the difference between 'private' and 'public' security actors was essentially non-existent; thus, in accounts given by Swedish officials, the contracting of private actors, even as they were granted diplomatic status, was rendered without controversy.[3]

The decision by the Ministry for Foreign Affairs in 2008 to hire a Swedish company – Vesper Group – to provide security coordinators to the embassies in Baghdad, Khartoum and Kabul was described as a 'pilot project'.[4] This indicates not only that the practice of using PMSCs in international operations is rather new, but also that recent experiences are seen as a test run that will help shape the ways in which Sweden deals with security contracting in the future. Afghanistan is thus *the* case in which Swedish state agencies join a growing number of state and non-state actors that rely on private-sector alternatives to provide security and protection for security–development efforts within their international operations.

Swedish contracting practices in Afghanistan

There is no doubt that in many ways the Swedish government finds Afghanistan exceptional, posing a number of unique challenges: civilian state agencies have only rarely operated in such volatile environments in the past. The uniqueness of the situation explains, in part, the willingness of Swedish government officials and organizations to accept the use of private security. According to the Swedish strategy for Afghanistan:

> To many of the insurgent groups in Afghanistan, the international community is a legitimate target for attacks. This creates new and increased demands for qualified resources for dealing with security issues, substantial resources for security-enhancing efforts and good coordination between state agencies.
>
> (Ministry for Foreign Affairs 2010)

The above statement seems to indicate that there is a demand for PMSCs, and declares the need for 'substantial resources' to be used to meet the new and increased demands for security. In terms of direct contracts with PMSCs, several steps have been taken since the initial contract in 2008.

Table 4.1 illustrates the use of PMSCs by Swedish state agencies. Owing to a lack of available information on contracts and costs, the table is not complete. However, it clearly shows that the reliance on PMSCs by Swedish state agencies is far from insignificant.

Vesper Group is formally under contract with the Ministry for Foreign Affairs in Stockholm, while Saladin (UK) has been contracted directly by the Swedish embassy in Kabul. The two companies provide security for Sweden's diplomatic staff, as well as for individuals working for Sida and other civilian agencies, and activities include providing armed personal security details and staff for static guarding duties. Formally, Sida is part of the Swedish foreign ministry. In Afghanistan, Sida is responsible for the development cooperation part of the Swedish efforts and works mainly through local and international partners. Sida has its offices at the Swedish embassy in Kabul and in Mazar-e-Sharif, where the Swedish Armed Forces are located.

The Swedish embassy in Kabul and the field office in Mazar-e-Sharif use Vesper Group staff as coordinators for security work for all state missions. Although formally under the command of the Swedish ambassador, Vesper's work essentially entails managing, vetting and organizing the guard force, supplying bodyguards and working with contingency planning, security analysis,

Table 4.1 Sweden's engagement in Afghanistan and use of PMSCs

Area	Main agencies	PMSCs	Services	Annual costs (€)*
Diplomacy	Ministry for Foreign Affairs	Vesper Group Saladin Track 24** plus subcontracting and indirect use of PMSC services***	Diplomatic security Security coordinators Bodyguards Site security Quick reaction force Tracking technology	Vesper: 1,500,000 Saladin: 235,000 Track24: n/a
Development cooperation	Sida (Swedish International Development Cooperation Agency)			
Civilian operation	Ministry of Justice Folke Bernadotte Academy Swedish Civil Contingencies Agency National Bureau of Investigation			
Military operation (ISAF)	Ministry of Defence Swedish Armed Forces (SAF)	Supreme Foodservice GmbH plus subcontracting and indirect use of PMSC services***	Logistics support and site management Access control personnel (ACP) within the SWECON ISAF area of operations	Logistics etc.: 983,000–2,457,000 ACP: 483,000

Notes: Data for the table draw on a number of different sources, including official documentation, original contracts, interviews and email correspondence with state officials. Still, several pieces of information on contracts etc. have not been made available, and the table is therefore incomplete. Unavailable information is marked 'n/a'.

* Costs for private security and support services are normally not specified in the budgets for Swedish Afghanistan missions. The figures reported here are taken mainly from the contracts or obtained from contract officers and should be read as an estimation of size/cost.

** The system from Track 24 is used to track embassy/Sida vehicles and serves here as an example of the use of security technology from a PMSC as part of the Swedish mission to Afghanistan.

*** Seconded staff from the Swedish Civil Contingencies Agency, for instance, rely on host organizations for their protection, such as the UN and EUPOL Afghanistan, both of which use PMSCs for site and transport protection. Also, Supreme subcontracts with another PMSC - Compass - to provide convoy/transport security.

intelligence gathering and liaising with the security details of other nations and embassies.[5] The embassy guard force is provided by Saladin, a UK-based PMSC that grew out of KMS Ltd. (Saladin Security n.d.). Saladin also organizes a quick reaction force, but this is mainly staffed by local Afghani employees.[6]

Depending on perceived threat levels, which in turn are determined by employees of Vesper Group, Sida and embassy staff sometimes travel with personal protection details, often in armoured cars without bodyguards. Since there is a lack of both vehicles and security staff, these assets are distributed according to rank and function at the embassy. In addition to personal protection, embassy vehicles also use equipment from Track24, a security company that specializes in developing tracking technology.[7] The field office in Mazar-e-Sharif houses a civilian high representative as well as staff from the Folke Bernadotte Academy and the Civil Contingencies Agency, along with a police adviser who works for the Ministry of Justice. As with the embassy in Kabul, the civilian staff in Mazar-e-Sharif have access to a security coordinator from Vesper Group.

In terms of Sweden's military component, the Swedish Armed Forces have been responsible for a Provincial Reconstruction Team (PRT) in northern Afghanistan since 2006 (SAF n.d.). The main camp, Northern Lights, is located in Mazar-e-Sharif and is shared with Finnish troops. The Swedish military contingent consists of about 650 troops (SAF n.d.). For some time before 2010, the camp was protected partly by locally hired Afghan guards, who were employed directly by the SAF. However, the Swedish government later decided that the military should not be allowed to hire and arm local guards, and the SAF had to abandon this practice.[8] Thus, in 2010, SWAFLOG (Swedish Armed Forces Logistics) contracted with Supreme Foodservice GmbH – a company that already supplied support services to the SAF.

Through the one-year contract, the guards formerly employed by the SAF were transferred to Supreme in order to serve as unarmed 'access control personnel' within the SWECON (Swedish Contingent) area of operations (SWAFLOG/FMLOG 2010). In addition to manning gates etc., Supreme supplies interpreters and logistical support services to the SAF, as well as a security manager who oversees the local guards and interpreters (Supreme n.d.). Yet, Swedish military personnel are ultimately responsible for site/camp security and armed response. Not primarily a security company, Supreme contracts with another PMSC – Compass – to protect its own transports.[9] This means that, as a subcontractor, Compass also helps secure the supply chain for the Swedish military effort in Afghanistan.

In terms of indirect contracting practices, the Swedish Civil Contingencies Agency (MSB), a Swedish state agency under the Department of Defence, supplies staff to various UN and EU missions such as the World Food Programme and the European Union Police Mission in Afghanistan (EUPOL Afghanistan). The agency as such does not contract for security, nor is it covered by the security arrangements made by Sweden's foreign ministry, but depends instead on arrangements made by host organizations. Since both the UN and EUPOL Afghanistan have contracted with PMSCs for site and transport protection, this means that the staff and mission of the Civil Contingencies Agency are indirectly dependent on the security solutions of the organizations with which it cooperates in the field.[10] Clearly, influence over the implementation, regulation and impact of these security solutions lies outside Sweden's jurisdiction, which raises further questions about authority and accountability in security governance.

While the costs of these combined contracts, subcontracts and indirect uses of PMSCs are difficult to estimate, the mounting expenses for security are increasingly seen as a concern. During an interview with a civil servant working in Afghanistan, the growing costs for private security arrangements was a theme that recurred repeatedly.[11] An additional sign of mounting costs for PMSCs can be seen in Sida's (2011: 9) budget plan for 2012–2014:

> During 2011, Sida will have drastically increasing costs for security in Afghanistan, both in Kabul and in Mazar-e-Sharif, as a result of the pressed security situation in the whole country. The costs for personal protection and security coordinators burden Sida's budget for overseas offices and thus Sida's administrative budget. … Sida estimates that these extraordinary security costs for having personnel in Afghanistan warrant an increase in resources of 9 million kronor [€998,000] per year.

This effectively means that Sida's perceived need for *additional* security will cost approximately €1 million per annum or €3 million for the whole period 2012–2014. These additional costs amount to about 1.4 per cent of the funds Sida spends every year in Afghanistan (Sida 2010b). Adding what we know about the costs for all security services contracted directly by Swedish agencies (see Table 4.1 above), the total cost per year is estimated as being at least €3 million. This, in turn, adds up to about 1.5 per cent of the total budget for the Swedish engagement in Afghanistan (Sweden in Afghanistan n.d.). The real cost for security services, however, is likely to be higher. For instance, in the case of Sida, it is not clear how much of the total programme budget for Sida's development-assistance programmes also pays for private security (contracted not by the Swedish embassy directly but by consultants working for Sida, or by partner organizations).

In sum, the Swedish efforts in Afghanistan are substantially and increasingly tied to the ability to use PMSCs either directly (as in the case of Vesper Group and Saladin) or indirectly (as in the case of security contractors working for partner countries and organizations). A Swedish PMSC is used to coordinate security through the Ministry for Foreign Affairs, which indicates that a certain degree of importance is ascribed to the 'Swedishness' of this company (Berndtsson 2012). In addition, these coordinators have been given diplomatic status, and have thus been turned into agents of the Swedish state rather than being merely PMSC employees. Several tasks of central importance, such as protection of diplomats and access control at the military camp in Mazar-e-Sharif, are handled directly by PMSCs. In addition, the security coordinators also govern the security work for the civilian state authorities, such as Sida.

Debate, silences and points of controversy

As indicated above, Sweden's increasing reliance on PMSCs in international operations has only rarely found its way into the political debate. In recent years, only two written questions – both concerning the subject of regulation of PMSCs – have been submitted in Parliament: one in 2007/08 and the other in 2009/10. While the domestic market for private security in Sweden is fairly strictly regulated, there is no national legislation specifically targeting PMSCs operating abroad (Bergman 2010). Judging from the answers to the two questions, there appears to be no ongoing political process to suggest this might change in the near future.

The first question observes that there are Swedish companies that sell security services in and around zones of armed conflict and asks Minister of Justice Beatrice Ask whether she will take action to ensure that those companies are regulated (Swedish Parliament 2007a). The answer essentially avoids the main topic and concludes that security companies registered and doing business in Sweden are regulated. Additionally, the minister observes that security services provided by commercial actors are acceptable as long as these services are supplied under state control, that the providers are 'responsible', and that they have 'the training that the task requires' (Swedish Parliament 2007b). However, she concedes, there are companies engaged in providing services in and around armed conflicts that are not controlled by the state, and this 'might be problematic'.

Ask, however, does not address the issue of Swedish companies providing such services, nor does she indicate any initiative to amend Swedish legislation. Instead, she points to the 'Swiss initiative' (of which Sweden was part) and simply states that she 'will follow this development with interest' (Swedish Parliament 2007b). This initiative came from the Swiss Federal Department of Foreign Affairs in 2006 and originally focused on starting a dialogue on the international legal rules that apply (or otherwise) to the private security sector. One result of the dialogues was the signing of the so-called Montreux Document in 2008, outlining the application of international humanitarian and human rights law to PMSCs (see Swiss Department of Foreign Affairs n.d.). The Swedish minister of justice's reply focuses on the areas that are regulated by the state, effectively restricting her answer to security companies authorized under Swedish law and operating in Sweden. She does not voice any need for amendment of Swedish law. Why she does not comment on Swedish companies operating abroad is not clear, but the silence on this issue indicates once more the lack of Swedish political interest in the question of the use of PMSCs in foreign operations.

The second question is addressed to Minister for Foreign Affairs Carl Bildt and concerns the Vesper Group contract. Observing that PMSCs sometimes pose serious problems to weak governments and that their activities sometimes border on mercenarism, the author of the question finds the granting of diplomatic immunity to Vesper Group personnel 'disturbing' (Swedish Parliament 2009a). In the light of this, he asks the minister what steps he has taken to ensure that Vesper Group does not violate Swedish, Afghan and international laws. In his reply, the minister observes that 'the security consultants are part of the Swedish mission and, like other embassy officials, they enjoy diplomatic status' (Swedish Parliament 2009b). Furthermore, he states, the security coordinators and the team of bodyguards that they supervise have pledged to abide by Vesper Group's code of conduct. 'The code', he assures us, 'states that security staff shall abide by Swedish and local [Afghan] regulation, as well as international law'. Again, no initiatives specifically targeting PMSCs are discussed, and neither minister touches upon the larger, ideologically charged aspects of security contracting alluded to in the questions.

Domestically, Swedish state authorities are no strangers to private security provision. Over the past decades, the use of security companies to provide protection at government offices, military installations, airports, ports and other public and semi-public areas has increased markedly (Munck *et al.* 2005; Berndtsson and Stern 2011). Yet, for Swedish government agencies involved in international operations, the practice of relying on PMSCs for protection is still novel, which to some extent explains the lack of political debate. However, the silence surrounding the issue appears to run much deeper.

The Swedish strategy for Afghanistan underlines the importance of openness and of explaining government methods (Ministry for Foreign Affairs 2010: 26). Apparently, and unfortunately, this does not include the contracting of PMSCs. In contrast to our previous experiences with research on security contracting, we have found conducting research on the subject of privatization in Swedish operations in Afghanistan to be problematic. The subject seems to be politically sensitive and to comprise both unchartered and untrodden terrain. Simply put, it has been exceedingly difficult to elicit responses to our questions. Our requests for information and interviews have often been sent from one official to another without landing on the 'proper' desk. Our impression is that many of those with whom we have spoken do not actually know what the procedures are for answering our questions on security contracting, or to whom we should be referred.

The answers we have obtained have often been curtailed, accompanied by the explanation that the minimization of risk requires that information not be spread indiscriminately, or that the 2009 Public Access to Information and Secrecy Act limits what we can be told. Alternatively (or additionally), the issue of security contracting may be so sensitive that few want to subject themselves or their institutions to inquiry. These difficulties, however, tell us something important about security contracting in this context: in both of these possible scenarios, the politics of commercial contracting has not been erased through routine technologization or successfully naturalized. Instead, the politics of security contracting is glaringly apparent in the silences and absences that surround our questions, as well as in the lack of comprehensive political debate.

Impact

How does the use of PMSCs impact upon Swedish international operations? To address this important question, we will consider the issues of coordination, the formulation of policy and security knowledge, and the implementation of peace and reconciliation efforts. However, our focus is not on the actual effect of the use of PMSCs in terms of the realization of the goals for/in Afghanistan. Instead, we address the ways in which the use of PMSCs informs the politics and the practice of peace and reconciliation strategies. As noted above, of particular interest is how the use of PMSCs in international operations reconfigures authority over security decisions and practices and poses wider questions about the changing politico-ethical landscape of security governance in Sweden, along with the ways in which we conceive of the security–development nexus more generally.

First, however, we pause to critically reflect on the role of PMSCs in the Swedish operations. Whether or not there is a role for PMSCs in promoting security and development in Afghanistan is a matter of debate. Additionally, while the contracts are quite specific (e.g. the embassy contract), it is unclear in practice what exactly private security companies do for the distinct Swedish engagements and how their authority should be defined: are those who are contracted by state institutions bodyguards who *only* provide protection for Swedish assets, or are they qualified security professionals with extensive security expertise (such as the security coordinators who work with risk assessment, intelligence gathering and knowledge of the cultural and political security situation)? Moreover, different regulatory systems are at play. Those contracted by the embassy for security coordination enjoy diplomatic status, while security guards who protect Sida personnel do not. A clear picture of by whom and how private security actors working in the different operations and with different tasks are regulated remains elusive.

Coordination

As noted above, one of the difficulties in most peace and reconciliation contexts is the lack of coordination of distinct security–development efforts – which, according to Swedish policy, make up a 'comprehensive approach'. The four pillars of Swedish involvement in Afghanistan are indeed separate, each with a distinct mandate, yet these mandates interrelate and overlap.

Ironically, while perhaps different missions lack coordination in important areas central to their aims, commercial security contractors do condition certain forms of coordination in the very practical carrying out of duties. Perhaps most strikingly, the contracting of security with Vesper Group (which subcontracts to Saladin) via the Ministry for Foreign Affairs creates a situation in which different Swedish authorities (e.g. Sida) and NGOs must go through the contracted security coordinator at the embassy in order to ascertain whether they are 'safe' or not and in order to be able to carry out their work. As noted above, they are then subject to a priority list deriving from the security coordinator, who decides who should be protected, how and when. If one is not high on the priority list, one can find oneself without security protection and without a car for transport.[12] Additionally, in response to the description of the 'security situation', different actors can choose/be forced to pool security solutions (guards, cars, etc.).

Measured in terms of the goals of a comprehensive commitment to security–development in international operations, increased coordination in relation to security provision among the distinct spheres of Sweden's involvement might indeed be a positive development. While such centralized coordination for the security of Swedish personnel is not necessarily due to the fact that the provision of security has been contracted to Vesper Group, that organization is a private company that seeks to make a profit through the provision of its services. That this coordination has been contracted out to a commercial company does raise questions about the influence of commercial actors on the coordination of Swedish security–development efforts.

Despite a massive demand for services, many critical voices lament the use of PMSCs and have raised the question of whether their use might hinder the coordination of peace and reconciliation efforts. One development consultant, for example, described the heavy reliance on PSCs and private bodyguards in Afghanistan as resembling a 'mass psychosis'.[13] To him, the perceived need for protection among organizations appeared vastly exaggerated. Also, the behaviour of some of these private actors, he said, might actually jeopardize the missions of many organizations, especially those working with reconstruction and develop-ment cooperation (implicitly including Swedish efforts for augmenting gender equality). A representative of the Swedish Committee for Afghanistan (SCA), an NGO with some 20 years' presence in the country, echoed this sentiment. While the SCA has people who work with security, these are locally employed Afghans who never carry weapons. 'We do not even have locks on our doors', the SCA representative explained, stressing that 'guns will not protect you in Afghanistan'. On the contrary, using armed guards could be counterproductive and put SCA people at risk.[14]

Given this line of thinking, some missions might suffer from the association with armed PMSCs. One Sida representative spoke of the private security con-sultants hired by USAID, who lack gender awareness and behave poorly (and in a 'macho' manner, in contrast with Swedish actors who show 'cultural sensitivity') towards the civil population when they accompany USAID personnel to the local villages. This representative explained that such behaviour 'stung her eyes', and that the Swedish (military and PMSCs) were more 'reasonable'. Sida personnel do not habitually bring their armed guards (Afghani, subcontracted by Saladin) with them if they do make a visit locally. The guard normally waits in the car, thus avoiding a potentially negative situation where the presence of a 'macho' security guard undermines the work being undertaken. Hence, the use of PMSCs informs both the possibility for and the nature of coordination within the concerted Swedish mission, as well as among international actors.

Formulation

The question of how the private contracting of security impacts upon the formulation of peace and reconciliation strategies and policy can be addressed at many different levels. We discussed above the question of regulation in government debates and how the Swedish government did not seem to be concerned with issues of regulation or the impact of PMSCs on Swedish operations abroad. We also discussed the lack of public debate (reflected also in the difficulty we have encountered in obtaining information) about the political and ethical implications of private security contracting in these contexts. This lack of open information, and therewith public debate about how, why and to what effect commercial security contracting occurs in a state that prides itself on its democratic values, invites even more questions about how political decisions concerning security are being made, what new forms of hybrid security actors are emerging, and what these developments might imply for security governance. We turn here, however, to the question of security knowledge and practice as formulated in the embassy contract with Vesper Group to flesh out some of these aspects of the politics of formulation.

As noted above, the security coordinator at the Swedish embassy assesses risk and formulates the security plan (which includes details of the security measures deemed necessary and how these measures are to be carried out for Swedish authorities and those who work under their auspices). The coordinator therefore produces the authorized and legitimate security knowledge (which, as we will recall, is usually the purview of the state security elite). The coordinator, who enjoys diplomatic status, works for a PMSC. He can thus be seen as a hybrid security actor. As part of his/her remit, the coordinator also requests security personnel to implement the security measures that are deemed necessary. As one Sida representative explained, this presents a situation of partiality and cost increase, to the detriment of security–development activities.[15]

The issue of cost due to security framing recurred often in this representative's narrative, hinting at a much larger question. It is explained as follows:

> We do not implement anything ourselves, but instead go through our partners, such as the Swedish Afghanistan Committee. In this way, (the use of PMSCs) influences even the NGOs with which we work. … There's a higher security cost. And there's a cost for other things. … When one works with civil society, usually one does not have weapons, but it can still cost because it's difficult to recruit people: salaries must increase for international employees and for Afghani ones. … There are many high costs. … There are more costs when one pays for private security companies.

It seems that what is of concern here is that a commercial logic is framing the security needs of all sorts of actors and rendering 'security' costly. Understood in this way, such commercial logics impact both the formulation of the security policy for the conditions of security–development work and the work that is to be carried out, at the very minimum through the allocation of resources from other areas towards 'security' procurement.

Implementation

The security requirements laid down by the Swedish embassy are expensive (drawing resources from elsewhere) and restrictive in terms of who can do what kind of work, how and when. The 'mass psychosis' of security thinking that 'necessitates' the use of PMSCs frames what kinds of activities can take place. Sida, for example (and to our surprise), rarely interacts directly with local organizations, but 'goes through their partners'. While this is also part of Sweden's 'partnership' policy, some of the explanation for this is framed in terms of 'security' – both for personnel who cannot travel without protection and for those working locally who might be placed at risk by this very protection.[16]

Another aspect that became clear is how security framing and consequent practices can be seen to hinder security–development work in general. Certainly, Afghanistan is at war, and undoubtedly a dangerous situation reigns. Nonetheless, the framing of security, which 'necessitates' security measures that PMSCs supply, limits the conditions of possible responses to the dangers that exist and the work that can be done. A Sida representative explained as follows:

> The overall security situation makes it so that ... it becomes a lockdown sometimes and one can't go out. ... I thought it was quite difficult when we were all supposed to have personal protection. Then there were not enough [guards for personal protection] for everyone. One couldn't go to all the meetings. ... Those who were lowest on the ladder had to fight for cars ... and we have curfews and ... they limit us ... they limit one's freedom of movement. ... The whole security situation ... maybe not so much with the security companies, but with the cordoning off of streets ... if one is Afghani and lives in Kabul, one can hardly get to work because streets are closed ... and half of the city is cordoned off because of some convoy ... of both Westerners, but also the president and ministers and Afghanis in high positions.[17]

This abundance of security measures is conceived of and implemented through a framing of security that includes commercial contracting. While such abundance is perhaps necessary to safeguard lives and property, it arguably also perpetuates a situation of insecurity and threat in the daily lives of people living and working in Afghanistan, and hinders peace and reconciliation operations.

Conclusions

As noted above, this chapter offers an empirically rich and much-needed overview of largely unchartered territory. Ironically, however, the difficulties we encountered in this unyielding terrain were perhaps one of the most telling research results – results that prompt us to think that investigating the politics of commercial security contracting in international operations promises rich knowledge about security contracting and about security–development governance, in the light of commercial contracting more generally.

Furthermore, our research has underscored how security–development efforts in Swedish peace and reconciliation activities comprise a contested field that warrants further exploration. Contestations occur not just in the more familiar sense of the competing mandates and spheres of activities of the different actors working to promote peace, development and stability. They also occur over the ways in which these different actors perceive their roles, and how they view 'security'. While many have explored the difficulties involved in the framing and practice of security–development efforts, little attention has been paid to the impact of commercial forms of security provision and expertise.

Additionally, the use of PMSCs spurs further questions in the light of the widespread embrace of the security–development nexus as a policy framework. While the mixing of the public and private has long been accepted in – indeed integral to – development efforts, the realm of security has long been assumed to be unique to public bodies – either states or international public bodies, such as the UN. What, for instance, happens to the unique position of the state in relation to the provision of security in security–development efforts? What logics or practices condition security–development efforts? And, what might the use of PMSCs *do* to peace and reconciliation missions? While this chapter only touches on these issues, it nonetheless points at the importance of further inquiry into the politics of commercial contracting in contemporary security–development governance.

Notes

1 Quotes and citations in Swedish have been translated into English by the authors.
2 Interview, Ministry for Foreign Affairs, August 2010.
3 Interview, Ministry for Foreign Affairs, August 2010.
4 Interview, Ministry for Foreign Affairs, August 2010; see also Berndtsson (2012).
5 Interviews, Ministry for Foreign Affairs, August 2010 and 29 October 2008; see also Berndtsson (2012).
6 Interview, anonymous, August 2011.
7 Interview, anonymous, August 2011.
8 Interview, anonymous, August 2011.
9 Interview, anonymous, September 2011.
10 Email correspondence, MSB, October 2011.
11 Interview, anonymous, August 2011.
12 Interview, Sida, August 2011.
13 Interview, anonymous, April 2011.
14 Interview, SCA representative, June 2011.
15 Interview, Sida, 26 August 2011.
16 Interview, Sida, 26 August 2011.
17 Interview, Sida, 26 August 2011.

References

Andrén, Nils. 1971. *Total Säkerhet*. Ystad: AB Aurora.
——1996. *Maktbalans och Alliansfrihet: Svensk utrikespolitik under 1900-talet*. Nordstedts: Stockholm.

Bergman, Andreas. 2010. 'The Regulation of Private Military and Security Services in Sweden', National Report Series 02/10. Florence: European University Institute.

Bergman, Annika. 2007. 'Co-constitution of Domestic and International Welfare Obligations', *Cooperation and Conflict* 42(1): 73–99.

Berndtsson, Joakim. 2012. 'Security Professionals for Hire: Exploring the Many Faces of Private Security Expertise', *Millennium Journal of International Studies* 40(2): 300–17.

Berndtsson, Joakim and Maria Stern. 2011. 'Private Security and the Public–Private Divide: Contested Lines of Distinction and Modes of Governance in the Stockholm–Arlanda Security Assemblage', *International Political Sociology* 5(4): 408–25.

Eliæson, Sven. 2002. 'Inledning', in Sven Eliæson and Hans Lödén, eds, *Nordisk Säkerhetspolitik inför nya utmaningar*. Stockholm: Carlsson Bokförlag, pp. 7–49.

FMV (Swedish Defence Materiel Administration). n.d. 'About FMV', available at: www. fmv.se/en/About-FMV/ (accessed 13 March 2012).

Hall, Stuart. 1996. 'Introduction: Who Needs "Identity"?', in Stuart Hall and Paul du Gay, eds, *Questions of Cultural Identity*. London: Sage, pp. 1–17.

Jervas, Gunnar. 1986. *Sweden Between the Power Blocs: A New Strategic Position?* Stockholm: Swedish Institute.

Lindqvist, Kent. 1982. *Program och parti: principprogram och partiideologi inom den kommunistiska rörelsen i Sverige 1917–1972*, Lund: Arkiv för studier i arbetarrörelsens historia.

Loader, Ian and Neil Walker. 2007. *Civilizing Security*. Cambridge: Cambridge University Press.

Ministry for Foreign Affairs. 2008. 'Contract with Vesper Group', Stockholm, 29 October.

——2010. *Strategi för Sveriges stöd till det internationella engagemanget i Afghanistan, Förhandskopia* [Swedish National Strategy for Afghanistan]. Stockholm: Utrikesdepartementet.

Munck, Jahan, Jan Vilgeus and Lena Carlberg Johansson. 2005. *Ordningsvakt och Väktare: Regler för ordningsvakter och bevakningsföretag*. Stockholm: Nordstedts Juridik.

Petersson, Magnus. 2011. 'Defense Transformation and Legitimacy in Scandinavia After the Cold War: Theoretical and Practical Implications', *Armed Forces & Society* 37(4): 701–24.

Petersson, Magnus and Olof Kronvall. 2005. *Svensk säkerhetspolitik i supermakternas skugga 1945–1991*. Stockholm: Santérus Förlag.

Polisen [the Police]. 2010. *Polisens årsredovisning 2010* [Swedish Police Annual Report 2010]. Stockholm: Polisen.

Saladin Security. n.d. 'Saladin: International Security and Risk Management Solutions', available at www.saladin-security.com/ (accessed 10 January 2012).

Sida. 2010a. 'Ett utvecklingssamarbete i förändring: Sidas resultat och prioriteringar', Sida report SIDA61289sv, available at, www.sida.se/Documents/Import/pdf/Ett-utvecklingssamarbete-i-f246r228ndring.pdf (accessed 13 March 2012).

——2010b. 'Utvecklingssamarbete med Afghanistan 2010', available at www.sida.se/Svenska/ Lander – regioner/Asien/Afghanistan/Samarbetet-i-siffror/ (accessed 12 January 2012).

——2011. 'Sidas budgetunderlag 2012–2014', Stockholm: Sida.

Statistics Sweden/SCB. n.d. 'Statistics Sweden: Trade in Goods and Services', available at www.ssd.scb.se/databaser/makro/start.asp?lang=2 (accessed 11 January 2012).

Stern, Maria and Joakim Öjendal. 2010. 'Mapping the Security–Development Nexus: Conflict, Complexity, Cacophony, Convergence?', *Security Dialogue* 41(1): 5–29.

Stockholm International Peace Research Institute (SIPRI). 2009. 'The SIPRI Top 100 Arms-Producing Companies, 2009', available at www.sipri.org/research/armaments/ production/Top100/2009 (accessed 10 January 2012).

Supreme. n.d. 'Job Description', available at www.supreme-group.net (accessed 22 March 2011).

SWAFLOG/FMLOG. 2010. 'SWAFLOG Contract 2010: Agreement: Purchase of the Service of Access Control Personnel. Case No. FM-1036-10', Stockholm: SWAFLOG/ FMLOG.

Sweden in Afghanistan. n.d. Official website for Sweden's role in the international involvement in Afghanistan, available at www.swedeninafghanistan.se (accessed 21 December 2011).

Swedish Armed Forces (SAF). n.d. 'Afghanistan – ISAF', available at www.forsvarsmakten. se/en/Forces-abroad/Afghanistan/ (accessed 21 December 2011).

Swedish Government. 1964. 'Government proposition 1964: 108', Stockholm.

——1978. 'Ordningsvakter. SOU 1978: 33', Stockholm.

——1990–91. 'Government Proposition 1990/1991: 102', Stockholm.

Swedish Parliament. 2007a. 'Written Question 2007/08: 1299', Stockholm.

——2007b. 'Answer to Written Question 2007/08: 1299', Stockholm.

——2009a. 'Written Question 2009/10: 629', Stockholm.

——2009b. 'Answer to Written Question 2009/10: 629', Stockholm.

Sweguard. 2011. 'Facts about the Security Business/Fakta om bevakningsbranschen', available at http://sweguard.se/index.php?option=com_content&view=article&id=52& Itemid=57 (accessed 21 December 2011).

Swiss Department of Foreign Affairs. n.d. 'Private Military and Security Companies', available at www.eda.admin.ch/eda/en/home/topics/intla/humlaw/pse.html (accessed 11 January 2012).

Tolgfors, Sten. 2009. 'Därför strider svenska soldater i Afghanistan', *Dagens Nyheter*, 29 July.

Towns, Ann. 2002. 'Paradoxes of (In)Equality. Someting Is Rotten in the Gender Equal State of Sweden', *Cooperation and Conflict* 37(2): 157–79.

5 Poland

Indirect and *ad hoc*

Marcin Terlikowski, Marek Madej and Beata Górka-Winter

A look at the Polish contingent's deployment within the ISAF operation in Afghanistan enables us to analyse the Polish military's indirect reliance upon private military and security companies (PMSCs). The specific model of relations this involves, we argue, stems from a lack of comprehensive strategy, policy and practice regarding the use of PMSCs to support the military, combined with popular perceptions of the role of armed forces within Poland, together with a state policy of relying on the direction of the lead nation in expeditionary deployments of Polish forces.

National context

In the case of Poland, existing legal frameworks, strategy, doctrine and practice regarding the use of the armed forces together create a rather unwelcoming environment for the commercialisation or privatisation of even minor aspects of military operations. This environment is driven by two cultural factors – the popular vision of the role of the armed forces within the state and the general approach to the privatisation of public services.

Perception of the armed forces and their role

Poland's military tradition is one of the key elements of the country's national identity. In the nineteenth century, when the political ideology of nationalism was emerging, Poland was non-existent as a state. During that period, memories of former military victories by the once-powerful Polish monarchy formed a crucial element of national heritage and identity. The special role of the military in terms of preserving Poland's national tradition during the 123 years of occupation (so-called Partitions) was further reinforced by the activities of Polish soldiers, who – driven by the hope of recreating Polish statehood with the help of a powerful ally, such as Napoleon – served under foreign command. The continuity of the Polish nation was also manifested by the insurgents who fought against various occupants in a series of uprisings. As a result, since the nineteenth century, the Polish military has been perceived as a 'carrier' of national identity and a symbol of national virtues (Siren 2009: 202; Davies 1994: 349).

The importance of the armed forces was reinforced after Poland recovered its independence in 1918. Even if this was more the result of political changes in the international order and the decisions of the great powers after the First World War than of Polish military efforts (though Polish units did serve in the armies of all three occupying countries – Prussia/Germany, Russia and Austria – as well as in the French army), the armed forces of the re-established Polish state (the so-called Second Republic, which lasted from 1918 to 1939) were commonly credited by Polish society with the recovery of Poland's independence and the securing of its borders – owing, for example, to the victory in the decisive Battle of Warsaw against the forces of Soviet Russia in August 1920 (Watt 2011: 134–8).

Poland's turbulent history also goes some way towards explaining the romantic nature of the Polish vision of the armed forces and the *gloria victis* mentality prevalent within both Poland's military and Polish society at large (Siren 2009: 210). And, within Poland's military tradition, landslide victories like that at Grunwald (1410) or the Battle of Vienna (1683) and 'glorious' but inevitable defeats like the uprising of 1830 or the defence of Westerplatte (1939) are celebrated equally. While the former are perceived as manifestations of Polish bravery and military genius, the latter exemplify Poland's determination and moral superiority over militarily powerful opponents. Moreover, within the same tradition, victories on the battlefield are celebrated and honoured even in cases when their strategic importance was limited (e.g. the attack of the Polish Napoleonic cavalry at Somosierra in 1808) or when long-term gains were largely disputable (e.g. Grunwald in 1410). This highlights the romantic character of Polish military tradition, in which symbols are generally valued more than economic and strategic efficiency.

Further, war fighting is understood in Poland primarily in terms of defending the country and nation against foreign aggression and occupation (Epstein 2006). Poland's self-perception as an innocent, non-expansive victim dominates. In social consciousness, the nation's history is virtually a series of defensive wars. Key elements of this vision are the German and Soviet invasions of 1939, together with subsequent Nazi atrocities and Soviet repression, but also the 'imperfect victory' of 1945, which led to the actual loss of sovereignty after the Second World War (Longhurst and Zaborowski 2007: 11; Niżyńska 2010: 470–1).

Further, even serving under foreign command is interpreted along similar lines – that is, as 'fighting in defence of a just cause' or to destroy a common enemy who constitutes a threat to international security. In line with this mindset, neither mercenarism – clearly condemned in Polish tradition – nor legal commercial services provided by military professionals – as in the case of the Ghurkas – find social approval. Even when under foreign command, Polish soldiers continue to be perceived as defenders of the nation and champions of universal values, rather than as professionals seeking financial benefits.

Accordingly, serving in the military has been traditionally seen in Poland as an honour and a noble duty for the citizen, as both a manifestation of patriotism and proper civic behaviour (Siren 2009: 211). It also constituted a 'rite of passage' to maturity and full participation in the national community. Thus, within Polish social consciousness, it is undeniably a unique activity, very different from a 'regular job' based on contracts and commercial logic. A military career should be first and foremost the result of a desire to fulfil civic obligations, with financial factors playing a secondary role.

Hence, Poland's strategic culture makes it hard to deviate from the axiom of state responsibility in the military domain. However, profound social changes – initiated by the transformation of Polish society and the economy towards a liberal and democratic model – began to challenge that scheme and opened the door for at least partial acceptance of the introduction of commercial logic and practices into the Polish military sector.

Perception of privatisation

Since the beginning of the shift in Poland's political and economic system in 1989, the issue of privatisation of state-run enterprises or public services has provoked ardent debate. Perhaps surprisingly given the country's 40 years of communist rule, attachment to private property is deeply rooted in Polish thinking on the economy. Positive attitudes towards private property lie deep within the national identity: even the communist government, for example, was unable to fully nationalise agriculture because of the resistance of peasants. Furthermore, shortages resulting from the centrally planned communist economy created a strong entrepreneurial drive within Polish society: against many odds, individuals learned to pursue any commercial opportunity they encountered. And, although private business was largely forbidden and pilloried in official propaganda, deficiencies in supply forced people to find other ways to access desired goods. As a result, a huge grey market emerged alongside the official system.

The entrepreneurial potential that accumulated during communist rule was released in 1989 when private business was allowed: more than half a million small and medium-sized enterprises were soon established. In the mid-1990s, the number increased fivefold, reaching 2.5 million. It now stands at 3.5 million (Chądrzyński 2004: 2–3). At the same time, within the popular mindset, the public sector has been somewhat neglected. The administration is largely perceived as being ineffective, badly managed and corrupt. State-run enterprises are viewed as operating chaotically and serving particular political interests, while the quality of state-provided services is generally regarded as unsatisfactory. In addition, Polish society lacks a sense of common responsibility for public infrastructure such as public transport, resulting in mismanagement, misuse and even deliberate damage to public facilities.

There are several reasons for such attitudes towards the public sector in Poland. During the period of the Partitions, public administration was seen as a symbol of foreign rule, and accordingly neither trusted nor respected. A more direct cause is the recent experience of communist rule, when the sector grew exponentially but was badly managed and disregarded by society at large. Presented in state propaganda as a common good, state-owned enterprises or infrastructure were instead seen as belonging to nobody. What followed was a waste of resources on an unprecedented scale: theft of public goods, corruption and carelessness on the part of managers, who lacked incentives for running enterprises properly, were common.

One might assume that such attitudes towards the public sphere would make privatisation a priority, but the situation proved more complicated. On the one hand, there is a general feeling that the private sector can provide higher-quality services or goods than the state, particularly in relation to healthcare, transportation or education at primary and secondary levels. On the other hand, there is deep suspicion towards the privatising of certain sensitive – or strategic – sectors of the state. Privatisation of public assets is also perceived as a murky business, which often ends up in asset stripping, leaving former employees jobless while enabling investors to enrich themselves. The core reason for negative attitudes to privatisation comes from experiences following the shift in Poland's economic and political system in 1989. A large number of public enterprises were then privatised. Many of these were in poor economic condition, so privatisation ended up in business closures, the sale of assets and mass lay-offs. The first wave of privatisation thus made the whole concept unpopular within Polish society. Subsequent privatisation initiatives did little to change the situation, since fiascos with the privatisation of large companies (e.g. shipyards, mines) overshadowed other efforts that proved more successful. Privatisation is still considered a non-transparent and politicised business, with polls taken in 2009 indicating that 30 per cent of Poles perceive privatisation as negative, and 20 per cent as positive, while over 40 per cent see it as bringing both benefits and costs (CBOS Report 2009).

The privatisation of public services is rejected in Poland even more strongly than privatisation in general. The privatisation of such services is commonly equated with the need to pay for something that used to be free. The strong opposition towards privatising public services in Poland therefore has more practical than ideological grounds: Polish society can accept that private entities might provide public services – or simply not care about the legal status of service providers – as long as such services remain free of additional charge.

Privatisation of the security and defence sector

Given generally sceptical attitudes towards privatisation within Poland, it is perhaps not surprising that the process of privatising the security and defence sector is not as advanced as in many other Western states. However, there appears to be a clear trend within the Polish military of adopting a modern model of privatisation/outsourcing in relation to some auxiliary services.

A distinctive feature of the Polish market for national security and defence services is that it has been growing asymmetrically: the defence segment – services offered to the armed forces and/or linked directly to the use of lethal force –

has remained almost non-existent, while the security segment – non-lethal services offered to both private and public entities – has flourished.

As a result, the majority of services offered on the Polish security market are provided by private security firms (PSCs – popularly dubbed 'security agencies' in Poland). Among other things, the portfolio of services includes guarding, electronic protection of facilities, operating CCTV systems, individual protection of persons, convoying sensitive goods, cash processing and the monitoring of vehicles. Clients include business entities (e.g. the banking sector), individuals (property protection) and the public administration (guarding).

As of 2009, the Polish security market was worth around €1.65 billion. By 2015, it is expected to double in size. There are over 3,000 PSCs in Poland, employing more than 300,000 people. The eight largest companies control 36 per cent of the market, making the level of concentration very low (in the largest EU economies, the respective figure is around 80 per cent).[1] These data reflect the general character of the Polish security and defence market: it is fragmented and shared mostly between inexperienced enterprises (the international leaders, such as G4 Securicor or Securitas, have not won a majority of the market so far), operating only at a regional scale and having little ambition either to expand abroad or to broaden the portfolio of services offered.

The defence segment is much less developed. Reportedly, the core of private military companies (PMCs) in Poland is made up of associations of former soldiers from the special forces, policemen from anti-terrorist police units or personnel from state protection agencies. A handful of such enterprises struggle with the general lack of interest on the part of the market: neither the military nor other entities are interested in complex services directly linked to the use of lethal force. Furthermore, it is widely believed that defence professionals can only find an appropriate job abroad, and this belief further impedes the development of the market.

While the private sector might simply not need the services of PMCs, the military's lack of interest in the outsourcing of tasks has deep roots. In 1989, Poland had a large armed force of around 280,000 soldiers. It was a Soviet-style military, meant to be self-sufficient – that is to say, to provide all kinds of maintenance, logistics and support services on its own. This self-sufficiency was achieved through the creation of special organisational entities within the military structure: cantinas, laundries, fuel-distribution stations, even publishing offices. Although such practices were common for the majority of armies based on conscription, even among liberal democracies, in communist regimes the necessity of self-sufficiency and institutional autonomy on the part of the armed forces had a different rationale. In centrally planned economies, the private sector was largely not permitted. Thus, outsourcing was simply impossible. Further, the armed forces were necessary for assuring the survival of the regime. Reliance on external (private) support could have severely reduced the ability of military to perform this particular task.

Over the 1990s, as a consequence of geopolitical changes, Poland's armed forces were reduced by 40 per cent, to around 150,000 soldiers. Nonetheless, the policy of self-sufficiency was largely kept, even despite the need to conform to NATO standards both prior to and after Poland's accession to membership of that organisation in 1999.

What changed the Polish military and its approach towards privatisation was the sharp growth of engagement in peace and stabilisation operations. In 2003, following Poland's engagement in Iraq, it was decided that the armed forces should be developed in a way that would ensure Poland could provide strong contributions to multinational military operations. This decision was followed by an intensive transformation of Poland's armed forces, which embraced four dimensions: an increase in the number of professional soldiers; the replacement of outdated equipment; improvements to the training system; and a reform of the military's organisational structure.

All of the above-mentioned developments slowly opened military planners for the privatisation of some services. The aim of the transformation process was twofold: to cut back on costs and to use human resources more effectively. Consequently, the decision was made to shrink the military in order to use available resources to build up an expeditionary capacity. Ultimately, this led to the suspension of conscription in 2008 and the first steps towards the building up of a fully professional army of 100,000 soldiers (Kościuk 2010: 152). The majority of organisational entities providing support services were closed down, and the lack of conscripts meant that 'free labour' – previously used to provide guarding, cooking, cleaning or equipment maintenance and repair services – was no longer available.

What followed was a gradual acceptance of the privatisation of maintenance, logistics and support services. Already at the end of the 1990s, private contractors began to guard military facilities. Currently, almost all such facilities are guarded by civil contractors, despite doubts over the quality of the services provided (Żemła 2011). Private firms are also used – albeit rarely – to provide advanced combat training. More common are cases involving civilians training soldiers in how to use advanced weapons or support systems. However, these individuals are generally employees of proper defence-sector companies and should not be considered defence contractors. Nor should the companies that provide catering, upkeep or maintenance for the military – the services that make up the bulk of the outsourcing effort of the Polish armed forces – be regarded as defence contractors: they are regular 'civilian' firms, working with a range of different clients, of whom the military is just one of many. In addition, relations between the military and the private sector are still perceived as being problematic and potentially leading to corruption. Such a view is epitomised by special anti-corruption regulation that strictly limits military-to-business dialogue, softened only recently following criticism that it was penalising even regular exchanges of information.[2]

The military's current approach to outsourcing and the lack of interest among private entities in the procurement of defence-related services has resulted in a slow pace of security-sector privatisation. This will have direct consequences for the deployment of Polish troops abroad: given the underdevelopment of its own security and defence market, Poland will be more likely to accept services offered by foreign PMSCs and PSCs.

Legal and doctrinal framework of participation of Polish Armed Forces in international missions

Legal framework. Apart from the Constitution, which sets out the general framework for the use of Poland's armed forces,[3] the basic rules and procedures regulating the involvement of the Polish military in international operations are defined in the Law on the Principles of the Use or Temporary Stay of the Armed Forces of the Republic of Poland Outside the Country's Borders.[4] This Act introduces a distinction between the use of and temporary stays by units of the Polish armed forces outside Polish territory. The first category includes three forms of engagement: participation in armed conflict or for reinforcement of allies; peacekeeping operations (including stabilisation or peace support missions); and actions aimed at preventing acts of terrorism or mitigating their consequences. The second category – temporary stays – is attributed to non-combat actions like participation in training and exercises, search and rescue missions, humanitarian operations, etc.

In the case of temporary stays, decisions about whether to send troops are made by the Council of Ministries or the minister responsible for particular forces (usually the minister of national defence). When the external use of armed forces is concerned – collective defence, peacekeeping, etc. – the final decision is made by the president on the request of the Council of Ministries. Notably, the Polish parliament is virtually excluded from the decision-making process.

Importantly, Article 6 of the Law of 17 December 1998 states that a deployed contingent may consist not just of soldiers on active duty, but also of civilian employees of the armed forces. In the context of the potential use of private contractors by Polish armed forces during foreign deployments, this is an important provision. The law provides the option of hiring civilian employees if specialised staff (such as interpreters, paramedics, etc.) are needed and unavailable among the ranks of the armed forces themselves. Such hiring can be carried out on the basis of contracts regulated by Poland's Labour Code, which means that employees are hired directly by the relevant state entity (i.e. the Ministry of Defence and/or other state bodies), not as personnel of private firms acting as subcontractors. This provision does not rule out the possibility of the armed forces acquiring services from private firms. However, the regulation illustrates that the most preferable option is to employ non-military specialists individually, as temporary employees of public institutions, not on the basis of a business contract with separate private or public legal entities.

Apart from the above-described case, the above law says nothing regarding the contracting of PMSCs. This is hardly surprising, given that it was enacted in 1998, before the dramatic increase in both the international activities of such companies and the expeditionary engagements of the Polish military.

Doctrinal framework. Fundamental Polish doctrinal documents covering the areas of security and defence – including the *National Security Strategy* of 2007 and the *National Defence Strategy* of 2009 – are very general in relation to expeditionary engagements (National Strategy 2007; Defense Strategy 2009). There is a confirmation of Poland's willingness and readiness to take part in such missions, together with lists of the types of operations in which Polish forces could participate (from peacekeeping and humanitarian operations, through anti-terrorist activities and other missions to counter asymmetric enemies, to stabilisation and peace enforcement actions). They also indicate the international institutions under whose auspices Poland is willing to act: NATO, the EU, the UN and 'coalitions of the willing'.[5]

In January 2009, the Council of Ministries adopted a document that deals specifically with Polish military engagements in international missions: 'The Strategy of Participation of Polish Armed Forces in International Operations' sets out the goals, principles and priorities of Polish military activities abroad. The document's key focus is on defining the conditions of Polish participation in international operations, and it emphasises such requirements as the compatibility of a given operation with Polish national interests, the probability of a mission's success, and the possibility of guaranteeing the 'visibility' of any Polish engagement. In addition, the strategy emphasises that Poland should benefit from its involvement in terms of an increase in the operational capabilities of its armed forces and/or a strengthening of Poland's position in the region of deployment or within the institution leading the operation.

The strategy is sparse in terms of details regarding the operational capabilities of the Polish armed forces. It defines Poland's level of ambition in terms of having 3,200–3,800 soldiers taking part in international operation(s) at the same time, prioritising NATO and EU missions as the best tools for strengthening Poland's position within those institutions. Specifications of requirements related to capabilities are limited to general phrases like 'securing the interoperability of the Polish armed forces'. Not surprisingly, the strategy document says nothing about possible cooperation between Poland's armed forces (or other state structures) and PMSCs in international operations (National Strategy 2009). Nevertheless, Poland has declared that it will abide by the principles of the 2008 Montreux Document.

The only official Polish document that explicitly mentions cooperation with private contractors is 'The Vision of the Polish Armed Forces in 2030', from January 2008. Paragraph 62 of this document envisages that the outsourcing of unspecified logistical services in support of combat forces would be a means of increasing the operational capabilities of Poland's armed forces, enabling them to perform their tasks 'irrespectively of the place, nature, intensity, duration and phase of the operation'. However, the relevance of that particular document is currently limited, since its crucial assumptions were overly optimistic and rather loosely linked to the Polish military's actual programmes for transformation.

Practice. Over the last decade, successive Polish governments have viewed involvement in expeditionary military operations in a rather instrumental fashion. In almost all of the significant foreign engagements since 2000 – Afghanistan (since 2002, Operation Enduring Freedom; later, also ISAF), Iraq (Operation Iraqi Freedom, 2003–08), the Democratic Republic of Congo (EUFOR, 2006) or Chad (EUFOR and MINURCAT, 2007–09) – the main rationale behind Polish involvement has been that of strengthening Poland's position among its allies and partners. More 'altruistic' factors declared as primary reasons for engagements – such as stabilisation or humanitarian necessity – were actually secondary, though not negligible. Poland's foreign and security interests in the country or region in which particular operations took place have also been of lesser importance for the decision-making process.

Poland's engagement in Iraq provides a perfect illustration. Undoubtedly, Poland was concerned about the Iraqi regime's alleged development of weapons of mass destruction. However, the decision to join the US-led coalition was made first and foremost with the aim of developing ties with the US (Kuźniar 2009: 329–39). Also important were hopes for economic gains from participation in Iraq's reconstruction.

Nor does the Polish engagement in missions in Afghanistan represent an exception to such a logic. Poland decided to participate in Operation Enduring Freedom less because of its desire to fight terrorism, and more in order to strengthen ties with the US. Even the increase of the Polish contingent within ISAF from 2006 onwards was to some degree motivated by a willingness to demonstrate Poland's reliability to the US, although the most important driver was the desire to build up Poland's position within NATO by demonstrating solidarity and responsibility for the mission (Madej 2011: 349).

Such an approach was to some degree a consequence of Poland's rather modest experience of expeditionary missions. Indeed, until the intervention in Iraq in 2003, Poland's experience in this sphere was limited to its involvement in UN peacekeeping activities, and, until the mid-1990s (UNPROFOR in Bosnia), solely within non-combat roles like logistics, engineering, etc. (Popiuk-Rysińska 2001). Accordingly, Poland could only offer rather limited military capabilities for international missions. This lack of experience also created a particular view of expeditionary engagements within Poland's political and military establishments, which saw them as relatively cheap, safe and easy to perform (as the UN reimburses its contributors), as well as a valuable tool for building up the international image of a country as an active member of the international community.

Such an 'instrumental' approach to expeditionary engagements naturally influenced the policies that were adopted. The first consequence was a sort of 'ad-hockery' in decision making regarding the use of the military. When building partnerships with allies is the primary reason for engagement, it is understandable that Poland would adapt to the strategies and plans of its partners, rather than set its own agenda. Second, in such circumstances, it is difficult to develop a strategy of foreign deployment other than of the type already adopted by Poland in 2009, focused on possible benefits for Poland rather than organisational and 'technical' issues, including the potential role of private contractors.

Poland in Afghanistan: a mission with hidden support from PMSCs

Based on a model of foreign deployment that assumes tight logistical reliance on the nation leading a given military operation, the Polish contingent in Afghanistan is heavily – though indirectly – dependent on PMSCs contracted by US public entities. As a consequence, various US and Afghan companies provide a wide range of auxiliary services to Polish troops, who for their part have little to say regarding the choice of these contractors and their performance. Notably, there are also numerous cases of civilians supporting the Polish contingent, though such contractors are largely employed on an individual basis by entities within Poland's public administration.

Polish military engagement in Afghanistan

For a relatively long period, the Polish presence in Afghanistan, which began shortly after the start of the US-led Operation Enduring Freedom, was limited. A modest contingent (about 100 troops) had operated on the ground since March 2002 and was tasked mainly with engineering, demining, chemical security and logistics in a Bagram base. In addition, a unit of special forces ('GROM') was engaged in combat operations against Al-Qaeda and the Taliban (Winid 2007; Górka-Winter 2009). From 2003, Poland also maintained some personnel within the ISAF operation's headquarters in Kabul.

Following a gradual scaling down of the Polish troop presence in Iraq, the possibility of engaging more substantially in Afghanistan emerged. In 2006, Poland thus decided to strengthen its contingent. By June 2007, the level of Polish forces was increased to up to 1,200 soldiers, operating in a number of different locations: Kabul, Mazar-e-Sharif, Ghazni, Paktia, Paktika and Kandahar (special forces). As the Polish government had decided against limiting the role of its contingent through 'national caveats', in the second half of 2007 significant numbers of Polish troops were engaged in kinetic operations.

This led to a situation in which the Polish contingent was operating in many regions (mainly within a US chain of command), which created serious problems of a political and logistical nature. The 'visibility' of the Polish effort in NATO was limited, as was its effectiveness. Moreover, in such circumstances, Poland was unable to create its own strategy for using its troops or to develop its own idea of a peace and reconciliation strategy. Therefore, in 2007 Poland changed the concept of its engagement in Afghanistan. It was decided to 'consolidate' the Polish contingent, and the government agreed to take over responsibility for Ghazni province. By the end of 2008, all Polish troop components in Afghanistan were concentrated in that province and began operating under NATO Regional Command-East (RC East).

This move allowed Polish commanders to have a greater impact on how the province was run, and to implement a comprehensive approach to Poland's engagement, as provided in the ISAF mandate. However, it required a substantial reinforcement of the Polish contingent, in terms of both manpower and military equipment. Initially, the Polish forces were upgraded to 1,600 soldiers. However, adverse conditions on the ground led to further increases throughout 2009 and 2010, with levels finally reaching around 2,600 troops at the start of 2011.

Along with the ISAF strategy, Poland also decided to go beyond military activity and engage more substantially in other tasks (Andrzejczak 2009: 18–23).

Owing to financial reasons and problems in cross-governmental coordination, the Polish authorities decided that Poland would not organise its own Provincial Reconstruction Team (PRT). However, since June 2008, Polish soldiers have been taking part in a US-led PRT in Ghazni, to which Poland contributes around 20 people, including a deputy commander for the PRT and eight civilian specialists. From the outset, Poland assumed that most of the contracts realised by PRTs – particularly with regard to infrastructure – would be implemented by local Afghan contractors. Efforts were also made to promote the values of democracy, freedom of speech, human rights and the rule of law through the training of local elites (Kulesa and Górka-Winter 2011: 218–9).

In spring 2010, the Polish government declared that it wished to end its troops' combat role in Afghanistan. At the beginning of 2011, following NATO's Lisbon summit, the government officially announced that during 2012 the profile of the Polish forces' mission would shift from combat to training and mentoring, and the mission would continue in that form until the end of 2014.

As far as the contingent's mandate is concerned, the most substantial part remains concentrated around military operations. The bulk of the Polish effort is directed towards securing safety and order on the strategic Kabul–Kandahar highway within Ghazni province, as well as challenging the activities of Taliban groups and common criminals in that area. As a rule, most of these actions are performed with US support and in cooperation with the Afghan National Security Forces.

Principles governing the use of PMSCs by Poland in Afghanistan[6]

In general, Poland does not use services offered by private contractors in its armed forces' expeditionary activities (ISAF included). With few exceptions, neither the Ministry of Defence nor any other Polish institutions have ever signed a contract for security-related services in Afghanistan with any private military or security company – Polish or otherwise. The principle of not using PMSCs in expeditionary missions, however, is somewhat loosely interpreted where local contractors (such as Afghan firms in the case of ISAF) are concerned.

There are several reasons for the adoption of such an approach by the Polish authorities. Some of these – such as the Polish military's tradition of 'self-sufficiency', the legal and doctrinal framework for military engagements, the weakness of the internal security and defence services market – have already been discussed.

The other factor, however, that seems to be crucial for the adoption of such a position is the technical model of Polish engagement in international missions, based on close cooperation with the US forces. This applies particularly to cases when Poland's contingent is numerous. Owing to the fact that such a pattern of engagement was largely invented during Poland's participation in Operation Iraqi Freedom, we might call it the 'Iraqi model'. This shows that the Polish armed forces' dependence on private contractors is far greater than is officially acknowledged, albeit generally indirect.

The 'Iraqi model': indirect use of private contractors

In this model, formulated during Operation Iraqi Freedom, Polish forces deployed in a particular area of operation rely on significant levels of support from their US allies as an indispensable element for the smooth functioning of the whole contingent. Such support is not limited to a co-financing of the Polish engagement, but also includes the provision of some basic services to ensure the sustainability of Polish forces in the area.

The reason for the development of such a pattern – acceptable and convenient for both Poland and the US – was rather prosaic. In Iraq, the US was striving for international legitimacy for its military activities. Having as many countries as possible involved militarily made it possible to claim that its invasion and subsequent occupation of Iraq was a multinational operation with broad international support. However, only a couple of countries willing to join the operation (UK, Australia, Italy and Spain) were able to offer significant forces. At that time, Poland was keen to provide a substantial presence, but had neither sufficient resources at its disposal nor adequate experience in international operations other than UN-type peacekeeping activities. The US therefore agreed to finance part of the cost of Poland's military engagement if Poland committed a larger number of troops. Ultimately, Poland decided to send around 2,400 troops to Iraq and to take command over the multinational division. However, more than 50 per cent of the overall cost of its engagement was financed from various sources by the US. In addition to some items of equipment (Humvees, etc.), the US provided logistical support and supplied Polish forces with oil, food and even entertainment (movies, communication facilities, etc.). It also took on responsibility for various engineering works and repairs in Polish bases. Obviously, without such support, the Polish contingent's strength and scope of tasks would have been much more limited. That would have had a negative impact on the credibility of claims that the intervention had an 'international character'. Thus, the somewhat peculiar Polish–US 'marriage of convenience' described above was contracted (Bratkiewicz 2004; Kulesa 2005).

As there seemed to be no organisational or economic reasons to build autonomous structures and networks of co-operators for the Polish forces in Iraq, the Polish contingent simply used the US' logistical system, within which a broad spectrum of support activities were provided by private contractors. As a result, without signing any contracts with PMSCs, the Polish contingent gained access to services offered by a range of firms hired by US institutions (the Department of Defense in particular). From the Polish perspective, it was of less importance who exactly provided a particular service – PMSCs or US forces – as long as the Americans accepted responsibility for its provision. Nevertheless, this meant that Polish forces in Iraq were *de facto* strongly dependent on private contractors, but lacked the ability to negotiate the details of the contracts with those companies. US forces played the role of intermediary, making decisions on all aspects of the services provided.

Afghanistan: the 'Iraqi model' slightly modified

A similar model of engagement has been implemented in Afghanistan. Here, a substantial share of the overall cost of the Polish engagement has been financed by the US on the basis of several bilateral arrangements and through Coalition Support Funds administered by the US Department of Defence.[7] However, these funds are generally not transferred to the Polish authorities, but are largely spent on support services offered to Polish forces in Afghanistan by PMSCs hired by the US. The main, though slight, modifications of the Iraqi model of engagement involve the smaller scale of US financial support (in Iraq, the US covered a much larger part of the Polish contingent's costs) and the increased – though still limited – use of Polish private entities to support the contingent (in Iraq, there were very few cases of outsourcing, while in Afghanistan there are more, although in absolute terms still not many). Accordingly, Polish forces in Afghanistan are supported by PMSCs on a much greater scale than is officially admitted. Private contractors who have received contracts to provide logistical support to the US armed forces in Afghanistan, in line with the abovementioned arrangements, also provide such support to several other allies, including Poland. Specifically, as in Iraq, all supplies of food and oil for the Polish forces in Afghanistan are provided by a private firm, which until 2010 was KBR, and since then Fluor Corporation. The latter company is also currently responsible for maintaining (i.e. repairs, resupplying, etc.) many facilities used by Polish units in Ghazni (Capaccio 2009). Private contractors hired by the Pentagon also provide communication services (internet, albeit in this case not exclusively) and even entertainment services, such as fitness clubs, cinemas, etc. Thanks to US support, the Polish contingent also has access to interpreters (from TITAN Corporation).

The situation is slightly different as far as transport is concerned. Although the vast majority of the Polish contingent's transport costs are financed by the US – and provided by companies granted contracts by US authorities – some flights are also performed by the Polish air force or via NATO mechanisms such as the Strategic Airlift Capability or the SALIS agreement. In the case of transport of non-lethal equipment within the area of deployment, when such services are not provided directly by Polish, US or other allies' forces, Polish units may request assistance from US logistics. The service would then be typically provided by local (Afghan) entrepreneurs, chosen and paid by the US (reimbursed later from the Coalition Support Funds).

Moreover, on the basis of Polish–American agreements on leasing specific equipment for Polish forces in Ghazni – 30 'Cougar' Mine-Resistant Ambush-Protected vehicles free-leased to Poland since 2008 – private contractors are responsible for service/repair and also provide services to Polish units without additional arrangements.

As these examples suggest, the majority of services provided to Polish forces by private contractors – indirectly, with US forces acting as an 'intermediary' – are or have been 'non-core military services' typical of so-called military support firms and far from the 'tip of the spear', to use P. W. Singer's (2008: 91–2) well-known metaphor. Poland also benefits to some degree, however, from services of a more military-specific character. Since the Polish contingent is dependent on US support in the area of ISR (intelligence, surveillance, reconnaissance), some data received from US forces is collected by private contractors. Additionally, some assistance from PMSCs was also provided in relation to the maintenance of the Boeing-made 'Insitu Scan Eagle' Unmanned Aerial Vehicle (UAV) system. This system was leased by the Polish Ministry of Defence from the US for a period of 12 months, starting from spring 2010. Private contractors provided by Boeing carried out the initial training and mentoring of Polish soldiers, who have since taken over full control of the system.

Unsurprisingly, all of the indirect support from PMSCs to Polish units in Afghanistan is provided through the infrastructure networks created for the US forces. Private contractors have developed no specific distribution systems to provide particular services to the US' allies. From the perspective of the Polish forces, this support is to a large degree simply something that is provided by the US authorities, and it is irrelevant whether the actual services are provided by a private contractor or by the US military.

Replicating the 'Iraqi model' in Afghanistan offers Poland several substantial advantages. Clearly, it makes Polish participation in ISAF cheaper: without US support, the contingent would have been significantly smaller, which would limit political gains. Moreover, it gives Polish forces the possibility of developing stronger ties with their US counterparts and deepens interoperability.

However, an unfavourable effect of copying the 'Iraqi model' is that again Poland is not involved in the selection of private contractors. Despite the fact that some of the services provided are critical for the performance of the contingent, Poland has no influence on the details of the actual contracts. The Americans manage contacts between the Polish forces and PMSCs. The US military administration sets priorities and makes decisions on the flow of the services. Thus, if the situation is deemed to require it and a given resource is scarce, the US can redirect available resources to its own units and make the allies simply wait. Such 'availability crises' have already happened, particularly in the context of transport to and from the area of deployment. In April 2010, some Polish soldiers got stuck in the US Manas base in Kyrgyzstan while on their way back from Afghanistan, since the transportation planes that were to carry them were directed to perform other tasks.

Nevertheless, the current model is probably still the best available. It enables Poland to maintain a much larger presence in Afghanistan than would be possible if it had a fully autonomous contingent. It also affects the performance of different activities on the ground – including these directly linked to peace and reconciliation – by allowing better allocation of the limited resources that Poland has at its disposal. The money that would normally cover logistics-related costs of the Polish deployment in ISAF, for example, can be spent on other purposes, such as training, procurement of equipment or projects conducted by PRT and CIMIC teams. If there were no such external support, the scale of Polish activities in the development and reconstruction domain – building roads, upgrading energy infrastructure, etc. – would be arguably smaller. Moreover, Poland has no viable alternative. Neither Polish state institutions, nor the Polish military, nor Polish security businesses (generally reluctant to engage in Afghanistan) could offer comparable capabilities. As a consequence, the 'Iraqi model' of engagement in international operations (and of arranging contacts with private contractors) will most probably be employed also in future deployments.

Direct use of PMSCs and civilians by Polish institutions

Even if the majority of services for the Polish contingent are provided by private entities only through the US, there are still some specific cases of direct out-sourcing. The scale and scope of such arrangements, however, is incomparable to the support provided by the Americans.

Maintenance of weapon and support systems. This is the main domain in which Polish forces rely on private contractors under agreements signed with them directly by the Polish Ministry of Defence (or another state entity). The most substantial and complex outsourcing relates to the 'Patria' Advanced Modular Vehicle (in Polish, *Rosomak*). Since the contingent began using these vehicles, a number of civilian technicians have been deployed to carry out maintenance and service tasks (for around 115 vehicles). These technicians (up to 20 people) are sent to Afghanistan by their own employers, responsible for servicing both the vehicles and their weapons systems. The contracted companies, however, are not genuine PMSCs but regular defence companies – WZM Siemianowice (vehicle), Bumar Łabędy (gun system), WB Electronics (internal communication) and AMZ Kutno (support elements).

Furthermore, there has been one peculiar case of the use of private contractors to operate a combat system – the 'Aerostar' UAV. In 2011, a team consisting of a couple of technicians were responsible for operating a set of vehicles and associated control-and-data-transfer stations, providing reconnaissance imagery for the Polish contingent. This was, however, the result of a breach of contractual obligations regarding the procurement of the system by the Polish Ministry of Defence from the Israeli corporation Aeronautics. The Israeli firm, which won the tender in 2010, failed to provide the Polish defence ministry with two sets of Aerostars according to the originally specified deadlines. As a penalty, it was requested to provide one set of the system to the Polish contingent free of charge. This system ended up being operated by private contractors, reportedly employees of a British PMSC, not Polish soldiers (Proceedings 2011). However, such assistance will be most probably terminated when – and if – the company manages to meet its contractual obligations (Ćwieluch 2012).

We should also note the use of the Polish-based information and communications technology company TS-2 to provide satellite communications, including a broadband internet connection. The services provided cover mainly entertainment and family contacts for soldiers, but still this is virtually the only Polish private firm that has succeeded in acquiring outsourcing contracts for a Polish contingent deployed abroad.

Training. There is a limited practice of outsourcing with regard to pre-deployment training of Polish forces. General courses – for example, linguistic or cultural – taking place in Poland, are led by civilians (e.g. university lecturers); again, though, these experts are not provided by companies, but contracted on an individual basis. On specific occasions, the Polish armed forces organise various training in Afghanistan, offered to members of the Polish contingent, soldiers from other countries, or local authority and security service personnel, etc. The majority of these courses are 'non-military-specific', but some could be more specialised (e.g. improvised explosive device awareness training). Nevertheless, even in such cases, civilian trainers are recruited mainly on an individual basis.

Security of Polish military bases and diplomatic posts. Some services are provided for Polish forces by local enterprises, including PMSCs. Afghan contractors are primarily contracted to secure the outer perimeters of Polish military bases and diplomatic posts. For instance, the protection of Polish diplomatic personnel is carried out by the Government Protection Bureau (GPB), which seeks to ensure a safe environment inside Polish bases and assists diplomatic personnel (the ambassador and other employees) during trips outside the embassy. However, the outer perimeter is monitored by Afghan contractors, who are hired directly (in a rare exception to the general pattern of avoiding direct links with PMSCs). Most prominent among these is the Asia Security Group (ASG), based in Sherpur, Kabul. A similar scheme applies to the military bases where Polish units are stationed. The outer perimeter of the main base of the Polish Task Force (near Ghazni) is monitored both by Afghan security forces and by private contractors. These entities are tasked with basic control of incoming vehicles and individuals, allowing Polish forces to concentrate on the actual defence of the base in the event of an armed attack (e.g. artillery shelling).

Contracts with individuals. A vivid example of the policy of preferring individuals over companies for the provision of military support services relates to emergency evacuation of sick or wounded personnel (medevac). Currently, a number of civilian paramedics have been deployed within the Polish contingent in Afghanistan, alongside military medical personnel. These have been contracted by the Ministry of Defence itself, using regular, individual contracts governed by the Labour Code. Therefore, this is a legal entity-to-private-person relation. Similar practices apply in the case of the civilian engineers (some ten persons) embedded in Polish elements of the PRT in Ghazni province. Obviously, neither of these cases provides a proper example of outsourcing. Nevertheless, they do illustrate the reluctance of the Polish armed forces to turn to private legal entities for acquiring support services (given the booming market for private health services in Poland, a bid to acquire medevac services commercially is conceivable, if certain problems – not least the lack of interest of the medical sector itself – were overcome).

Conclusions

For years, the military has been perceived by Poles as one of the most trustworthy and respectable groups within society. The image of the Polish armed forces has remained untarnished, even after combat failures. Interestingly, even during the communist period, when the Polish army was in fact directly tasked by Soviet generals in Moscow (as a consequence of Polish participation in the Warsaw Pact) and was used to suppress democratic opposition in Poland, it managed to preserve its privileged position in people's minds. Despite its involvement in the intervention in Czechoslovakia (1968), the suppression of public protests in Gdańsk (1970) and the implementation of martial law (1981–83), the military did not lose much of its support. The main reason seems to be the cherished romantic vision of the military as the only force able to preserve national identity and defend the state. It should be noted that no other uniformed state entity (the police, the military police, etc.) has been able to gain such status and respect.

Such a cultural background leaves little space for privatising or outsourcing military-related activities. Even if private entities end up accessing the space traditionally reserved for the military and are allowed to perform some tasks within the armed forces' usual scope of activity (guarding, catering, training, etc.), this should be seen as a consequence not of ideological change but rather of economic realities. Following the decision to transform the force into a fully professional army, subsequent Polish governments have walked a tightrope trying to balance scarce resources with growing demands. Privatisation of some basic support services offered a way of bypassing this problem, but at the same time it was resource scarcity that drove the scope and pace of the process.

Further, external premises do not create favourable circumstances for greater reliance by the Polish army on PMSCs. The Polish policy on international missions is characterised by a preference for state-to-state cooperation (preferably relying on the 'lead nation') and for executing missions primarily with military tools. This is mostly due to the fact that Polish contributions have in most cases only formed a limited part of a greater effort by different countries or organisations, which took the primary decisions regarding the execution of the relevant operations, including setting the role for private contractors. The Polish authorities usually sign a contract with private firms (not necessarily, and in fact not primarily, with PMSCs) only when there is no other viable alternative and when the issue of the contract is of minor importance.

The current practice in relation to the use of PMSCs is determined largely by the experience of participation in Operation Iraqi Freedom, the first international operation other than UN peacekeeping activities in which Polish forces took part on a significant scale. The fact that this was a mission performed by a US-led coalition proved to be decisive for elaborating a specific model of Polish expeditionary engagement. The replication of this model in Afghanistan, however, suggests that Poland favours such a pattern of engagement. Nevertheless, the practice of relying on stronger partners is in fact neither a consequence of strategic considerations followed by the adoption of a long-term plan for performing international operations nor a thoroughly elaborated model, but rather the result of *ad hoc* decisions and a desire to exploit available opportunities.

The Polish model of engagement in international operations assumes that Poland's own resources can only partially guarantee the sustainability of a Polish deployment. This results in dependence on allies for the provision of support related to vital aspects of the functioning of Polish contingents, which could further lead to substantial – albeit indirect – reliance on private contractors hired by those allies. Nevertheless, even if such indirect dependence is serious, Poland has a disproportionally small influence on the performance of the private partners on which its forces rely (at least as long as Poland is not contributing to their costs).

Therefore, as of today, Poland has not developed a coherent strategy on cooperation with PMSCs in international operations. Furthermore, the possibility of adopting any new policy in this domain is diminishing owing to three factors. First, there are no signs that Poland's authorities, military or civilian, have any interest in changing the current situation. Present patterns of engagement in international missions seem to be widely accepted by Polish decision makers, which may also be due to the fact that Poland's military and civilian authorities seem not to be fully aware of the effects caused by the implementation of the current model of engagement. Second, decisions concerning the most obvious cases of potential outsourcing – such as the guarding of military bases on Polish territory – have already been implemented as part of the military transformation process. The current government is more focused on implementing these decisions than developing them, unless the situation demands the latter. Third, the compelling need to direct all efforts into the acquisition of capabilities for the military (within a difficult context of economic crisis) rather than engaging it abroad rules out the possibility of sending large contingents to any new international operations, even within the NATO framework (as was shown recently in the case of Libya).

Further, nothing suggests that Poland will change its instrumental approach to peace and stabilisation operations. The current Strategy for the Participation of the Polish Armed Forces in International Operations enjoys silent but wide support and understanding across divergent political sectors in Poland. The concept of engaging forces in foreign deployments to build up Poland's political position on the international arena has become a kind of dogmatic assumption, one that is widely shared. The absence of any wider motivation for participation in foreign operations will thus hamper the development of any peace and reconciliation strategy.

Changes in Polish policy on that issue will only be possible if the professionalisation of the Polish armed forces progresses. This process will probably cause increased pressure to outsource some aspects of the functioning of the Polish armed forces in the future. However, achieving a level of outsourcing comparable to that of the most advanced NATO members, such as the US and the UK, seems improbable. If it were to occur, it would undoubtedly involve a rather long process of change, and it seems possible that outsourcing will not be initiated in response to changes in Polish expeditionary activities, but may be triggered by other factors. One that is especially worth mentioning is the coming generational shift. People born in the 1990s and 2000s will be the first generations since the Second World War that have no formal obligation to serve in the army (the draft was suspended in 2008). Consequently, they will perceive the armed forces more as a professional than a 'societal' entity, which could make them more prone to favour a more commercialised logic in relation to military operations. Additionally, structural changes in the army (including changes to the pension system announced recently by the government) will cause many soldiers – some well trained, highly qualified and experienced in foreign deployments – to leave the military.[8] It cannot be ruled out that their skills will end up being utilised by new PMSCs that might emerge as a response to the in-flow of such specialists into the market. Only if a new model of thinking on peace and stabilisation operations is gradually established by the Polish strategic community will it be possible for Poland to develop a coherent peace and reconciliation strategy, one that would put considerable emphasis on the capabilities of private actors.

Notes

1 See *Konsalnet łączy agencje ochrony*, available at http://biznes.gazetaprawna.pl/artykuly/420961, konsalnet_laczy_agencje_ochrony.html (accessed 7 February 2012).
2 Decision of the Minister of National Defence no. 16/MON, 9 January 2007.
3 The tasks of the Polish armed forces are defined in Article 26 of the Polish Constitution (1997); see www.sejm.gov.pl/prawo/konst/angielski/kon1.htm (accessed 7 February 2012).
4 'Ustawa o zasadach użycia lub pobytu Sił Zbrojnych Rzeczypospolitej Polskiej poza granicami państwa', *Dziennik Ustaw*, 1998, No. 162, Item 1117.
5 See *National Security Strategy of the Republic of Poland*, Warsaw 2007, available at: http://merln.ndu.edu/whitepapers/Poland-2007-eng.pdf (accessed 7 February 2010); *Defence Strategy of the Republic of Poland*, Warsaw 2009, available at: www.bbn.gov.pl/portal/pl/475/2826/Strategia_Obronnosci_Rzeczypospolitej_Polskiej.html (accessed 7 February 2010).
6 Except where indicated otherwise, this subsection is based mainly on the authors' interviews with officials from Poland's Ministry of Defence and Ministry of Foreign Affairs, in particular with former Special Representative of the Polish Ministry of Defence for the Polish military contingent in ISAF Col. Piotr Łukasiewicz; Secretary of the Afghanistan Interagency Coordination Group Piotr Krawczyk; and several officers from the special forces (GROM) under the condition of anonymity.
7 In 2011, Poland spent from its budget PLN 413 million (ca. US$ 153 million) on maintaining its 2,600-strong contingent in ISAF (purchase of equipment excluded; total budgetary appropriations for 2011 were PLN 1,060 million). Additional US support – estimated as less than US$100 million in total (precise official data are unavailable) – constituted therefore up to 40 per cent of the overall costs of the Polish engagement.
8 See: *7 tysięcy żołnierzy mniej* at: www.rp.pl/artykul/317607,768106.html?p=1 (accessed 7 February 2012).

References

Andrzejczak, Rajmund. 2009. 'Wejść do głów', *Polska Zbrojna*, 6 December.
Bratkiewicz, Jarosław. 2004. 'Poland's Engagement in the War and Stabilisation in Iraq'. In *Yearbook of Polish Foreign Policy 2004*, 25–40.Warsaw: PISM.
Capaccio, Tony. 2009. 'DynCorp, Fluor Win Afghan Work Worth $7.5 Billion'. www.bloomberg.com/apps/news?pid=newsarchive&sid=aMvHvWx8Ra0c (accessed 23 February 2012).

CBOS Report. 2009. *Prywatyzacja – oceny, skojarzenia, oczekiwania i obawy*, Raport BS 133/ 2009, Warszawa: CBOS.

Chądrzyński, Mariusz. 2004. 'Zarejestrowane i aktywne małe i średnie przedsiębiorstwa w Polsce w latach 1994 – 2004'. www.ae.katowice.pl/images/user/File/katedra_ekonomii/ M._Chadrzynski_Zarejestrowane_i_aktywne_msp_w_Polsce_w_latach_1994_2004.pdf (accessed 23 February 2012).

Constitution. 1997. *Konstytucja Rzeczypospolitej Polskiej* [Constitution of the Republic of Poland], 2 April, *Dziennik Ustaw*, 1997, nr 78, poz. 483.

Ćwieluch Juliusz. 2012. 'Drony tanie niesłychanie', *Polityka*, 18 January.

Davies, Norman. 1994. *Boże igrzysko. Historia Polski*, vol.II. Kraków: Znak.

Decision. 2007. 'Decision of the Minister of National Defence no 16/MON', 9 January.

Defense Strategy. 2009. 'Strategia Obronności Rzeczypospolitej Polskiej' [Defence Strategy of the Republic of Poland], www.bbn.gov.pl/portal/pl/475/2826/Strategia_Obronnosci_Rzeczyp ospolitej_Polskiej.html (accessed 23 February 2012).

Epstein, Rachel A. 2006. 'When Legacies Meet Policies: NATO and the Refashioning of Polish Military Tradition', *East European Politics and Societies* 20 (2): 254–285.

Górka-Winter, Beata. 2009. 'Udział Polski w operacjach pokojowych i stabilizacyjnych'. In *Rocznik Polskiej Polityki Zagranicznej 2009*, Warszawa: PISM, 15–32.

Kościuk, Lech. 2010. 'Przełom w transformacji', *Kwartalnik Bellona* 42 (4): 151–159.

Kulesa, Łukasz. 2005. 'Poland's involvement in Iraqi Stabilisation in 2004'. In *Yearbook of Polish Foreign Policy 2005*, 161–170. Warsaw: PISM.

Kulesa, Łukasz and Górka-Winter, Beata. 2011. 'From Followers to Leaders as "Coalition Servants": The Polish Engagement in Afghanistan'. In *Statebuilding in Afghanistan, Multinational Contributions to Reconstruction*, edited by Nikola Hynek and Peter Marton, 212–226, London: Routledge.

Kuźniar, Roman. 2009. *Poland's Foreign Policy after 1989*. Warsaw: Scholar.

Law. 1998. 'Ustawa o zasadach użycia lub pobytu Sił Zbrojnych Rzeczypospolitej Polskiej poza granicami państwa' [Law on principles of use and stay of the Armed Forces of the Republic of Poland outside state borders], *Dziennik Ustaw*, nr 162, poz. 1117.

Longhurst, Kerry and Zaborowski, Marcin. 2007. *The new Atlanticist: Poland's foreign and security policy priorities*. London: Blackwell Publishing.

Madej, Marek. 2011. 'Poland in the fight against international terrorism'. In *Poland's Foreign Policy in the 21st Century*, edited by Stanisław Bieleń, 339–361, Warsaw: Difin.

National Strategy. 2007. National Security Strategy of the Republic of Poland, Warsaw, http://merln.ndu.edu/whitepapers/Poland-2007-eng.pdf (accessed 23 February 2012).

Niżyńska Joanna. 2010. 'The Politics of Mourning and the Crisis of Poland's Symbolic Language After April 10', *East European Politics and Societies* 24 (4): 467–479.

Popiuk-Rysińska, Irena. 2001. 'The United Nations in Poland's Security Policy'. In *Poland's Security Policy 1989–2000*, edited by Roman Kuźniar, 378–403, Warsaw: Scholar.

Proccedings. 2011. 'Proceedings of National Defence Commission of Polish Parliament No 4983/VI', http://orka.sejm.gov.pl/Biuletyn.nsf/0/C5ADAB2FA918A44DC125788C00 47B282/$file/0498306.pdf (accessed on 23 February 2012).

Singer, Peter W. 2008. *Corporate Warriors. The Rise of the Privatized Military Industry*. Ithaca, NY: Cornell University Press.

Siren, Torsti. 2009. *State agent, identity and the 'new world order': reconstructing Polish defence identity after the Cold War era*. Helsinki: National Defence University.

Strategy. 2009. 'Strategia udziału sił zbrojnych Rzeczypospolitej Polskiej w operacjach międzynarodowych' [The Strategy of Participation of Polish Armed Forces in International Operations], www.bbn.gov.pl/download.php?s=1& id = 6585 (accessed 23 February 2012).

Vision. 2008. 'Vision of the Polish Armed Forces 2030'. Warsaw: Ministry of National Defense, www.dt.wp.mil.pl/en/78.html (accessed 23 February 2012).

Watt, Richard M. 2011. 'Gorzka chwała. Polska i jej los 1918–1939'. Warszawa: AMF Plus.

Winid Bogusław. 2007. 'Udział Polski w działaniach stabilizacyjnych w Afganistanie', *Polski Przegląd Dyplomatyczny* 35 (1): 5–19.

Żemła, Edyta. 2011. 'Wojsko fatalnie chronione', *Rzeczpospolita*, 25 March.

6 Hungary

From outsourcing to insourcing

Krisztian Varga

Introduction and overview

With its accession to NATO membership in 1999, Hungary attained one of its most important security goals since the time of transition: to become part of the North Atlantic defence community. The foundation of the country's long-term defence was thus established. The issue of NATO membership had been a matter of political consensus within Hungary since the mid-1990s. However, the ending of conscription and the politics of various missions in the Balkans, Iraq and Afghanistan did stir public discussion. It is precisely these issues that pushed successive governments towards considering outsourcing and the use of private companies in the field of defence.

Private companies make an important contribution to the activities of the Hungarian Defence Forces (HDF). Beyond playing a role in guarding and protecting army bases in Hungary proper, such companies are also present in the logistical support of international operations, thus enabling a leaner – even if not necessarily a 'meaner' – military to fulfil its role in the service of an alliance that is considered vital in terms of Hungary's foreign policy objectives. Four months after joining NATO, the first Orbán government (Conservative) issued Decision 2183/1999 (VII. 23), which set out revised basic principles for defence development and planning.[1] One of the main principles outlined concerned the future involvement of Hungary's private sector in the logistical support of the army (Jároscsák 2002). This was intended to improve cost-efficiency.

Conscription had existed in Hungary for 156 years prior to 2004. When it ended on 4 November 2004, significant additional costs were imposed on the Hungarian military. The end – or, more precisely, suspension – of enlisted military service generated additional demand for services. Previously, conscription had provided Hungary's armed forces with an abundance of cheap labour. Enlisted soldiers joined the military's ranks for a year or more, and after a few months of basic training were employed in tasks on-base, including in the maintenance and protection of military facilities. This cheap, conscripted workforce also saved the military from having to spend on cleaning, gardening and other simple tasks. For all of these tasks, private contractors would now need to be hired, as professional soldiers are generally unwilling to perform such menial work. For these types of tasks, the Hungarian Ministry of Defence preferred its own companies as principal contractors, and these were at the same time supposed to find themselves a viable place within the market. In parallel to these developments, NATO commitments generated demands related to capability development and logistics services for deployments to international operations. These kinds of services are generally provided by foreign companies through NATO/EU or allied cooperation.

Military outsourcing was initially viewed as a largely technical (organizational and financial) issue, and as such remained under the radar of public discourse. No philosophical or practical discussion of the state's monopoly over the use of force – or the implications of the lack thereof – took place. However, interest groups around the outsourcing business tended to make the technical approach more complex than was initially intended, which began to draw matters to the public's attention, mostly in relation to concerns over cost-efficiency stemming from questionable pricing practices. In the summer of 2010, the second Orbán government began to review the outsourcing business from such a perspective, with a view to tackling corruption and improving capability development and economic efficiency. Public debate has never really moved beyond these more mundane – albeit important – aspects of the issue, and ethical considerations are thus largely restricted to the ethics of the government's use of the public purse.

The first section of this chapter introduces the reasons behind the start of privatization in the Hungarian defence sector, and describes the emergence of a semi-outsourced sphere of activities dominated by enterprises owned by the state/ Ministry of Defence. The second section explains how these structures tend to impose negative externalities on their environments (i.e. subcontractor chains and society) in various ways. To an extent, the third section then examines contrary experience in the context of the HDF's international operations, while the fourth section provides further detail in the form of a case study of the Afghanistan mission. The final section returns to the original thread of the discussion – namely, the challenges involved in domestic security commercialisation – and offers a preliminary assessment of the Hungarian government's attempt to address these through a set of reform measures that may offer interesting food for thought in reflection on the general merits and possible downsides of privatization and outsourcing, as well as a reversal of these processes.

The Hungarian context: Ministry of Defence-owned companies

During the Cold War, Hungary was a member of the Warsaw Pact, along with countries such as Poland and Romania. As a result of the socialist system's centrally planned economy, the state was the sole owner in all sectors, including security and defence. For this reason, there were no private companies specializing in security and defence before the transition. The Hungarian People's Army was self-supporting. In other words, it had its own service, maintenance and technical–development capacities, as did the armed forces of all the Warsaw Pact countries.

Military outsourcing was viewed by governments from the end of the 1990s to 2010 as a tool for easing the effects of military downsizing and defence budget cuts. This may be referred to as a kind of semi-outsourcing, since the internal market for services was created through government defence reforms in two ways. First, these reforms made available a large number of former military personnel with special expertise after the HDF's strength was slashed from 155,000 to 26,500 between 1989 and 2010 (Honvedelem 1994: 62; Ministry of Defence 2011: 51). Second, the downsizing occurred in parallel with the NATO accession and the suspension of compulsory military service, which both resulted in an increased demand for services. The latter would permit the military to focus more on its core combat and combat-support tasks. However, as this section demonstrates, the transformation has not come without complications.

In 1992–93, Hungary's Ministry of Defence established its own state-owned defence industrial companies on the basis of the defence forces' existing repair and technical–development capabilities, with many of these new firms including 'HM' – that is, 'Ministry of Defence' – within their official names. These would provide maintenance and repair services both for the military and for the ministry as a whole. The rationale behind the creation of these limited companies was to maintain existing capacities for the repair and modernization of the HDF's mainly Soviet-made technical assets (ÁSZ 2005: 16). The initiative was driven by two key factors: first, it was hoped that the move would make it possible to downsize the military without loss of existing capacity; second, state-owned companies could be forced to open up towards the civilian market as a way of utilizing spare capacity.

With a view to their role in defence matters, these Ministry of Defence-owned limited companies were deemed the property of the state under the terms of Act XXXIX of 1995 on privatization. In 2000, the defence ministry also created a number of public companies for activities that, strictly speaking, do not belong to the military, such as recreation or cultural activities within the armed forces. In Government Decision 2183/1999 (VIII, 23), the first Orbán government ruled that the Ministry of Defence should re-examine what its core competencies were. The aim was both to strengthen the military and to enable improved conformity with NATO requirements by externalizing tasks that did not, in a direct sense, constitute core defence functions (Honvedelem 2006: 107). Accordingly, in 2000 and 2001, a number of 'public benefit companies' were created, with the Ministry of Defence acting as the source of institutional financing for these.

The MoD Electronics, Logistics and Property Management Company (MoD EI) is the largest of the Ministry of Defence companies that provide services for the HDF and the ministry – both in terms of revenue (€153 million in 2009) and in terms of number of employees (hmei.hu). It is a textbook example of a company responsible for semi-outsourced activities. In 2011, it was providing services to the HDF/Ministry of Defence in two main areas: property management and

Table 6.1 Hungarian Ministry of Defence companies in 2010

Type	Activities	Established
Defence industrial		
MoD Electronics, Logistics and Property Management Company (MoD EI) www.hmei.hu	Property management and property protection/security. The main services provided by MoD EI are logistics support for military exercises; maintenance of law enforcement, military health and civilian facilities; dwelling-house management (Ministry of Defence-owned blocks of flats and apartment houses for service personnel); and comprehensive security services.	January 1993
MoD ArmCom Communication-Technical Co. Ltd. (MoD ArmCom) www.armcom.hu	Maintenance, renewal, installation and control of stable and mobile communications equipment and cryptographic devices. Logistics support and the renewal of special-purpose vehicles for engineering, ambulance and CBRN defence troops.	April 1992
MoD Currus Combat Vehicle Technique Company (MoD Currus) www.currus.hu	Logistics support, maintenance, repair and development services for its military vehicles (tanks, combat vehicles, military trucks, etc.).	December 1992
MoD Arzenál Electro-Technical Company (MoD Arzenal) www.hmarsenal.hu	Overhaul, repair and technical inspection of missiles and missile systems, fire control systems, radar, and other additional equipment.	April 1992
Forestry		
MoD Verga www.verga.hu MoD Kaszó www.kaszort.hu MoD Budapest www.bp-erdo.hu	Forestry and game management in forested and agricultural areas around large military facilities (shooting ranges, driving ranges, training facilities, command and control sites).	January 1993 January 1993 January 1993
Service provider		
MoD Zrínyi Media www.honvedelem.hu	Publishing journals and other print publications, film-making and documentation. Editorial office and the website of the online magazine.	2000
MoD Bessenyei György www.stefania.hu MoD Topographic Ltd. www.topomap.hu	Recreation: owning and running hotels and resorts. Producing maps, topographical data and related materials.	2000 2001

Source: Homepages of Ministry of Defence companies; Hanitz (2011a, 2011b).

property protection/security. There is limited competition within the Hungarian market for military-related services. The state prefers its own companies as key contractors. State-owned firms regularly acquire contracts through public procurement tenders, and can generally count on acting as the lead contractors (ÁSZ 2004). Private actors can primarily only compete for sub-contractor positions. The most important client in the market is the state. Around 70 per cent of the annual turnover of companies owned by the state – with the exception of forestry companies – derives from commissions from the military (ÁSZ 2005). In 2007, Ministry of Defence companies received €135 million for their services from the ministry, while their annual turnover reached €179 million (ÁSZ 2009).

A problem in terms of the viability of these companies is that while their capacities may extend beyond the limited demands of the state, their assets cannot be flexibly converted to serve other purposes, and the costs involved in maintaining existing capacities make it very difficult for these companies to diversify their product lines. It is thus very difficult for them to fully utilize any spare capacity (ÁSZ 2005). Nevertheless, the Ministry of Defence companies operate outside of the strict budgetary control of the ministry and government, and thus can take loans and hire or lay off personnel more freely than the latter, which permits a more flexible approach to wage costs. This has expanded the room for manoeuvre enjoyed by the Ministry of Defence during the downsizing of the armed forces, for example in relation to the guarding of HDF facilities. Within the personnel of Hungary's defence- and security-related private companies, former military, police and penal-enforcement personnel are over-represented, illustrating the effects of the downsizing and reorganization of the state security sector.

In terms of issues affecting the viability of these companies, a look at the role of so-called service pensions may be useful to illustrate how far-reaching the state's impact has been in shaping their opportunity structures. Until the end of 2011, personnel serving within the military, police or penal enforcement were entitled to retire after 25 years of service, the reason given for this being the lack of employment prospects for officers in the shrinking military. According to esti-mates by the trade unions of services personnel, up to 40,000 people under the age of 57 may have benefitted from Hungary's early-retirement pension scheme (Duna TV 2011a). For these former military and police personnel, now receiving service pensions, working for reduced wages may be an attractive proposition. Companies can thus benefit from the experience and professional knowledge of former military personnel at a reduced cost. Serving in this way is even con-sidered to be a kind of 'second service'. And, given the availability of well-trained personnel, companies' training costs are also lowered. Needless to say, this has created an intricate regime of companies dependent on a state lifeline and an uncomfortable sensitivity to changes in regulation whose importance ought not to be a central concern for supposedly independent companies. The following sec-tion sheds further light on how the undesired implications of such a situation manifest in market practices.

The Hungarian market for military services

The HDF outsources services in three main areas: the maintenance of barracks; guarding and protection services for HDF bases; and facilities and logistics services for Hungarian troops engaged in international operations.

Tasks related to maintenance began to be commercialized in 1997 (Jároscsák 2006: 83), when the MoD EI Company was awarded an open tender for services connected to the maintenance of HDF barracks. Since January 2000, the Ministry of Defence has relied on private companies for the maintenance of nearly all its military bases and barracks (Honvedelem 2006: 162–3), after the defence ministry signed a contract for the long-term maintenance of its facilities with its own company, MoD EI, with authorization from the Defence Committee of the National Assembly. The open-ended contract was awarded through the public procurement process (Honvedelem 2006: 162–3). Since 2005, however, almost all of the bases, barracks, hotels, buildings, dwelling-houses and service apartments of both the armed forces and the defence ministry have been operated and guarded by MoD EI (Honvedelem 2006: 109). In turn, MoD EI employs subcontractors to perform various contract-related tasks. Between 2005 and 2010, MoD EI used two main subcontractors: Kipszer Co. Ltd. and Mega-Logistics Co. Ltd. Kipszer was contracted primarily for management, maintenance and repair work worth approximately €15 million per year (Hír TV 2011b). Contracts typically did not set out in specific terms the concrete tasks required as part of their implementation, but rather contained only general terms and conditions regarding the performance of management-related services. Verifying implementation would accordingly prove problematic. For example, MoD Topographic Ltd. paid a flat-rate price for the facility-management services of MoD EI. Prices rose steadily from the first year on. In 2005, MoD EI's services cost a gross total of €300,000. By 2010, this figure had increased by 320 per cent (Haraszti 2011).

After conscription was terminated in 2004, soldiers continued to perform guard services at strategically important buildings of the Ministry of Defence and the military. Protection of the remaining facilities – including those left empty as a result of the reduction of the armed forces – was outsourced to private actors. MoD EI has since become the main contractor for the guarding and protection of defence sites (securifocus.hu 2004). Through the Ministry of Defence's decision to favour its own company, MoD EI has become one of the principal actors in Hungary's private security market. The company has been able to fulfil its increasing role by employing additional personnel and hiring other Hungarian private security firms to carry out particular tasks. Through its strong market position, MoD EI could apply for contracts for other guarding tenders as well. The main client and provider of 'life support' within the Hungarian private security market is thus the state, through its guarding and protection contracts tendered by the Hungarian State Holding Company (NPV Zrt). Besides state-owned firms, various banks and the Hungarian Oil and Gas Company are the most important customers. More recently, major Western firms have also offered high-value contracts to Hungarian security firms, for example related to investments in the automobile industry. According to the former owner of one security company, the annual turnover of the Hungarian market for private security is approximately €700–800 million.[2] Overall, around 2,500 property-protection enterprises compete with one other, but the market is highly concentrated, with 94 per cent of the actors on the market being small enterprises with a total annual revenue of below €1 million. Because of their limited capacities, these small companies compete primarily for subcontractor positions. For these reasons, long subcontractor chains are a key characteristic of the Hungarian security market. According to May 2011 data from the Hungarian Chamber of Bodyguards, Property Protection and Private Detectives (SZVMSZK), 116,568 persons have permission to participate in these types of activities (SZVMSZK 2011). Approximately 80 per cent of those working in private security are former soldiers and policemen.[3]

A large percentage of Hungarian property-protection firms are characterized by the presence of former leaders or mid-level managers from the ranks of the military or various law-enforcement agencies, either within their management or among their owners and/or shareholders. One example of this is MoD EI's director for guarding and protection, Ret. Lt. Gen. Ferenc Győrössy, the former commander of the Hungarian military's Land Forces Command (see: www.hmei. hu). Or, the director of strategy at In-kal Security 2000 is Ret. Lt. Gen. István Bökönyi, the former commander of national penal enforcement (inkal.hu 2011). In this way, Hungarian security companies occupy a gatekeeper position within the Hungarian market. Any foreign investor seeking to establish a private security business – for example, related to investments in car manufacturing – would most likely need to buy a Hungarian private security company and employ its management for the work.[4] Through the outsourcing of guarding and protection tasks, direct costs for the procurer may be diminished. Costs and benefits tend to be increasingly unevenly shared the further one moves down the subcontractor chain. Actual service providers may reduce costs by, for example, only registering their employees as employed for six or four hours a day instead of eight (Farkas 2011), lowering entrepreneurs' tax and benefit costs. Through employing private companies, state institutions can thus reduce the costs appearing in their official budgets under the headings for guarding and protection-related tasks. However, at the same time, state revenues are lost in the form of taxes and benefits that go unpaid, while many of the previously incurred costs are externalized and imposed upon those that have no say in the matter – for example, subcontractors and their employees (napi.hu 2011). A 2010 audit by the National Tax and Custom Administration (NTCA) found that around 40 per cent of the approximately 300 private security companies examined had contravened Hungary's taxation laws to a combined value of €25 million. The NTCA accordingly imposed fines to a value of €20.5 million (napi.hu 2011). This is the other side of the privatization coin: a state shedding competencies and responsibilities in ways that have imposed undue burdens both on some companies and employees involved in subcontractor chains, and on society as a whole in terms of lost tax revenue.

Contribution to international operations

A more positive experience related to PMSCs is in the field of international operations. Small states, such as Hungary, may rely primarily on two principal means for furthering their security interests in international relations: (1) through working (and voting) in international organizations, taking part in their decision making; and (2) through troop contributions to international operations. The role and importance of PMSCs in relation to the latter need to be assessed in the light of Hungary's basic foreign policy interests.

As of November 2011, around 1,000 Hungarian soldiers were engaged in tours of duty in ten countries on three continents (Ministry of Defence 2011). In line with Hungary's national interests, the main thrust of the HDF's efforts has been in the Western Balkans and Afghanistan. Approximately 430 Hungarian soldiers were engaged within NATO's ISAF operation in Afghanistan at the end of 2011. The size of this deployment illustrates NATO's relative importance vis-à-vis other commitments within Hungary's foreign policy. The system of national logistics support is vitally complemented in the area of operations by multinational logistics – that is, the logistics supply system of the lead nation or leading organization behind a given mission, for example one or more of Hungary's NATO partners (Jároscsák 2006: 100). As a matter of basic principle, Hungarian contingents should receive logistics support through a national supply system. In reality, the situation in Afghanistan is that, at least in relation to some services, it is rather the national support system that complements multinational support.

Various companies have contributed to the HDF's activities in international operations in the field of logistics support. From December 1995, MoD EI was commissioned by the Hungarian government to provide complex logistics support as part of the host-nation support provided to IFOR and later SFOR forces stationed in and transiting through Hungarian territory. The company also provided logistics services (purchasing of goods, transportation and food supply) for NATO peacekeeping forces in Croatia and Bosnia and Herzegovina (see: www.hmei.hu). The logistical support of the HDF's Iraqi logistics battalion in 2003–04 proceeded in line with general NATO procedure. Several technical assets were provided by the US for the Hungarian military. Everyday personal and work-related needs were supported, within the framework of the LOGCAP treaty, by the US company KBR (Hautzinger and Bakó 2006: 156–7). KBR was also involved in servicing the 109 vehicles provided to the battalion for transporting both shipments and personnel (Sramkó 2004: 38). Assets and vehicles used by the HDF would otherwise be repaired and maintained in Hungarian bases. In Iraq, personnel from the Hungarian firm MoD Currus joined the battalion for the purpose of carrying out repairs (Sramkó 2004: 37–8).

Through the use of private military companies within its international operations, the Hungarian military is able to operate with a higher number of active-duty troops in any given operation. When a deployment is being assembled, the number of personnel involved in support tasks can be minimized, and thus the troops who contributed to a military operation have greater combat strength.

Furthermore, when military capability development is achieved through the market, PMSC employees are not included and do not appear in the official numbers for the HDF contingent approved by the parliament. This is the case even with Hungarian firms, not just foreign suppliers, which contributes to the overall more positive record of security commercialization in this context. As a case study, the following section examines this experience in the context of the HDF's operations in Afghanistan. In addition, in relation to the more general theme of the present volume, it includes a brief discussion of whether any of this experience may be of relevance for peace and reconciliation strategies in Afghanistan.

The Hungarian engagement in Afghanistan

Hungary's participation in ISAF operations in Afghanistan is primarily about NATO, and only secondarily related to the ongoing challenges in Afghanistan (Szlankó 2011: 193; Marton and Wagner 2011: 197). A look at Hungary's Afghanistan policy reveals that what is perhaps most important is conforming to NATO's expectations vis-à-vis the organization's needs in Afghanistan, and thus conveying to its partners the image of Hungary as a good ally.

The main thrust of Hungarian activities in Afghanistan takes place within the framework of the Provincial Reconstruction Team (PRT) in Baghlan Province. Alongside the 240 troops manning the PRT, there are only two civilians in the contingent. A political advisor has been involved since October 2006, and a development advisor was incorporated within the PRT staff only from October 2011. The reason for the predominantly military composition of the PRT is that the Hungarian government undertook to carry out the role of lead nation essentially in order to increase the visibility of the Hungarian flag on the ISAF placemat. Prime Minister Ferenc Gyurcsány's Socialist–Liberal government could thus demonstrate the importance it attaches, as a good ally, to the objectives the alliance is seeking to achieve in its most important foreign mission. Within Hungarian politics, the PRT has since become firmly established as being *de facto* a Ministry of Defence project (Marton and Wagner 2011: 202). And it was within the Ministry of Defence that the idea of taking over the leadership of a PRT first arose, back in 2005. Because of the institutional ownership of the project, there is a huge discrepancy between military and development budgets, the latter being considerably more modest. The defence ministry spent €32 million in 2009 to maintain its presence in Afghanistan, while the Hungarian development budget for activities in Afghanistan at that time was only €1.6 million (Wagner 2010b).

Without the logistical supply system of the NATO framework, the HDF would have difficulties deploying and maintaining troops in international operations thousands of kilometres from Hungarian territory. In order to improve the coordination of logistics support for Hungarian contingents, the 35 members of the HDF National Support Element Afghanistan (HDF NSE) were deployed to Mazar-e-Shariff and Kabul in summer 2010. Before that, this type of activity was performed by the PRT Logistic Branch and National Logistic Element in Mazar-e-Sharif.

Table 6.2 Hungarian Defence Forces deployments to Afghanistan in November 2011

Contingent	Location	Since	Activities
Provincial Reconstruction Team (PRT)	Baghlan Province	2006	Coordination and participation of development in the province and providing military support for those who work in it.
Operational Mentor and Liaison Team (OMLT)	Baghlan Province	2009	Training and mentoring the Afghan National Army (ANA) with Ohio National Guard under NTM-A.
Special Operation Team		2009	Special operation tasks with US forces under ISAF.
Mi-35 Air Mentor Team	Kabul (capital)	2010	Training and mentoring Afghan Air Force (AAF) Mi-35 gunship pilots and ground crew under NTM-A.
Mi-17 Air Advisory Team	Herat Province	2011	Training and mentoring AAF Mi-17 pilots and ground crew under NTM-A.
Logistics Mentor Team	Kabul (capital)	2010	Teaching and mentoring ANA soldiers at NATO ISAF Combat Service Support (CSS) Logistics School under NTM-A.
National Support Element	Kabul (capital), Balk Province	2010	Providing logistics support for all Hungarian contingent under ISAF.
Staff officers	Kabul (capital), Balk Province	2003	Various tasks.

Source: Ministry of Defence Press Office hand-out

The supply of HDF contingents engaged in international operations is mainly carried out using air transport from Hungary because of the country's centralized public procurement procedure. As a result, contingent commanders have very limited freedom in terms of procuring what they might need from the local market. Even blank sheets of paper for printing and copying are delivered to the troops in this way, over a distance of 4,500 km – and this is only one of the many items that make supplying Hungarian contingents unduly expensive (Solymosi and Révész 2011: 81). Catering services for the troops and maintenance of barracks represent exceptions to this strict procurement rule. Yet, the system of logistics supply for Hungarian contingents is bureaucratic, and regulations have not kept up with the growing needs of the armed forces since the NATO accession (Szlankó 2011: 114–6). For these reasons, strategic airlift capabilities are extremely important in terms of enabling the HDF to participate in international operations.

Indirect contracting: logistics support to contingents involved in international operations

NATO's 1999 Strategic Concept placed considerable emphasis on the alliance's ability to engage in out-of-area operations. In response to this new challenge, member states needed to take steps to improve their expeditionary capabilities (Szarvas 2007). Hungary's armed forces are equipped with Antonov An-26 medium-range transport aircraft, which generally permit only tactical airlift. Yet, the Hungarian military ended up having to use these to transport a small amount of supplies, along with some of its troops, to the Afghan theatre (MNO 2007). A number of opportunities exist for loaning transport capacity on the basis of bilateral military agreements. The Hungarian military has technical agreements of this nature with NATO's Allied Joint Force Command Brunssum, as well as with the German, Canadian and Romanian armies and the armed forces of the Netherlands (Szarvas 2007: 21–2). In these cases, a 'one-way ticket' to the Afghan theatre costs approximately €500–600 (Orosz 2009: 7). Between 2005 and 2009, the HDF paid around €3–3.5 million for passenger charter services and €3 million for freighter services to Hungary's NATO allies (Orosz 2009: 7). Currently, there are two multilateral programmes providing NATO member states with missing strategic airlift capability. One of these is the Strategic Airlift Interim Solution (SALIS), the other NATO's Strategic Airlift Capability (SAC), provided by NATO's Heavy Airlift Wing (HAW). These will be discussed in turn below.

The Hungarian military leases 25 flight hours per year from RUSLAN–SALIS GmbH, at a total cost of €615,000 between 2006 and 2009 (honvedelem.hu 2006). Within the framework of the SALIS programme, one hour of flight time (in the case of An-124 Ruslans) costs around €23,000, all expenses included (Szarvas 2007: 20). According to Szarvas, given the large quantities of cargo shipped and the fixed price, this has in fact been a fair rate. When Hungary took over the leadership of its PRT in Afghanistan in 2006, the military flew most of the assets and equipment it would need using SALIS capacities, just as it did for the return leg, when the by-then redundant materials and equipment of the Light Infantry Company, a Hungarian unit deployed to Afghanistan earlier on, needed to be brought home (Szarvas 2007: 20). Given the size and the weight of such transport assignments, once again the only realistic option was to rely on the An-124 under the SALIS framework.

SAC is a long-term programme of cooperation in the field of strategic airlift, envisioned to last for up to three decades. The 12 participating countries have created a jointly owned, maintained and operated fleet of three Boeing C-17 transport planes. These aircraft arrived at Pápa Airbase in Hungary in 2009. Hungary provides host-nation support to the HAW's operations. Accordingly, these C-17 aircraft are registered in Hungary and flown under Hungarian insignia. The joint air fleet is the most cost-efficient way of providing for strategic airlift capability. In total, Hungary's demands for flight time and cargo capacity constitute no more than 2 per cent (50 hours) of the capacities made available by these aircraft, and the country's share of the financial burden related to the SAC closely matches this, at exactly 2 per cent. An example of when the SAC proved useful to the Hungarian military was when one of these C-17s carried members of the HDF's Staff Officer Group to Kabul for their mission at Kabul International Airport (KAIA) on 21 September 2010 (regiment.hu 2010).

Besides air transport, PMSCs provide services related to catering for troops and maintaining barracks through indirect contracting. These companies are directly hired by major contributors to ISAF, such as the US, Germany or Italy. In military encampments under ISAF Regional Command-North (RC-N), the PMSC Supreme Global Services provides services related to the operation of bases. The nations contribute to financing related costs depending on the number of personnel required and the quantity and quality of the services delivered. HDF NSE Afghanistan's main task is to coordinate orders and payments related to the provision of housing, catering or laundry services for the Hungarian contingents and staff soldiers throughout the country, and to manage the transportation of soldiers when they are on leave in Hungary. Since HDF NSE deployed to Afghanistan, it has been responsible for managing the full scope of logistics support for Hungarian contingents in ISAF (Solymosi and Révész 2011: 80–1). At Camp Pannonia, the home of the HDF's PRT in Pol-e-Khomri, Baghlan Province, some services (catering, maintenance, laundry, etc.) have been provided by Supreme Global Services. The company provides catering for around 300 (Hungarian, Croat, Montenegrin and Albanian) soldiers, and also carries out repair and maintenance work in the camp (Turzai 2010). Supreme's employees are not included in the official numbers for the HDF contingent approved by the Hungarian parliament. In this way, the number of personnel involved in support tasks can be minimized within the HDF contingent, increasing the overall combat strength of the military personnel contributed to the operation. Other HDF contingents are mostly accommodated in camps at Mazar-e-Sharif, Kabul, Khilagay and Shindand, where PMSCs provide similar services. HDF NSE pays for the services that Hungarian soldiers receive in these bases (Solymosi and Révész 2011: 80).

Direct contracting: capabilities directly from the market

In addition to autonomous national capacities and cooperation with allies on a bilateral or multilateral basis, it is possible for the HDF to have direct participation from the market. It is the task of the HDF's Military Transportation Centre (MH Katonai Közlekedési Központ) to award public procurement contracts for the leasing of sufficient charter-flight capacity to support the airlift of personnel and supplies to the area of operations. In these cases, for example, a flight to the Afghan theatre costs approximately €600–750 per soldier (Orosz 2009: 7). HDF demand is equal to about 20 chartered flights per year. Air Bucharest is the main contractor for chartered flights to Afghanistan. In another example of direct contracting related to deployments but not from the open market, each HDF contingent includes a number of soldiers specialized in providing technical support for military vehicles or other technical assets, but these sometimes require outside professional assistance.

Two of the Ministry of Defence companies discussed earlier – MoD ArmCom and MoD Currus – are involved in the support of HDF contingents worldwide. According to its own website, MoD ArmCom provides services related to the maintenance and control of communications equipment and cryptographic devices for HDF forces engaged in international operations (see: www.armcom.hu). For its part, MoD Currus provides technical assistance and servicing of military vehicles used by HDF personnel in international operations around the world, and its civilian employees are sent out to the appropriate units to carry out this work (see: www.currus.hu). Their travel is organized and paid by the HDF. The remaining two Ministry of Defence companies – Arzenal and EI – are not involved in activities associated with the HDF's international operations. While MoD Arzenal specializes in different missile systems, radar and other related equipment, there are currently no Hungarian troops using those kinds of systems in international operations (see: www.hmarsenal.hu). MoD EI has widespread experience in the field of maintenance and armed protection of army bases, but the firm currently only provides services within Hungary and is not involved in activities in Afghanistan (see: www.hmei.hu).

HDF contingents can obtain services directly from the market through HDF NSE. Owing to rising demand for road transportation services, HDF NSE hired the Mazar-e-Sharif-based firm Sadiqzada Construction Company in January 2011 to deliver international aid and shipments to its contingents for €65,000 (Honvédelmi Közlöny 2011/2: 269; Honvédelmi Közlöny 2011/3: 337). Because of growing demand, HDF NSE increased its own transport capacity when seven new Raba armoured military trucks arrived from Hungary in May 2011 (Kormany.hu 2011). Through the use of private companies, the military can respond faster to demands that occur during an operation. However, only limited information is available on the commercialization of security in the context of the HDF's engagement in Afghanistan. Guarding and protection services for the Hungarian PRT base was strengthened in early 2010 through the arrival of a platoon of the Montenegrin Defence Forces. Afghans carry out security tasks at the outer perimeter of Camp Pannonia (Turzai 2010; Szabó 2010: 22). Turzai (2010) notes that these Afghan guards are under the command of the PRT Force Protection Company (Turzai 2010), but does not say whether they are armed or unarmed, or whether they are members of the Afghan security forces, civilian employees of a PMSC or even locals hired by the PRT. Other sources have indicated that these guards are local Afghan civilians, familiar with the region (Ambrus 2010: 161). The practice of employing locals for security at the outer perimeter is common among many other countries, such as Italy.

Two NGOs involved in development assistance in Baghlan Province – Hungarian Baptist Aid (Baptista Szeretetszolgálat) and Hungarian Interchurch Aid (Magyar Ökumenikus Segélyszervezet) – have been employing unarmed local Afghans to assist them with their activities. HDF troops are responsible for the security of the staff members of these Hungarian NGOs. However, NGO personnel are often reluctant to accept protection from the military, which they see as being potentially counterproductive for their operational security. Maintaining a low profile, staying unarmed and working with Afghan staff, they feel safer, and therefore only regard the PRT's main base in Pol-e-Khomri as a 'safe house' in the event of an extreme contingency, where they might seek shelter as a last resort.

Implications for peace and reconciliation strategies

In official Hungarian political discourse, the term 'Afghanistan strategy' refers primarily to a document officially entitled 'Hungary's Role in Afghanistan: Mid-Term Strategic Outlook' (from here on referred to as the Mid-Term Strategic Outlook), which was published in November 2009 (MFA 2009). The key objective formulated in this document is the creation of the conditions necessary for Hungary's responsible exit from its area of operations. For the period 2010–15, the Mid-Term Strategic Outlook identified three key components of Hungary's efforts: military operations, assistance with training law-enforcement personnel, and development cooperation. The discussion of the latter makes reference to various goals that are presented as strategically significant: poverty reduction, amelioration of living conditions, creation of employment opportunities, assistance to the democratic functioning of local institutions of government, improving the situation of women, etc. However, it does not in a clear manner set out means for achieving all of these objectives, and is rather vague in terms of the delimitation of competences and responsibility for measurable success.

The Mid-Term Strategic Outlook does not deal with matters of peace and reconciliation strategy in any explicit form, and peace and reconciliation efforts form no explicit part of Hungary's exit strategy. This is partly a manifestation of the prevailing sentiment in Hungary – that is, that the country does not necessarily have direct stakes in the success of the Afghanistan mission. Rather, the mission is seen as fulfilling alliance requirements. Given this, what passes for strategy in Hungary's case is a largely technical approach to matters in which the country adapts to its partners' requirements. Thus, strategy is not built on a genuine notion of conflict with enemies of values considered dear, and in fact the mission is seen largely as an apolitical humanitarian and peace support mission by a small country whose effort may be noble but does not count in terms of the bigger picture. From such a framing of the mission, there stems no firm conviction of having to play an active role in reconciling with any party – be that of the Taliban or any of the other insurgent factions opposing the current Afghan government.

New developments in the field of outsourcing since 2010: insourcing

The second Orbán government is seeking to reform Hungary's defence system. Restructuring and reorganization have been salient items on the agenda, the explicit aim being to address the downsides of the operations of the state-owned enterprises discussed earlier. A White Paper presented in June 2011 sets out a number of key issues related to the management of firms operating under the

Ministry of Defence. Early on, it is emphasized that the new political leadership of the Ministry of Defence does not support 'irrational' forms of outsourcing. In other words, the Ministry of Defence does not favour outsourcing activities to the market if a Ministry of Defence company has the capacity to provide the services in question (WP 2011: 5). The White Paper also highlights the Ministry of Defence's inadequate outsourcing practices between 2005 and 2010. Tenders were restricted, and only partners already in a contractual relationship with one of the Ministry of Defence companies were invited to participate. This meant that there was no real competition among market actors for the outsourced services. In connection with various management and maintenance subcontractor agreements, MoD EI paid out a total of €54 million (according to rates valid as of mid-2010) to its contractors for related activities (WP 2011: 6). Contracts between MoD EI and these subcontractors were at first signed for one or two years, and subsequently extended to five years. Throughout the five-year period, rates were not renegotiable – which created extra profits for the subcontractors (WP 2011: 7). In all major procurements, the same enterprises participated regularly as applicants and were subsequently awarded contracts (WP 2011: 9). The majority of the highest-value contracts were in fact awarded through restricted tendering by reference to Government Decree 143/2004 (IV. 29), which specifically exempts such procurements from the terms of the Public Procurement and Transparency Act. On the basis of the available documentation for the relevant cases, it is impossible to ascertain whether reference to Decree 143/2004 was warranted. However, through such a method – technically expanding the authority of the Government Decree in particular cases – the level of competition in the market was limited.

From 2005 to the first half of 2010, the MoD industrial companies and service-provider firms were allegedly responsible for losses in the range of €6.7 million on the part of the Hungarian Ministry of Defence as a result of the inadequate out-sourcing techniques described above (WP 2011: 14). Alongside inadequate tech-niques, corruption was also a problem between 2004 and 2010 in relation to military outsourcing. According to investigations led by the Military Prosecutor Service in 2010 and 2011, at least 18 Ministry of Defence officials – including high-ranking military officers and civil servants – were allegedly engaged in cor-ruption in connection with requests for an 'extra service fee' of around 5 per cent from subcontractors who had secured low-value contracts (Origo.hu 2011). Such practices also hindered genuine competition within the market. A key motive driving the second Orbán government's current endeavours in this area is thus the goal of reducing costs through a re-examination of the system of outsourcing that has led, under previous governments, to the widespread use of contractors and corruption in the field of national defence. In addition, it is hoped that the level of services that will need to be provided by these companies will more rea-listically reflect the demands of a significantly reduced military following the lat-ter's gradual downsizing over the course of the last 20 years. According to ministerial guidance, services that can be provided by the Ministry of Defence's own firms will no longer be outsourced to contractors – the aim being to break away from a system of operation characterized by redundancies and the wasteful use of resources of Ministry of Defence firms.

Lajos Móró, the new CEO of MoD EI, stated that his company was conforming to the Ministry of Defence's expectations and had the following key objectives, in line with which a renegotiation of the existing service contract would have to take place (Magyar Demokrata 2011): (1) to achieve a 10 per cent reduction in prices without compromising the quality of service provided (Hír TV 2011a); and (2) to in-source those areas – i.e. guarding facilities – that were contracted out to service providers. On 31 December 2010, MoD EI did not renew contracts issued to its 18 private security subcontractors. All currently operational military sites have been in the care of MoD EI's Armed Security Guards (Fegyveres Biztonsági Őrök, FBŐ) since January 2011. This organization's 2,049 guards are all employees of MoD EI, the majority of them former soldiers and police personnel. In the words of Minister of Defence Csaba Hende: 'It was not befitting of the military to guarantee its safety through private security actors. This is something the military has to handle on its own, and it will do so in the future' (Farkas 2011).

The status of the security guards serving as FBŐ is much different from that of other personal- and property-protection personnel employed in Hungary's private security sphere. Their legal status, rights, duties and equipment, as well as their authorization to act, differ markedly. FBŐ's activities are regulated by Act CLIX of 1997 on Armed Security Guards and Environmental Protection and Rural Guards, while personal and property protection personnel fall under the terms of Act CXXXIII of 2005 on Security Services and the Activities of Private Investigators. FBŐ provides for the protection of critical infrastructure, including the Paks nuclear power plant, and FBŐ staff serving at these sites are employed as employees of the organizations they protect.

MoD EI's FBŐ staff are also registered as 'defence reservists' by the HDF. As reservists, they can be called on to perform active duty when the need arises – for example, in disaster-relief mission (Farkas 2011). Along with the insourcing of the protection of military sites, the new leadership of the Ministry of Defence has successfully rationalized related activities. In contrast with earlier entrepreneurial practices, the guards now enjoy greater security. Their employer, MoD EI, pays all taxes and benefits related to their work. In addition, the use of MoD EI's FBŐ staff as volunteer defence reservists represents a new capability for the Hungarian military. As Chief of Hungarian Defence General Tibor Benkő concludes:

> If we were to keep active 2,000 volunteer reservist soldiers, they would cost money. In this way, however, we can have the same personnel serve in double roles. This has to be taken into account and noted as a really cheap solution.
>
> (Duna TV 2011b)

Conclusions

The Hungarian market for military services is characterized by limited competition, and the most important client in the market is the state. The state prefers its own companies as key contractors, and firms owned by the Ministry of Defence regularly acquire contracts through public procurement tenders and can count on serving as lead contractors. Around 70 per cent of the annual turnover of these Ministry of Defence-owned companies derives from commissions from the military, and former military personnel are over-represented within both the management and the staff of these firms, which are mainly involved in providing services within Hungarian territory, such as guard services and services related to the management and maintenance of facilities.

The new Conservative government is attempting to approach the issue of defence reform from the perspectives of both capability development and economic efficiency – partly incompatible objectives that will be challenging to reconcile. Developing an assessment of the system of ministry-owned companies and how they should transform existing outsourcing practices is a part of this agenda. The ministry is seeking to utilize its own companies to meet the HDF's existing demands, while at the same time reducing costs and eliminating corruption. It therefore no longer favours outsourcing to subcontractors in cases where one of its own companies has the capacity for a particular task. This can be seen clearly in current policies on the guarding of HDF facilities within Hungary.

In relation to the commercialization of international operations, the supply of HDF contingents engaged abroad is mainly carried out using air transport from Hungary owing to the regulations governing Hungary's centralized public procurement procedure. The HDF would face difficulties in deploying and maintaining troops in Afghanistan without the current NATO framework. Hungary is a participant in NATO's SALIS programme and currently houses NATO's Heavy Airlift Wing to support strategic transport capability. Meanwhile, Hungarian contingents within ISAF are stationed in camps that are maintained by international PMSCs contracted by allied forces. Hungary's practices in the field of defence outsourcing appear to have no direct implications for its peace and reconciliation strategies in Afghanistan. Moreover, there is no explicitly formulated Hungarian peace and reconciliation strategy as such. Accordingly, Hungary cannot claim to have a significant role in consciously shaping peace and reconciliation efforts within its area of operation or elsewhere in Afghanistan. The key aim of Hungary's Afghanistan policy is to conform to NATO's expectations vis-à-vis the alliance's needs in Afghanistan, and thus to convey the image of Hungary as a good ally.

Outsourced activities are secondary in importance to conventional military tasks, which enables the HDF to focus on core functions and capabilities in terms of both combat and combat support. In some cases, the question of whether to retain particular military capabilities has become a matter of technical issues related to financing procedures. In cases where military capability development is achieved through a resort to the market, the employees of PMSCs do not appear in the official numbers of HDF personnel approved by the Hungarian parliament. This expands the room for manoeuvre enjoyed by the government and the Ministry of Defence.

The debate on the commercialization of military services thus runs in two different ways. The rationales behind outsourced services – such as guarding and maintenance of facilities in Hungary – are questioned mainly because of corruption and the defence ministry's own internal capabilities. Within EU/NATO operations, commercialization has remained a largely technical issue and is still more or less under the radar of public discourse. The present Conservative government is interested in addressing the unintended consequences of using private companies within the military, an intention that was also signalled when Hungary became the Montreux document's thirty-sixth participating state on 1 February 2011.

Notes

1 The first Orbán government was in power between 1998 and 2002, while the second came into power in May 2010.
2 Interview with the former owner of a Hungarian security company, Budapest, 24 March 2011.
3 Interview with the former owner of a Hungarian security company, Budapest, 24 March 2011.
4 Interview with the former owner of a Hungarian security company, Budapest, 24 March 2011.

References

ÁSZ. 2004. 'Jelentés a Magyar Honvédség közbeszerzései rendszere működésének ellenőrzéséről'. *Report No. 0451 of State Audit Office of Hungary 2004* [Report on the Audit of the Operations of HDF Procurement System]. www.asz.hu/jelentes/0451/jelentes-a-magyar-honvedseg-kozbeszerzesi-rendszere-mukodesenek-ellenorzeserol/0451j000.pdf (accessed 22 April 2011).
——2005. 'Jelentés a Honvédelmi Minisztérium fejezet működésének ellenőrzéséről'. *Report No. 0535 of State Audit Office of Hungary 2005* [Report on the Audit of the Chapter operation of the MoD]. www.asz.hu/jelentes/0535/jelentes-a-honvedelmi-miniszterium-fejezet-mukodesenek-ellenorzeserol/0535j000.pdf (accessed 22 April 2011).
——2009. „Jelentés a Honvédelmi Minisztérium fejezet működésének ellenőrzéséről. *Report No. 0905 of State Audit Office of Hungary 2009* [Report on the Audit of the Chapter operation of the MoD]. www.asz.hu/jelentes/0905/jelentes-a-honvedelmi-miniszterium-fejezet-mukodesenek-ellenorzeserol/0905j000.pdf (accessed 22 April 2011).
Ambrus, Péter. 2010 *Az igazi misszió*. Budapest: Alexandra.
Farkas, Cintia. 2011. *Nem „szekus' őrzi végre a katonákat* Figyelonet.hu, *3 March*. www.fn.hu/belfold/20110228/nem_szekus_orzi_vegre/ (assessed 15 March 2011).
Hanitz, Zsolt. 2011a. 'A HM kezelésű társaságok bemutatása'. Zrínyi Miklós National Defence Universitiy Electronic Library. http://193.224.76.4/download/konyvtar/digitgy/publikacio/hanitz_zsolt01.pdf (accessed 21 May 2011).
——2011b. 'A HM vagyonkezelésű ipari társaságok 2009-es tevékenységének elemzése'. Zrínyi Miklós National Defence University Electronic Library. http://193.224.76.4/download/konyvtar/digitgy/publikacio/hanitz_zsolt02.pdf (accessed 21 May 2011).
Haraszti, Gyula. 2011. 'Trükkös HM-es ingatlanüzemeltetés', *Magyar Nemzet*, 3 May.
Hautzinger, Gyula and Bakó, Antal. 2006. 'A nemzetközi ('lengyel') Közép-dél hadosztály logisztikai támogatása a Magyar szállítózászlóalj részvételével a koalíciós "Iraki szabadság" műveletében'. *Katonai Logisztika* 2006/2: 146–174.

Honvedelem. 1994. 'A honvédelem négy éve 1990–1994'. Budapest: Zrínyi Kiadó.

——2006. 'A honvédelem négy éve 2002–2006'. Budapest: Zrínyi Kiadó.

Honvedelem.hu. 2006. *Lipcsében a közigazgatási államtitkár.* www.honvedelem.hu/hirek/kul foldi_hirek/lipcseben_a_kozigazgatasi_allamtitkar (accessed 17 March 2011).

Inkal.hu. 2011. Webpage of In-kal Security 2000 Kft. www.inkal.hu/index.php?page=ve zetok (accessed 21 February 2011).

Jároscsák, Miklós. 2002. 'A fogyasztói logisztikai rendszer fejlesztésének irányai'. *Hadtudomány* 2002/1: 30–44.

——2006. 'Nemzetközi feladatokban résztvevő Magyar katonai kontingensek logisztikai támogatása'. *Katonai Logisztika* 2006/1: 92–109.

Kormany.hu. 2011. *A biztonságot tovább fokozva.* Webpage of the Hungarian MoD 12 May. www.kormany.hu/hu/honvedelmi-miniszterium/honved-vezerkar/hirek/a-biztonsagot-tovabb-fokozva (accessed 12 May 2011).

Magyar Demokrata. 2011 *A honvédelem nem lehet kockázatos üzlet.* Interview with Lajos MORÓ, CEO of MoD EI Company. *Magyar Demokrata.* 6 April.

Marton, Peter and Wagner, Peter. 2011. *Hungary's involvement in Afghanistan Proudly going through the motions? State building in Afghanistan: Multinational contribution to reconstruction.* New York: Routledge.

MFA. 2009. *Hungary's Role in Afghanistan: Mid-Term Strategic Outlook.* www.mfa.gov.hu/NR/rdonlyres/534F1052–1EAF-4B89–8F2D-3B4DC651CF25/0/AFG_strat_1118.pdf (accessed 15 September 2011).

Ministry of Defence. 2011. 'Facts and Figures on Hungarian Defence Forces 2011'. Budapest: Hungarian MoD. MoD Press Office hand out to journalists on HDF involvement in international operations. Meeting with the press representatives on 14 December.

MNO. 2007. 'Afganisztánba is szállíthatnak majd az AN 26-osok'. *Magyar Nemzet Online* 11 February. www.mno.hu/portal/396571 (accessed 8 January 2011).

NAPI.hu. 2011. *Ezeken a cégeken kaszált nagyot az adóhivatal.* 7 February. www.napi.hu/default.asp?cCenter=article.asp&nID=473073&place=kepes2 (assessed 8 June 2011).

Origo.hu. 2011. 'Közös kalapba gyűlt a HM-es kenőpénz az ügyészség szerint'. 16 March. www.origo.hu/itthon/20110316-tizenmyolc-ember-ellen-emeltek-vadat-a-hm-korrupcios-botranya-ugyeben.html# (assessed 17 March 2011).

Orosz, Zoltán. 2009. 'Szállítórepülők alkalmazásának aktuális kérdései a Magyar Honvédség missziós feladat rendszerében'. *Repüléstudományi közlemények.* 2009/2 special edition. www.szrfk.hu/rtk/kulonszamok/2009_cikkek/Orosz_Zoltan.pdf (accessed 15 May 2011).

regiment.hu. 2010. *Pápáról Kabulba.* 23 September. www.regiment.hu/hirek/paparol_k-abulba (accessed 24 September 2011).

Securifocus.hu. 2004. *Őrző-védőket keres a HM EI Rt.* 1 September. www.securifocus.com/portal. php?pagename=hir_obs_reszlet&szokod=16007&cikk=2&56&i=504 (accessed 16 May 2011).

Solymosi, Ferenc and Révész, Gyula. 2011. 'Nemzeti támogatás a megalakító szemszögéből'. *Sereg Szemle* 2011/2: 79–82.

Sramkó, Mátyás. 2004. 'Az MH szállítózászlóaljának az iraki misszióban való alkalmazásával kapcsolatos tapsztalatok'. *Katonai Logisztika* 2004/4: 33–46.

Szabó, Csaba. 2010. *Fél év Afganisztánban.* Budapest: Ad Librum.

Szarvas, László. 2007. 'A Magyar Honvédség nagytávolságú szállítási lehetőségei'. *Katonai Logisztika* 2007/2. MH ÖLTP: 9–31.

Szlankó, Bálint. 2011. *Maximum nulla áldozattal.* Budapest: Atheneum.

Szvmszk. 2011. 'Webpage of Hungarian Chamber of Bodyguards, Property Protection and Private Detectives'. www.szvmszk.hu (accessed 15 May 2011).

Turzai, Zsolt. 2010. 'Akikkel együtt szolgálunk'. Honvedelem.hu, 11 August. www.honvedelem.hu/cikk/21429/akikkel-egyutt-szolgalunk (accessed 15 November 2011).
Wagner, Péter. 2010a. 'Az afganisztáni nemzetközi fejlesztési együttműködés'. *Magyar Külügyi Intézet*. www.hiia.hu/pub/displ.asp?id=SRGIEV (accessed 15 September 2011).
———2010b. *The Background of the Hungarian Activities in Baghlan Policy Brief 2010/3*. Hungarian Institute on International Affairs. www.hiia.hu/pub/displ.asp?id=NBWWAE (accessed 15 September 2011).
WP. 2011. 'Honvédelmi Minisztérium Fehér Könyv: Korrupció, átvilágítás és büntetőjogi konzekvenciák' [MoD White Paper: Corruption, vetting and criminal law consequences]. www.kormany.hu/download/3/52/40000/Honv%20Min%20-%20Feh%C3%A9r%20k%C3%B6nyv.pdf#!DocumentBrowse (accessed 29 September 2011).

TV reports and interviews

Duna TV. 2011a. Interview with Péter KÓNYA, chairmen of FRDÉSZ (Joint Trade Union of Service Personnel) Közbeszéd, Duna TV. 9 May.
Duna TV. 2011b. Interview with GEN. Tibor BENKŐ, Chief of Defence. Reggel a Dunán, Duna TV. 9 May.
Hír TV. 2011a. Híradó. *Hír TV.* 15 March.
Hír TV. 2011b. Célpont. *Hír TV.* 26 March.

Regulations

1995. évi XXXIX. törvény *az állami tulajdonban lévő vállalkozói vagyon értékesítéséről.* [Act XXXIX of 1995 on the Sale of State-Owned Entrepreneurial Assets].
1997. évi CLIX törvény *a fegyveres biztonsági őrségről, a természetvédelmi és a mezei őrszolgálatról* [Act CLIX of 1997 on Armed Security Guard and Environmental Protection and Rural Guards].
2005. évi CXXXIII. *törvény a személy-és vagyonvédelmi, valamint a magánnyomozói tevékenység szabályairól* [Act CXXXIII of 2005 on Security Services and the Activities of Private Investigators].
143/2004. (IV. 29.) kormányrendelet *az államtitkot vagy szolgálati titkot, illetőleg alapvető biztonsági, nemzetbiztonsági érdeket érintő vagy különleges biztonsági intézkedést igénylő beszerzések sajátos szabályairól* [Government Decree 143/2004. (IV. 29.) on the special rules of procurements affecting a state secret or service secret, a fundamental security or national security interest or calling for a special security measure].
2183/1999. (VIII. 23.) kormányhatározat *a NATO 1999. évi védelmi tervezési kérdőívére adandó magyar válaszról, a 2001–2006. közötti időszakra szóló NATO haderő-fejlesztési javaslatokkal kapcsolatos magyar álláspontról, valamint a honvédelmet érintő egyes kérdésekről* [Government Decision 2183/1999 (VIII. 23.) on Hungary's response to NATO's defence planning questionnaire of 1999, on Hungary's opinion with regard to NATO's military development proposal for 2001–06 and on certain issues regarding national defence].

Military bulletins

Honvédelmi Közlöny (H.K. 2) 2011 2. szám. www.kozlonyok.hu/kozlonyok/Kozlonyok/13/PDF/2011/2.pdf (accessed 18 November 2011).
Honvédelmi Közlöny (H.K. 3) 2011 3. szám. www.kozlonyok.hu/kozlonyok/Kozlonyok/13/PDF/2011/3.pdf (accessed 18 November 2011).

Webpages of Ministry of Defence companies

MoD Electronics, Logistics and Property Management Company: www.hmei.hu.
MoD ArmCom Communication-Technical Co. Ltd.: www.armcom.hu.
MoD Currus Combat Vehicle Technique Company: www.currus.hu.
MoD Arzenál Electro-Technical Company: www.hmarsenal.hu.
MoD Verga: www.verga.hu.
MoD Kaszó: www.kaszort.hu.
MoD Budapest: www.bp-erdo.hu.
MoD Zrínyi Media: www.honvedelem.hu.
MoD Bessenyei György: www.stefania.hu.
MoD Topographic Ltd.: www.topomap.hu.

7 Romania

The high and low politics of commercialization[1]

Liliana Pop

In the case of Romania, the national context for the commercialization of security has been closely reflected in the patterns of engagement in Afghanistan. In both cases, the decisive structuring element has been Romania's decision to pursue NATO membership. This has driven military reform in Romania and has set the context for the emergence of security services as a legitimate economic activity. It has also been the main motive behind Romania's engagement in Afghanistan. Numerous small private and military security companies have participated in the maintenance and upgrading of military hardware and the provision of IT services for Romanian troops deployed in Afghanistan. However, these actors did not have an impact on the crucial decision to participate either in Operation Enduring Freedom or in the International Security Assistance Force (ISAF). Rather, those decisions were state-led and reflected a perception that it was in Romania's national interest to establish credibility as a prospective NATO member and a reliable ally.

At the same time, in the first decade of the twenty-first century, Romania was still very much struggling to overcome some of the difficult legacies of the communist regime, especially in terms of economic reform and development. As a result, domestic processes of change were piecemeal and protracted. Internationally, unlike the other European countries studied in this volume, Romania did not have the resources for and did not seek to pursue a leading role in Afghanistan. While Romania responded to allied requests for military involvement, it did not wish to lead a Provincial Reconstruction Unit, for instance. Accordingly, rather than trying to achieve large aims through significant and concentrated deployment of troops and resources, Romania has played a combat and supporting role under the leadership of other allies, such as the US, Germany and the UK, in various geographical and operational areas of Afghanistan.

Thus, Romania's military engagement in Afghanistan has consisted of the performance of materially small but symbolically high-impact combat missions as well as support missions, involving such tasks as VIP protection, the training of the Afghan military and police, and liaison with Afghan civilians. In these latter functions, Romanian military personnel have performed roles that might otherwise have been contracted out. On the whole, though, the Romanian contingent in Afghanistan depended on the existing logistical infrastructure – in terms of catering and housing, for instance – in which foreign contractors played a large part, and in this sense it implemented and coordinated the wider allied strategies regarding the use of private military and security companies.

In addition to military involvement, Romania has been an active participant in the diplomatic efforts surrounding the building and maintenance of consensus around the international intervention, its scope, aims and duration. In this capacity, Romania contributed to the legitimization of a maximalist under-standing of the international alliance's responsibilities for peace and reconciliation in Afghanistan. This has indirectly created opportunities for the involvement of private contractors.

The national context for the commercialization of security and international intervention

As with so many relatively recent European states, the prevalent national-identity narratives in Romania are focused on the major episodes of state building in the modern era: the union of the principalities of Moldova and Valachia in 1859; the war of independence against the Ottoman empire in 1877–78; the First World War, followed by the 'great union' in 1918 – which was recognized by the Treaty of Versailles – when Transylvania, Bessarabia and Dobrogea became parts of Romania; and finally the post-Second World War border changes, especially in the east, when Bessarabia became part of the USSR. Romania's history is one of struggle for an autonomous identity against neighbouring empires, where the ingenuity and even cunning of the local elites, and later the state, won out in the long term, against extraordinary odds and through great sacrifice. During the communist era, this narrative was overlaid with the well-known teleological interpretation according to which socialism was the culmination of human his-tory. Romania's history supposedly culminated in the realization of another major historical project – a society without classes, peace loving, opposed to nuclear armament, active in forging alliances across the globe and fully developed, under the leadership of the communist party.

The abrupt collapse of Romania's communist regime naturally reopened the discussion over many of these interpretations and, amid political struggles over the legacy of the communist era, a clear and nuanced view of Romania's national identity and role in world affairs has been slow to emerge. A core orientation, however, has been shared by all political parties and the population: a retreat from the ambitious agenda of Nicolae Ceaușescu's regime, which cultivated alli-ances within the Non-Aligned Movement, the Middle East and Africa, alongside the historical relations with European powers and the communist bloc. Instead, the focus has become NATO and EU membership, pursued at first haltingly but from the mid-1990s with some decisiveness and success.

The decision to pursue such a strategy was inseparable from systemic trans-formations at the domestic level, as Romania shifted towards a market economy and democracy. Perhaps inevitably, given the scale of these changes, policies and strategies for reform emerged relatively slowly through a process of trial and error, and were shaped both by targeted state action and by resistance and initiative from below. The competition between political parties took place over differences of emphasis, style and speed of reform implementation against a broad agreement about the overall objectives (Pop 2006, 2007, 2009; Pridham 2007; Schimmelfennig *et al.* 2006; Vachudova 2005).

This pattern is also reflected in the empirical record of the process of commercialization of security, which has involved relatively few overarching, clearly formulated and systematically pursued strategies. In this context, the strategies that do exist are implicit in the practice and result out of improvisation and post-hoc rationalization. Delays, reversals and retracing of steps are common, even as it is possible to identify several moments and decisions when the course of commercialization is set for a given period of time.

On the day of the terrorist attacks on US soil, 11 September 2001, Romania was already far advanced in the orientation of its security strategy towards integration into NATO. Among the first to sign up for the Partnership for Peace programme, the cooperation framework with former communist states set up by NATO in 1993–94, Romania carried out extensive reforms of its military and security apparatuses throughout the 1990s. However, these ultimately fell short of NATO expectations, and the country was not included in the first wave of post-communist enlargement in 1999. Romania hoped, however, to be invited to join the organization at the November 2002 summit in Prague, with membership to take effect from 2004. To achieve this, the government redoubled its reform efforts. These included a firm commitment to international NATO-led missions, and on 19 September 2001 the Romanian parliament agreed to triple the number of Romanian troops deployed in the Western Balkans as part of KFOR and SFOR (MOR 2001c), which freed up other NATO forces for redeployment in Afghanistan.

Thus, the political reaction to the 9/11 attacks was swift and unequivocal: to affirm Romania's 'support for the large international coalition against terrorism and the decision to continue to behave as a strategic partner for the USA and a *de facto* member of NATO' (MIP 2001). Romanian troops were deployed in Afghanistan in January 2002, and since then Romania has consistently supported its allies not just militarily but also diplomatically in various forums, especially the UN (Paşcu 2008). This commitment, firmly expressed in the early weeks and months of the post-9/11 era, and reflected in actual material support, confirmed for NATO the logic of its Eastern enlargement. In turn, Romania did become a NATO member in 2004, and an EU member in 2007 – major foreign policy achievements that were highly acclaimed both by the country's political classes and by the general public.

The transformation of the military: state and private actors in Romania's security field

The introduction of new private–public distinctions following the breakdown of the communist regime has affected several major areas related to the armed forces: the defence industry, the recruitment of personnel, and the content and procedures for acquisitions of armaments and services. The defence industry was put under civilian control but was left out of the privatization process in the early 1990s owing to its political sensitivity. As a result, it suffered from lack of investment and rapid shrinkage of the domestic and international markets as the army was downsized and Romania signed up to various non-proliferation agreements (Şcheianu 2001). According to one estimate, while prior to 1989 the defence industry exported the equivalent of €590 million of equipment and ammunition annually, by 2010 the total production, domestic and export, was worth only €170 million, less than one-third of its former value (Matache 2011). Five companies so far have been privatized. The ten that are still state owned accumulated losses of around €230 million during the 2000s, while providing employment for only 1,700 people. Cancellation of this debt in 2011 may revive their prospects for privatization or partnerships with foreign investors (Mediafax 2011).

As part of the NATO accession process, the army also changed its basis for recruitment, from conscription to professionalization and contracting. In 1989, there were over 115,000 conscripts in the army, out of 220,000 personnel (Barbu 2002: 82). As a result of demographic decline, a reduction in the length of military service and the multiplication of types of exceptions to it, the numbers decreased over time. From 2007, conscription was abolished and the army came to rely on voluntary, paid soldiers and personnel (Ciungu 2007). The blueprint for the force is a total of 90,000 personnel with an optimal composition of 75,000 armed forces and 15,000 civilian staff (Barbu 2004). In effect, more than half of the positions in Romania's land, air and sea forces were eliminated between 2001 and 2007–08 (MApN 2009c: 22).

The involvement of the private sector in servicing the army expanded slowly, owing to modest defence budgets, difficulties with the development of procedures for procurement, and mismatch between demand and supply. Thus, in spite of formal commitments to allocate 2.38 per cent of GDP to the defence budget, Romania's relatively buoyant economic performance until the onset of the economic crisis in 2009 and the evident need to provide for the troops deployed abroad, the Ministry of Defence budget was a modest 1.85 per cent of GDP in 2006 and shrunk even further to 1.4 per cent in 2009. Alternative ways of funding large purchases, through borrowing and multi-annual budgetary planning, were set up in 2006 (MOR 2008), but did not become operational until 2009 (Tudor 2009; MApN 2009a).

Imports for the army and the exports of the defence industry have been traditionally handled by Romtehnica, an autonomous structure within the Ministry of Defence that was first established in 1950 and became a national company owned by the defence ministry in 2001. In addition, the ministry contracts services and purchases goods through 29 of its departments, from the armaments, logistics and medical departments through to the military-technical academy and the national office for the cult of heroes (MOR 2011a). As a result, the range of acquisitions is very broad, according to official data, available since 2004. Contracting of IT services is particularly well developed, involving private security companies such as UTI, Romsys, Interactive Systems and Business, and Bidtdefender, and covering such diverse areas as security systems for military sites, supply and maintenance of equipment to protect the international communications network in the Ministry of Defence, handling of radar images, and intranet services (MApN 2005, 2006, 2007, 2009b, 2011a).

However, it remains the case that a significant number of calls for bids for security services advertised by the defence ministry could not be filled. A review of cancelled procedures for the award of contracts and the reasons for cancellation highlights the mismatch between supply and demand, as well as bureaucratic difficulties in aligning procedures and practice. In 2008, of the 66 cancelled procurement processes, lack of any bids or inadequate bids represented 41 cases, nearly two-thirds of the total. Another significant category of failures pointed to incorrect administration of procedures (17 cases), as revealed in decisions by the National Council for the Resolution of Contestations in response to various complaints (MapN 2009b). In 2009, the number of cancelled procedures was 35, and the vast majority of these – some 29 cases – were the result of inadequate offers. In 2010, no suitable contractor could be found to provide security for 21 military bases (39 contracts were awarded) (MApN 2011a).

Catering services have been among the first to be externalized, starting in 1999. By 2005, catering had been externalized in 160 military units through individual contracts managed by the units in question, with mixed results in terms of quality and continuity of service. Experiments were also being carried out in other areas, especially in relation to laundry and equipment maintenance (Nedelcu 2005). Following a critical review of the quality of services in catering and static security, a new strategy was launched in the summer of 2011. Two new companies, Ro Army Catering and Ro Army Security, have been set up within Romtehnica to take over these services for all army bases by the end of 2014. The army expects to save around 20–25 per cent of current costs by contracting the services of these two companies. Ro Army Catering and Ro Army Security will create some 6,000 new posts for reservists (MApN 2011b).

The Ministry of Defence also owns other assets, some of which are run on a semi-commercial basis, including the Army Press Trust (TPA), several museums, an art gallery, the Collective Artistic Ensemble of the Army and the Research Agency for Military Technique and Technology. The TPA has its own website, launched in 2002, and is responsible for several publications and a publishing house, in addition to producing TV and radio programmes broadcast on national channels. In 2001–03, the TPA attracted around €190 million from advertising and sponsorships, nearly one-third of its total income (MApN 2004). The defence ministry also has a sports team, as well as its own network of military hospitals and training schools and facilities across the country.

Thus, some aspects of Romania's military reform process – for example, massive downsizing – have been completed, and their relative effect on the size and composition of the market for private security should become apparent over the next few years. More evident at this stage is the fact that the state is still fine-tuning its procedures and practices for involving the private sector in the effective provision of security. In some cases, as with the examples of catering and static security discussed above, it appears that the Ministry of Defence is bringing these services in-house, albeit organized on a commercial basis. Such a relationship with the private sector is similar to what we observe in Hungary.

The emergence of the private security market

A market in private security emerged in the early 1990s somewhat independently of reform in the state sector. The first private security companies operated according to the general laws regulating the setting up of private enterprises and specialized in the static security of buildings and surveillance. From 1996, specific legislation has expanded the market for security by setting high standards for security for economic actors and has regulated the operations of private security firms. Under the current law – Law no. 333/2003 regarding the safety and security of sites, persons and goods – the police are responsible for issuing licenses to PMSCs. Licenses have to be renewed every three years, and plans for the static security of buildings have to be approved by the police. At the end of October 2011, there were 1,295 companies licensed to provide static security and other forms of protection, 1,176 companies licensed to install alarms, and 402 surveillance monitoring centres. In total, private security companies are estimated to employ around 100,000 people (Apostol 2008). Relations between these companies and the police have been generally cooperative, with numerous examples of joint actions, the temporary rental of cars by the police from the security companies, and protection services carried out by the gendarmerie for private clients (SEESAC 2005, 71–2).

The majority of the private security firms operating in Romania are small or medium-sized, employing fewer than 100 guards. Even the largest companies, such as G4S, BGS, Securitas Services Romania, Rosegur and UTI, which employ more than a thousand people, have relatively small market shares of 7 per cent or less. Some of the larger companies, initially set up by local entrepreneurs in the 1990s, have been bought by multinationals a decade later. For instance, G4S, the Danish company, entered the Romanian market in 2002 by purchasing a six-year-old local start-up, APS Valachia. It now operates through G4S Secure Solutions and G4S Cash Solutions. According to records filed at the Ministry of Finance, in 2010 the turnover for the two companies was about €82 million. While Cash Solutions, employing 5,408 people, operated at a loss of €1.56 million, Secure Solutions, which employs 3,772 people, made a profit of almost €2 million. Its clients include banks (Alpha Bank, Raiffeisen, CEC, ING, Banca Romaneasca, RBS, Banca Transilvania) and large companies such as Petrom and the Romanian Post Office.

Rosegur, owned by the Spanish Prosegur and GED I Eastern Fund since 2005, was funded in 1992 as Dragon Star Guard Srl. In 2010, it had 2,972 employees and made a profit of €39,000 on a turnover of €18 million. Its cash services operation is small, representing only 9 per cent of its total business, while the most important activity is static security (65 per cent), followed by monitoring and intervention (16 per cent), and installation of alarms and protection systems (10 per cent) (Florea 2010).

Securitas Services Romania is the local branch of the Swedish Securitas AB. It was set up as CPI Security Services in 1995, but Securitas AB acquired 55 per cent of the shares in 2007, becoming the sole owner in 2009. In December 2010, Securitas purchased another local firm, Cobra Securities, from UTI, for a reported €3 million. In 2010, Securitas had a turnover of almost €22 million, made a profit of €1.5 million, and employed 3,642 personnel.

There are also several significant private security companies that are still owned by their original founders. The security division of BGS, which also owns investigations, disasters intervention and medical businesses, employed 2,945 people in 2010, and had a turnover of €23.6 million and a profit of €322,000. The business was established in 1994 by three brothers, Bogdan, Daniel and Costin Oprea, and remains a family business, although it has been seeking stock-exchange listing in New York and Bucharest. Clients include OMV Petrom, Coca-Cola HBC, Banca Carpatica, Orange Romania, Oracle Romania and commercial centres Plaza Romania and Vitantis Shopping Centre.

Tiberiu Urdăreanu (son of a retired army general of the same name), Lucia Urdăreanu and Dumitru Aelenei built up UTI starting in 1990, seeking to meet the emerging security needs for static security and protection. The divestment of the Cobra unit in 2010 signals the commitment of the company to what has emerged as its strength, a focus on information technology and communications (IT&c) security solutions for complex systems such as the Bucharest underground (including CCTV, radio communications and fire-detection solutions), the Henri Coandă airport in Bucharest, Bancorex and the Romanian Commercial Bank. Its homeland security and defence line of business was responsible for €34.8 million in turnover in 2010, while commercial and industrial security accounted for €9.7 million (operating profit for the two divisions was €7.7 million). Total turnover was €158.9 million, and it employed 3,219 people.

According to Schreier and Caparini (2005: 27), 160 private security firms in Romania were run by former Securitate or military intelligence personnel in the early 2000s. Thus, they have had to overcome the deep distrust and public opprobrium that surrounded those institutions. They have also been suspected of using their strong links with the state bureaucracy to cover up improper conduct in regard to privacy laws and taxes (Prisăcariu n.d.). However, this migration of personnel from the state apparatus to the private sector, which has been the result of individual decisions, may be taking on a more purposeful character under the auspices of the Ministry of Defence through the establishment of Ro Army Catering and Ro Army Security.

Struggling to meet the domestic demand for private security, Romania's PMSCs have had little involvement abroad beyond occasional incursions in the Balkans related to post-conflict stabilization efforts in that region. Romanian legislators have given no specific attention to the need to regulate foreign operations by Romanian PMSCs, and the country has not signed up to the existing, informal, international codes of conduct, such as the Montreux Document.

Romania's engagement in Afghanistan

As already mentioned, Romania's engagement in Afghanistan was clearly defined as a crucial step in relation to the overall objective of joining NATO. To demonstrate *de facto* membership even before the invitation to join had been extended (which would be at the Prague summit in November 2002) required decisive and unequivocal action. This was clearly understood by the Romanian government and parliament in the discussion over the participation of Romanian troops in combat missions, as will be shown below. In addition to military involvement, Romania developed bilateral diplomatic ties with Afghanistan and extended a certain amount of aid. Romania also provided significant diplomatic support for UN and NATO positions.

Military intervention

The immediate response in Romania to the 9/11 terrorist attacks in the US was to implement the terms of UN Security Council Resolution 1333 from 2000, including bans on military and security cooperation with the Taliban government, freezing of its financial assets abroad and restrictions on the freedom of movement of Taliban officials (MOR 2001a). On 19 September 2001, taking account of NATO's decision to invoke Article 5 of its constitutive treaty, the parliament decided that

> Romania, as a strategic partner of the USA and member of the Partnership for Peace, will participate, as a *de facto* NATO ally, together with the NATO member-states and their other partners and allies in the effort to combat international terrorism, by all means necessary, including military means.
>
> (MOR 2001b: Article 1)

They also gave transit rights over its national territory to alliance forces.

On 21 December 2001, the parliament agreed to Romanian participation in ISAF, constituted on the basis of the Bonn Convention on Afghanistan two weeks earlier, with 15–20 military doctors, a company of 70 troops, 25–30 military police, a 170-strong company of special forces and a Hercules C-130 airplane (MOR 2001d). The Romanian delegation was thus among the first 16 nations to sign up officially for ISAF, at the London conference in January 2002. In the event, ISAF requested only 48 personnel at this stage, mostly military police, along with a C-130 plane and three liaison officers.

In April 2002, at the request of the US, the Romanian parliament decided to approve the deployment of a battalion of combat troops as part of Operation Enduring Freedom. The parliamentary debate surrounding this decision, which took place on 30 April, is significant because it specifically addresses the motivation for Romania's involvement in Afghanistan. Both houses of parliament – that is, the Senate and the Chamber of Deputies – were convened, and the discussion raised the full spectrum of issues associated with intervention. The stated aim of the intervention was 'to execute missions of protection, control of sensitive areas, humanitarian support, the neutralization of Taliban and Al-Qaeda forces and participation in military operations in Afghanistan' (CDR 2002a). Since not all of the NATO member states were participating in the intervention in Afghanistan, some deputies disputed the necessity of linking Romania's NATO aspiration to participation in the war effort. Deputies speaking for the opposition – for example, Cornel Boiangiu (Independent), Sorin Frunzăverde (Democratic Party) and Norica Nicolai (Liberal Party) – raised concerns about the cogency of the overall strategy in Afghanistan, the measures taken to ensure the safety of the troops and the clarity of the cooperation agreements with the allies (CDR 2002a, 2002b).

The prevailing point of view, articulated by Defence Minister Ioan Mircea Paşcu, conceded that Romania had no direct interest in the Afghan region and that the question of participation in the allied effort only arose in the context of the post-9/11 'war against terrorism'. Paşcu argued that participating in a NATO deployment that involved real risks would have a powerful effect: it would establish in the eyes of the NATO allies that Romania was a genuine partner, one that would not shrink from doing the difficult and dangerous work. This would demonstrate Romania's commitment to the NATO alliance, as each member should be ready to defend the security of the others and to be a provider, not just a consumer, of security (CDR 2002b). This reference to being a provider and/or consumer of security is a direct reflection of the tenor of discussions within NATO at the time, reiterated time and again in different NATO meetings and conferences and aimed at establishing something like a fair principle of judgement for the accession applications of prospective members and a norm regarding good behaviour as a member.

In effect, Romania's military planning was assuming low actual risk of casualties or even involvement in fighting. The Romanian battalion was to replace a Canadian unit that had encountered no attacks and sustained no casualties during its deployment; moreover, overall, the allied troops had incurred an insignificant casualty rate of only 1 per cent, mostly due to accidents rather than enemy fire. The Romanian authorities argued that these risks were far outweighed by the importance of the mission: to support the setting up of a viable political process in Afghanistan. Specifically, international troops were necessary to ensure the peaceful elections on 6 June 2002 of representatives to the Great Afghan Jirga and the Afghan National Transitional Authority (CDR 2002b).

The battalion sent to join Operation Enduring Freedom, in Kandahar, was the largest single deployment by Romania in the early years of the intervention. From July 2006, as the ISAF mandate expanded to southern Afghanistan, the Romanian troops were placed under ISAF leadership and transferred to Zabul, a border province with Pakistan, where, together with US troops, they were responsible for providing the security backing for the efforts of the Provincial Reconstruction Team in that area. After the NATO withdrawal from Iraq, the intensification of the Taliban insurgency and the allied 'surge' in Afghanistan, the commitment of Romanian troops also increased. From 2010, a second battalion was sent to Zabul, alongside four Operational Mentor and Liaison Teams, a garrison team and a supporting combat team. Securing the A1 road to Kandahar is one of the top priorities in this particular region. Accordingly, the number of Romanian military troops increased from 1,020 at the end of 2009 to 1,800 in October 2011.

Especially during their time as part of Operation Enduring Freedom, the Romanian troops participated actively in seeking out and disarming Al-Qaeda and Taliban fighters. For instance, during Operation Carpathian Thunder in March 2003, Romanian troops searched out and destroyed a complex of caves in the Red Mountains, up to an altitude of 2,700 metres, identified by Predator reconnaissance. A few days later, acting in a support capacity in the US-led Operation Valiant Strike, the Romanians participated in the arrest of 16 terrorist suspects and the discovery and destruction of important caches of ammunition, including 107-mm rockets. On 5 October 2005, a Romanian–American team accompanied by 261 Afghan troops seized 3.3 tonnes of marijuana, tens of grenades, 15,000 bullets and other heavy armament in Paktia, 100 kilometres south of Kabul.

On occasion, travel to or from such missions, as well as the routine patrols on the A1 road, proved dangerous. The first incident involving a Romanian transport vehicle that passed over an improvised explosive device (IED) occurred in Kalantar Kalay, near Kabul, in October 2003. There were no casualties then, but less than a month later two Romanian soldiers died as a result of fighting in an incident in Spin Puldac, in the south of Afghanistan, near the Pakistan border. By the end of October 2011, 19 Romanian soldiers had lost their lives in Afghanistan and 59 had been injured.

Bilateral diplomacy and aid

An early initiative to open a Romanian embassy in Kabul in 2004, for which the parliament had in fact issued a decision, was not implemented, and at the time of writing Romania's diplomatic presence in Kabul is minimal, consisting of a two-person legation. The Afghan embassy in Warsaw handles Afghanistan's diplomatic and consular affairs with Romania. Even so, the diplomatic record shows a number of visits to Romania by Afghan officials and bilateral meetings on the fringes of large international summits or during visits by Romanian officials to meet the troops. Such meetings have been opportunities to restate the unity of purpose around the internationally accepted objectives, to work towards peace and stabilization in Afghanistan.

In terms of aid, as a contributor to international organizations with responsibilities in this area, not least the United Nations Development Programme, the World Health Organization and UN-HABITAT, Romania has had an indirect impact on the development effort in Afghanistan. Romania has also made direct contributions and donations. On 14 February 2002, the Romanian government decided to give to the National Guard of Afghanistan a quantity of goods and materials (MOR 2002b). By May, Romania had put 1,000 AK-74s at the disposal of ISAF for the Afghan army, together with tents and other materials necessary for army training (MApN 2002). On another occasion, on 21 January 2004, Romania's Supreme Defence Council decided to donate 50 T-55 tanks to the Afghan army (CSAT 2005).

The largest aid package of just over €2.3 million euro was awarded on 7 November 2002 and consisted of: medicines; six full university scholarships (in civil engineering and electronics/computing); feasibility studies for transfer of communications technologies and complex industrial projects, including electrification, hydroelectric plants and water wells; technical assistance to build car and other machinery plants (the largest component, with a value of €2.1 million); military uniforms; tents; and foodstuffs (MOR 2002c). About 160 tonnes of food were collected from Romanian farms and enterprises and dispatched to Afghanistan from January 2003 (MAAP 2003). Further funds for five university scholarships, for six years starting from the academic year 2004/05 and in areas of interest to the Afghan government, were allocated in August 2004 and September 2005 (MOR 2004, 2005).

During 22–25 March 2004, a delegation of Afghan experts visited Romania, holding meetings at a number of ministries, including those of defence, health, transport, construction and tourism, and agriculture, forestry and rural development, as well as at Uzinexport. The purpose of the visit was to tailor ways in which Romania might participate in reconstruction efforts within the existing Regional Reconstruction Teams in Afghanistan, reaffirm its commitment to participating in the ongoing reconstruction and stabilization efforts in that country, as well as ISAF and Operation Enduring Freedom, and continue to support the operationalization of the Afghan army through training and donations of equipment (MAE 2004a). The Afghan delegation was especially interested in Romania's expertise in agriculture, the setting up of a pilot programme to counter opium production in Afghanistan, the petroleum and gas sectors, and various other industrial projects, including the construction of a cement factory. These areas of interest were reaffirmed at the Berlin conference on 'Afghanistan and the International Community: A Partnership for the Future', held on 31 March–1 April that year (MAE 2004b).

Multilateral decision making: the UN and NATO

During 2004–05, Romania was a non-permanent member of the UN Security Council, and was thus at the forefront of diplomatic efforts to shore up international approval and legitimacy for the intervention in Afghanistan. In this capacity, Romania chaired two committees – the 1540 Committee dealing with non-proliferation of weapons of mass destruction and the 1518 Committee on Iraq – and it also held the vice presidency of the 1267 Committee on Al-Qaeda and the Taliban. Romania co-authored Resolution 1546 on Iraq, which formally ended the occupation of that country and handed authority to the interim government from 30 June 2004. During its presidency, Romania organized a July 2004 seminar on the relationship between the UN and regional organizations in stabilization processes, which led a year later to Resolution 1631, which calls on the

UN to integrate consultation with regional organizations in its routine decision making for dealing with conflict and stabilization.

A number of other resolutions were passed during this period with the effect of continuing the status quo of the United Nations Assistance Mission in Afghanistan (Resolutions 1536 and 1589), expanding the geographical reach of ISAF (Resolutions 1563 and 1623) and prolonging the international presence in Iraq (Resolutions 1538, 1546, 1619 and 1637). Here, Resolution 1623 is especially worth noting, as it articulates a particularly strong view of the desirable end-state of intervention in Afghanistan. It stresses:

> [T]he importance of extending central government authority to all parts of Afghanistan, of respect for democratic values, of *full* completion of the disarmament, demobilization and reintegration process, of the disbandment of illegal armed groups, of justice sector reform, of security sector reform including reconstitution of the Afghan National Army and Police, and of combating narcotics trade and production.

During the same period, the Security Council also passed a number of resolutions condemning acts of terrorism (Resolutions 1526, 1530, 1535, 1566, 1617, 1618 and 1624) and set up a new Peacekeeping Commission (Resolution 1645); together, these steps contributed to maintaining the high profile of the issue of terrorism and reinforcing the premise that the 'war on terror' was necessary.

After becoming a NATO member in 2004, Romania naturally began to take part in the political and military decision-making processes within the organization. There are two clear initiatives that reflect Romania's learning and an active attempt to shape peace and reconciliation strategies in Afghanistan. One is at the highest level of decision making in NATO, the annual meeting of heads of state, and the other is a proposal for organizational development.

First, then, in April 2008 Romania hosted the NATO Summit of Heads of State, which was, by all accounts, the largest in the history of the organization up to that moment in time. Moreover, in a separate, parallel forum, the Romanian authorities brought together all the nations participating in ISAF, as well as prominent international diplomats, including UN Secretary-General Ban Ki-moon, his Special Representative to Afghanistan Kai Eide, EU Commission President José Manuel Barroso, EU High Representative Javier Solana, World Bank Managing Director Ngozi Okonjo-Iweala, Japan's Deputy Foreign Minister Kenichiro Sasae and Afghanistan's President Hamid Karzai.

Romania's President Traian Băsescu (2008) was very clear about his objectives for the summit:

> We hope that this NATO summit will be able to make a commitment to a vision regarding Afghanistan, a vision that will cover the military dimension, the economic dimension, the social dimension, the institutional dimension. Otherwise, NATO's success in Afghanistan will be put in question.

A pre-summit conference organized in February 2008 in Iaşi, entitled 'NATO Lessons in Afghanistan', had also supported the view that to consolidate military gains, further inroads would have to be made in reform in the social sphere. Corneliu Dobriţoiu, a junior minister within the Ministry of Defence, spelled out the conclusions of the conference for Romanian national radio: before the US troops could safely withdraw, as they were showing signs of wanting to do, present military gains would have to be consolidated through efforts to address social and developmental needs (RRA 2008).

In addition to the NATO Summit Declaration, in which the priorities of securing Afghanistan were reiterated, there was a separate declaration on Afghanistan by the ISAF contributing nations. This is also optimistic and maximalist in terms of its expectations of what could and should be achieved in Afghanistan. It subordinates ISAF activities to the strengthening of the capacities of the Afghan authorities to govern and to provide both security and development. At the same time, it articulates the need to strengthen cooperation between the UN, ISAF and the Provincial Reconstruction Teams, to deliver to the greatest extent possible on the Afghanistan Compact and the priorities of the Afghan authorities. In sum:

> We as Allies and Partners stand united in our firm commitment to support the Afghan people fulfil their aspirations for a better life. The Afghan Government and people are taking increasing responsibility for the country's security, reconstruction and development. Together we will ensure they achieve the future they have long been denied and thereby bring greater security to all of our people.
>
> (ISAF 2008)

Second, in terms of NATO organizational development, Romania initiated the setting up of a centre of excellence in intelligence from human sources (HUMINT) in March 2010 in Oradea, with sponsorship from Greece, Hungary, Slovenia, Slovakia, Turkey and the US. The centre aims to train NATO personnel and to develop NATO policies and strategies in this field. Explaining the origins of the idea, President Băsescu has emphasized that the experience of the Romanian troops in Afghanistan and Iraq was remarkable for bringing attention to the role of intelligence from human sources in the pursuit of peace and stabilization strategies. According to him, the presence of the Romanian intelligence officers in the field led to a new policy for intelligence gathering. The former overreliance on data gathered by satellites was replaced by a recognition that obtaining intelligence from human sources is vital. In Băsescu's (2010) words, 'the Romanian army was probably the best prepared army from this point of view in Iraq and Afghanistan'.

Thus, Romania's intervention in Afghanistan reflects certain ambitions and limitations. Symbolic, high-impact actions, such as making available troops for combat missions and carrying out a significant amount of diplomatic work across a variety of forums, not least the UN and NATO, coexist with modest material commitments: comparatively small amounts of aid and limited troop numbers. While Romania achieved its aim of joining NATO, its diplomatic efforts had a mixed impact on the nature of the intervention in Afghanistan itself. In some sense, especially at the April 2008 NATO and ISAF summits in Bucharest, Romania gave high priority to Afghanistan and the renewal of international commitment to a maximalist peace and reconciliation agenda in that country. At the same time, in other initiatives – such as UN Resolution 1631, which calls for a greater role for regional organizations in conflict resolution – and in its emphasis on intelligence from human sources as a means of war – Romania might be seeking to temper some of the worst excesses of unilateral and technologically driven intervention.

Contracting practices and peace and reconciliation in Afghanistan

Even though Romania is not a major and direct user or promoter of contractors and contracting services, its engagement in Afghanistan illustrates several aspects of this issue. For example, Romanian troops have relied mostly on their own weaponry and supplies, regularly sent from home. In this sense, they import into Afghanistan the kind of relationship that the Romanian army has with private suppliers in the domestic context. In addition, the specific needs of adapting machinery to the conditions in Afghanistan have required modifications such as the installation of air conditioning for armoured vehicles. Specialized personnel from SC U.A. Moreni SA, a Romanian state-owned supplier, provided this in theatre in Afghanistan on several occasions – in August 2002, in 2003 and in July 2004.

Parliamentary and press debates point to concerns about the safety of troops and the availability of equipment and services capable of minimizing risk. Anti-bullet vests and headgear have been the immediate concerns behind such discussions. Purchases of these vital items have been slow and encumbered by complex bureaucratic structures, and were still in the process of being resolved in April 2006 (Atanasiu 2006). The quality of Romania's armoured vehicles has also been a recurring issue. By November 2008, when ten soldiers had already lost their lives in Afghanistan and Iraq, the minister of defence could reply to another tabled question that 31 Piranha III, 8x8 armoured vehicles had been purchased from Mowag. Deliveries and deployment in theatre had started, but would not be complete until October 2010. The purchase also included 4x4 armoured and unarmoured cars (20 and 40, respectively, VAMTAC S3 series) from URO Vehicles Especiales, but the procedures for strategic acquisitions of this type were only then being drawn up (Meleşcanu 2008).

In some cases, Romanian troops make use of services and goods provided by allies on a commercial and contractual basis, according to terms stipulated in accords such as the Acquisition and Cross Servicing Agreements (ACSA) or Lift and Sustain and Coalition loans. They also have access to Morale, Welfare and Recreation (MWR) facilities on the bases they share with allies. Most importantly, Romanians loaned a variety of armoured vehicles, including HMMWVs (high-mobility multi-purpose wheeler vehicles). From April 2010, the US provided on loan 60 MRAP (mine-resistant ambush-protected) vehicles. The premise of all of these agreements is that the Romanian army will pay the same price the allies pay to their contractors or a fair price linked to real costs. Judging by press reports from the field, the Romanian troops tend to be fairly self-reliant in terms of cooking, cleaning, etc., and thus less reliant on the 'invisible army' (Stillman 2011) of contract workers from the developing world that provide these types of services on US bases in Afghanistan. From 2011, the Romanian forces have had their own Reception, Staging and Onward Integration (RSOI) facilities, built by their own means (Tănase 2011: 167).

In their support roles, Romanian troops have also carried out activities that might have otherwise been contracted out to PMSCs. For instance, in April 2003 Romania approved the participation of six officers who were specialists in civil–military cooperation, along with ten specialists in military and civilian construction, in the Provincial Reconstruction Teams (CDR 2003a). Ten officers and 15 technical staff were mobilized for the training of the Afghan army and police in May 2003 (CDR 2003b). In March 2004, 30 military intelligence officers were sent to the NATO–ISAF headquarters, and nine specialists in logistics, demining and healthcare were attached to the German Provincial Reconstruction Team in Kunduz (CDR 2004a). In September 2004, the team of military instructors was supplemented with a support team of 25 personnel. Romania also participated in the British Provincial Reconstruction Team in Mazar-e-Sharif with a liaison officer and a mobile observation unit of six men (CDR 2004b). In February 2005, 12 more military personnel were sent to the Guard and Protection Service of the UN mission in Afghanistan, the 45-strong demining team from Operation Althea was withdrawn, but two HUMINT teams of five troops each and a three-man explosive-ordnance team remained in theatre (CDR 2005).

At especially sensitive moments, such as the elections in 2005 and 2009, additional troops were mobilized for three-month periods. During the deployment in 2005, the Romanian battalion operated as part of the Multinational Force in Kabul and had the US Dragon Company under its command. Providing technical and administrative personnel to handle the traffic at Kabul's airport was also an important task. Starting in April 2006, a 49-strong team was deployed for four months and again for a whole year in 2011. About 230 Romanian troops were also part of the SEEBRIG Brigade, a collective effort by Albania, Bulgaria, Greece, Italy, the former Yugoslavian Republic of Macedonia, Romania and Turkey, deployed in Kabul in February 2006. Romania is a contributor to the latest effort by the European Defence Agency in the area of counter-IEDs, to set up a field laboratory in Afghanistan to investigate data collected from explosion sites (MOR 2011b).

As has been the case in conflicts elsewhere, for instance in Kosovo (Huysmans 2002), NATO has combined humanitarian and combat objectives. Press releases from the Romanian Ministry of Defence often mention the involvement of troops and the use of military resources in humanitarian activities. Examples include the use of the C-130 Hercules plane to transport medicine, food and other necessities in the wake of the earthquake in Mazar-e-Sharif in early March 2002, and participation in symbolic gestures that reinforce respect for local traditions and the 'friendship between the Afghan and the Romanian peoples'. In addition, visits by high-level officials from Romania to meet the troops and activities to mark various national holidays or specifically army holidays sometimes include local communities through donations of foodstuffs, toys and school materials for children. On 1 June 2006, the SEEBRIG team in Kabul opened a new park and recreational area they had built for children in Kabul in cooperation with a local NGO, in the presence, among others, of the city's mayor.

Other types of missions carried out by troops include patrols, data gathering, security for logistical operations, VIP escorts and also, specifically, aid distribution. 'Village teams' have not only distributed aid but have also consulted and collected locals' views on developmental needs, given out information about the aims of both ISAF and the Taliban, as well as provided medical assistance. Military medical teams have also visited villages to provide surgeries. For instance, during 12–15 October 2006, over 400 Afghans from Zabul received medical care from a Romanian–American team. NATO has, of course, a distinct civil–military (CIMIC) doctrine and methodology, which has been incorporated by the Romanian army (Udrea 2003a, 2003b, 2003c).

The setting up of the Afghan army and police has been a major priority within the overall international effort. Romanian experts were part of this complex process, which entailed training in a variety of kinds of armament and types of operations, the drawing up of organizational statutes, management of the acquisition programmes and donations, recruitment, inspection and maintenance of equipment, and so on. Sometimes, the choice of Romanian trainers was due to their experience in handling particular kinds of weapons that were unfamiliar to US soldiers. The quality of the rapport between the Romanians and their Afghan colleagues, as it comes through in Afghan testimonies, might also have been a factor. Especially in the context of common missions, it transpires that cultural differences remain, but emotional distances are not impossible to bridge. The Romanians seem to have provided desirable and at the same time accessible role models, on the model of 'older brothers'. Their competence and material superiority established, they were also perceived as sensitive and respectful of cultural difference. An important point seems to have been the scheduling of activities to allow for the Afghan routine of prayer five times a day.

Thus, on the whole, the case of Romania shows that states may participate in both direct and indirect ways in the commercialization of security in the peace and stabilization efforts in Afghanistan. As a result of its political ambitions – to join NATO and to play a visible role in the diplomatic community – Romania has contributed to the legitimation of the international intervention in Afghanistan and indirectly has created opportunities for the expansion of opportunities for private contractors there. At the same time, in the low-profile roles they have actually performed, Romanian troops have carried out functions that might have otherwise been contracted out. In such advisory capacities, Romanian troops might continue to contribute to a 'downsized war' (Malkasian and Weston 2012) in Afghanistan after 2014.

Note

1 The author would like to thank the editor of this volume, as well as Claudiu Degeratu, Elke Kaufmann, Stefano Ruzza and all the other participants in the project for their comments and questions.

References

Apostol, D. 2008. 'Cum arată primul trimestru pentru afacerile de securitate', 23 April, www.wall-street.ro/articol/Companii/41089/Cum-arata-primul-trimestru-pentru-afacerile-de-securitate.html, accessed 31 May 2011.

Atanasiu, T. 2006. 'Răspuns la interpelarea formulată de dl deputat George Scutaru', 27 April, www.cdep.ro/interpel/2006/r1416B.pdf, accessed 26 September 2012.

Barbu, V. 2002. 'Restructuring and modernization in the human resources field'. In C. Moştoflei (ed.) *Romania – NATO 1990–2002*, Bucharest: The Academy for Advanced Military Studies, pp. 77–78.

——2004. 'Restructurarea resurselor umane', www.presamil.ro/SMM2004/03–04/pag% 2023–27.htm, accessed 24 May 2011.

Băsescu, T. 2008. 'Joint Press Conference of the Romanian and Afghan Presidents, Traian Băsescu and Harmid Karzai', 2 April, www.summitbucharest.ro/ro/doc_171.html, accessed 26 September 2012.

——2010. 'Annual Evaluation Meeting, Ministry of Defense, 5 March', www.presidency. ro/?_RID=det& tb=date& id=11896&_PRID=search, accessed 26 September 2012.

Camera Deputaţilor României (CDR). 2002a. 'Transcript parliamentary debate, 30 April, Point 2' [Deputies Chamber, Parliament of Romania], www.cdep.ro/pls/steno/steno. stenograma?ids=5263&idm=2&idl=1, accessed 26 September 2012.

——2002b. 'Transcript parliamentary debate, 30 April, Point 3', www.cdep.ro/pls/steno/ steno.stenograma?ids=5263&idm=3&idl=1, accessed 26 September 2012.

——2003a. 'Transcript parliamentary debate, 17 April, Point 4', www.cdep.ro/pls/steno/ steno.stenograma?ids=5417&idm=4&idl=1, accessed 26 September 2012.

——2003b. 'Transcript parliamentary debate, 7 May, Point 2', www.cdep.ro/pls/steno/ steno.stenograma?ids=5457&idm=2&idl=1, accessed 26 September 2012.

——2004a. 'Transcript parliamentary debate, 2 March, Point 2', www.cdep.ro/pls/steno/ steno.stenograma?ids=5621&idm=2&idl=1, accessed 26 September 2012.

——2004b. 'Transcript parliamentary debate, 9 Sept, Point 6', www.cdep.ro/pls/steno/ steno.stenograma?ids=5720&idm=6&idl=1, accessed 26 September 2012.

——2005. 'Transcript parliamentary debate, 3 Feb, Point 2', www.cdep.ro/pls/steno/ steno.stenograma?ids=5790&idm=2&idl=1, accessed 26 September 2012.

Ciungu, M. 2007. 'Profesionalizarea armatei – implicaţii asupra marilor unităţi şi unităţi din Forţele Terestre', *Gândirea militară românească* 1: 74–79.

Consiliul Suprem de Apărare al Ţării (CSAT). 2005. 'Hotărîri adoptate de CSAT în 2004', http://csat.presidency.ro/documente/Hotararile_CSAT – 2004_5ro.pdf, accessed 14 September 2011.

Florea, L. 2010. 'Primul şef roman al companiei de pază Rosegur: E dureros că trebuie să ofertăm la preţuri foarte mici', 22 December, www.wall-street.ro/articol/Companii/ 96969/Primul-sef-roman-al-companiei-de- ... , accessed 25 October 2011.

Huysmans, J. 2002. 'Shape-shifting NATO: humanitarian action and the Kosovo crisis', *Review of International Studies* 28: 599–618.

International Security Assistance Force (ISAF). 2008. 'ISAF's Strategic Vision'. Declaration by the Heads of State and Government of the Nations contributing to the UN-mandated, NATO-led ISAF in Afghanistan, 3 April, www.nato.int/cps/en/natolive/official_texts_8444.htm, accessed 26 September 2012.

Malkasian, C. and J. K. Weston. 2012. 'War downsized: How to accomplish more with less', *Foreign Affairs* 91 (2): 111–21.

Matache, C. 2011. 'Industria de apărare trage cu gloanţe oarbe', 16 September, *Săptămîna Financiară*, www.sfin.ro/articol_24415/industria_de_aparare_trage_cu_gloante_oarbe. html, accessed 26 September 2012.

Mediafax. 2011. 'Schimbări la fondul de salarii şi la numărul de angajaţi din industria de apărare', 21 January, www.mediafax.ro/social/fondul-de-salarii-si-numarul-mediu-de-angajati-in-industria-de-aparare-au-fost-majorate-cu-peste-7-9201479/, accessed 10 October 2011.

Meleşcanu, T. 2008. 'Răspuns la întrebarea adresata Ministerului Apărării de domnul deputat Ovidiu Muşetescu', www.cdep.ro/interpel/2008/r5288A.pdf, accessed 26 September 2012.

Ministerul Afacerilor Externe (MAE). 2004a. 'Press release, 22 March', www.gov.ro/ comunicat-de-presa – 11a27071.html, accessed 21 September 2011.

——2004b. 'Press release, 30 March', www.gov.ro/comunicat-de-presa – 11a27392.html, accessed 21 September 2011.

Ministerul Agriculturii, Alimentaţiei şi Pădurilor (MAAP). 2003. 'Press release, 15 January', www.gov.ro/comunicat-de-presa – 11a15830.html, accessed 21 September 2011.

Ministerul Apărării Naţionale (MApN). 2002. 'Press release, 27 May', www.gov.ro/comu nicat-de-presa – 11a10369.html MApN 2009, accessed 21 September 2011.

——2004. 'Press release, 16 January', www.gov.ro/comunicat-de-presa – 11a24908.html, accessed 25 September 2011.

——2005. 'Buletinul Contractelor de Achiziţii Publice' [Public Acquisitions Bulletin], No. 1, Year 1, 9 March, www.dpa.ro/rp/publicatii/buletine/bc2005_1.pdf, accessed 25 September 2011.

——2006. 'Buletinul Contractelor de Achiziţii Publice', No. 1, Year 2, 18 May, www.dpa. ro/rp/publicatii/buletine/bc2006_1.pdf, accessed 25 September 2011.

——2007. 'Buletinul Contractelor de Achiziţii Publice', No. 1, Year 3, 15 January, www. dpa.ro/rp/publicatii/buletine/bc2007_1.pdf, accessed 25 September 2011.

——2009a. 'Biroul de presă, Drept la replică', in *Săptămîna Financiară*, 20 February, www. sfin.ro/articol_15451/drept_la_replica.html, accessed 25 September 2011.

——2009b. 'Buletinul Contractelor de Achiziţii Publice', No. 1, Year 5, 11 June, www. dpa.ro/rp/publicatii/buletine/bc2009_1.pdf, accessed 25 September 2011.

——2009c. 'Planul Strategic al Ministerului Apărării Naţionale 2010 – 2013', [Strategic Plan for the Ministry of National Defense 2010–13] Bucharest: www.mapn.ro/despre_ mapn/informatii_generale/documente/plan_2009.pdf, accessed 23 June 2011.

——2011a. 'Buletinul Contractelor de Achiziţii Publice', No. 1, Year 7, 3 May, www.dpa. ro/rp/publicatii/buletine/bc2011_1.pdf, accessed 26 September 2011.

——2011b. 'Press release no. 77, 1 June', www.mapn.ro/cpresa/13668_COMUNICAT-DE-PRESĂ, accessed 26 September 2011.

Ministerul Informatiilor Publice (MIP). 2001. 'Press release, 7 October', www.gov.ro/comunicat-de-presa – 11a6976.html, accessed 25 September 2011.

Monitorul Official al României (MOR). 2001a. 'Hotarâre 918 din 13 septembrie 2001 pentru aplicarea Rezoluţiei nr. 1.333/2000 a Consiliului de Securitate al Organizaţiei Naţiunilor Unite privind situaţia din Afganistan', No. 602/25, September, Bucharest: MOR Press.

———2001b. 'Hotarâre 21 din 19 septembrie 2001 privind participarea României, impreună cu statele membre ale NATO, la acţiunile de combatere a terorismului international', No. 589/20, September, Bucharest: MOR Press.

———2001c. 'Hotarâre 22 din 19 septembrie 2001 privind suplimentarea participarii Romaniei la Forta de Stabilizare din Bosnia-Hertegovina (SFOR) si la Forta de Mentinere a Pacii din Kosovo, Republica Federala Iugoslavia (KFOR), cu forte din Ministerul Apararii Nationale', No. 589/20, September, Bucharest: MOR Press.

———2001d. 'Hotarâre 38 din 21 decembrie 2001 privind participarea României în cadrul forţei internaţionale de asistenţă din Afganistan, precum si împuternicirea Guvernului de a stabili forţele, mijloacele, finanţarea si condiţiile în care se va asigura participarea la aceasta misiune', No. 832/21, December, Bucharest: MOR Press.

———2002a. 'Hotarâre 133 din 14 februarie 2002 privind donarea unor bunuri aparţinând domeniului privat al statului pentru Garda Naţionala a Afganistanului', No. 143/25, February, Bucharest: MOR Press.

———2002b. 'Hotarâre 15 din 30 aprilie 2002 privind participarea României la Operaţia 'Enduring Freedom' din Afganistan', No 293/30, April, Bucharest: MOR Press.

———2002c. 'Hotarâre 1.261 din 7 noiembrie 2002 privind acordarea de catre România de asistenţă cu titlu gratuit pentru ajutorarea Afganistanului', No. 832/19, November, Bucharest: MOR Press.

———2004. 'Hotarâre 1347 din 26 august 2004 privind acordarea de catre statul român de asistenţă cu titlu gratuit pentru Afganistan, in vederea formării de specialişti in domenii de interes pentru partea afgană', No 811/2, September, Bucharest: MOR Press.

———2005. 'Hotarâre 1.076 din 15 septembrie 2005 privind asistenţa acordată de statul român, cu titlu gratuit, pentru Afganistan, în vederea formării de specialişti în domenii de interes pentru acest stat', No. 853/21, September, Bucharest: MOR Press.

———2008. 'Ordonanţa de urgenţă privind finanţarea unor proiecte de investiţii care necesită o perioada mai lungă de un an pană la finalizare, oug nr. 111/2006', No. 246/28, March, Bucharest: MOR Press.

———2011a. 'Ordin pentru modificarea anexelor nr. 1 şi 2 la Ordinul ministrului apărării nr M31/2008 privind competenţele de achiziţie a produselor, serviciilor si lucrărilor în cadrul Ministerului Apării Naţionale', No. 563/8, August, Bucharest: MOR Press.

———2011b. 'Hotarâre 915 din 14 septembrie 2011 pentru aprobarea participării României la Iniţiativa Agenţiei Europene de Apărare privind dislocarea in Afganistan a Laboratorului de nivel teatru pentru investigarea probelor rezultate în urma incidentelor cu folosirea dispozitivelor explozive improvizate şi a plăţii contribuţiei financiare a României la bugetul comun al acestei iniţiative', No. 667/20, September, Bucharest: MOR Press.

Nedelcu, I.-M. 2005. 'Preocupări concrete în modernizarea Forţelor Terestre. Interlocutor generalul de brigadă Neculae Oţelea, şeful resurselor din SMFT', www.presamil.ro/OM/2005/23/pag%206.htm, accessed 26 September 2012.

Paşcu, I. M. 2008. *Bătălia pentru NATO*, Bucharest: Tritonic.

Pop, L. 2006. *Democratising capitalism? The political economy of post-communist transformations in Romania 1989–2001*, Manchester: Manchester University Press.

———2007. 'Time and crisis: Framing success and failure in Romania's post-communist transformations', *Review of International Studies* 33: 395–413.

———2009. 'Strategic action is not enough: A Bourdieuian approach to EU enlargement', *Perspectives on European Politics and Society* 10: 254–267.

Pridham, G. 2007. 'The scope and limitations of political conditionality: Romania's accession to the European Union', *Comparative European Politics* 5: 347–376.

Prisăcariu, C. n.d. 'Romania: New system, same players', www.reportingproject.net/security/index.php/stories/7-romania, undated blog, accessed 31 May 2011.

Radio Romania Actualități (RRA). 2008. 'România va cere aliaților o mai mare implicare in Afganistan', www.summitbucharest.ro/documente/fisiere/ro/iasi%20romana.pdf, accessed 26 September 2011.

Schimmelfennig, F., S. Engel and H. Knobel (2006) *International Socialization in Europe: European Organizations, Political Conditionality and Democratic Change*, London: Palgrave.

Schreier, F. and Caparini, M. 2005. 'Privatising security: Law, practice and governance of private military and security companies', Geneva Centre for the Democratic Control of Armed Forces, Occasional paper no. 6, www.dcaf.ch/content/download/.../op06_privatising-security.pdf (accessed 20 June 2011).

South Eastearn Europe Clearing House for the Control of Small Arms and Light Weapons (SEESAC). 2005. 'SALW and private security companies in South Eastern Europe: A cause or effect of insecurity', SEESAC, August, www.isn.ethz.ch/isn/Digital-Library/Publications/Detail/?ots591=0c54e3b3-1e9c-be1e-2c24-a6a8c7060233&lng=en&id=13719 (accessed 22 June 2011).

Șcheianu, D. 2001. 'Probleme ale pregătirii economiei și teritoriului pentru apărare (III)', *Gândirea militară românească* 3: 77–86.

Stillman, S. 2011. 'The Invisible Army', *The New Yorker*, June 6, www.newyorker.com/reporting/2011/06/06/110606fa_fact_stillman, accessed 26 September 2012.

Tănase, M. 2011. 'Cu echipa de rotire a OMLT in Afganistan, Interviuri GMR', *Gîndirea Militară Românească* 2: 152–181.

Tudor, R. 2009. 'Înzestrarea armatei, un faliment garantat', *Săptămîna Financiară*, 13 February, www.sfin.ro/articol_15343/inzestrarea_armatei_un_faliment_garantat.html, accessed 26 September 2012.

Udrea, F. 2003a. 'Cooperarea civili-militari – componentă a misiunii fiecărui militar', *Gândirea militară românească* 2: 40–45.

———2003b. 'Cooperarea civili-militari – în operațiile de sprijin al păcii', *Gândirea militară românească* 3: 106–11.

———2003c. 'Cooperarea civili-militari – în operații umanitare', *Gândirea militară românească* 4: 51–5.

Vachudova, M. A. 2005. *Europe Undivided: Democracy, Leverage and Integration after Communism*, Oxford: Oxford University Press.

8 France

Making both ends meet?

Christian Olsson

Introduction

Issues related to the French private military and security sector remain within a cloud of elusiveness. Indeed, it is difficult to define what one is really looking for and how one might assess its significance. This predicament can be illustrated through three apparent paradoxes.

First, sociological–historical accounts of French state formation tend to insist on the early and thorough accumulation of coercive means within the purview of the crown (Tilly 1992; Elias 2000). Yet, while the French state is today traditionally described as being averse to the delegation of 'royal functions' (*fonctions régaliennes*), the country is generally among the first to come to mind when the topic of post-colonial mercenarism is under consideration (Musah and Fayemi 2000). This has especially been the case in relation to francophone Africa, where, since decolonization, mercenarism has been used to further French influence and circumvent international law.

Second, while one might consider the French take on the issue during the last 50 years to highlight both a propensity to make use of 'murky mercenaries' and an aversion to 'corporate PMSCs', one of the first French mercenary 'corporate firms', la Société Générale Comorienne, was founded by Bob Denard in the Comoros back in the 1980s as a way of managing his pool of old-school 'dogs of war' (Chapleau 2011). We might also note that one of Denard's collaborators, François-Xavier Sidos – incidentally also a right-wing extremist – was a few years ago still active in attempting to lobby against the French law 'on the suppression of mercenary activity' of 2003.

Third, and finally, while the public debate on military contracting seems to be gaining traction, the main international operation carried out by French troops – France's contribution to the NATO/ISAF operation in Afghanistan – remains ambiguous in this regard. On the one hand, French troops are heavily dependent on private actors for logistics either directly, through their own contracting practices, or indirectly, through their allies. On the other hand, there is very little in terms of French PMSCs in-country, because much of the contracting concerns local firms. Furthermore, even though military contracting is increasing within national borders, the use of actual force, particularly in the context of international operations, is generally viewed as one of the domains that cannot be outsourced.

This chapter will attempt to unpack these three paradoxes in order to show what is at stake. It is divided into two main parts. Drawing on the insight that the French PMSC business has largely preceded the formal contracting practices of public institutions,[1] we seek first to analyse the small realm of French PMSCs. Then, we look at the contracting practices of French defence institutions. Here, we will seek to highlight the role played by private operators in the context of international operations, with a particular focus on the French contribution to ISAF. This second part will also illustrate a number of current trends and debates.

Commercial security in the cradle of the Weberian state: an 'exception française' regarding private security?

In relation to his misdeeds in Africa, Bob Denard used to claim that he had received a 'yellow light' from official services. This meant either that operations were condoned at the highest levels but that the executive would deny responsibility if they were uncovered, or that French services were simply reluctant either to condone or to condemn beforehand. In any event, with its inherent ambiguity, Denard's metaphor applies just as much to the official stance of recent French governments towards PMSCs. Indeed, there is no such stance. There is neither significant support (in terms of demand) nor opposition (through rules, regulations) to PMSCs. In fact, there is no consistent policy on the issue at all at present, although that situation is rapidly changing. This absence of a clearly identified policy – neither prohibiting nor regulating – sheds light on many of the features of France's PMSC microcosm.

A controversial microcosm

France is often considered the cradle of the modern nation-state as constructed by and through war. Indeed, the French Revolution built further on the centralizing impetus of the absolutist state (de Tocqueville 1955), allowing for the *levée en masse* of 1793 and later for Napoleon's armies, both laying the foundation of the myth of the armed forces as 'the nation in arms'. The construction of the 'Revolutionary Wars' as the foundational moment of the French Republic means that Tilly's (1975: 42) famous reasoning that 'war makes the state and the state makes war' became not only an accurate description but also a constitutive part of French patriotism: the public monopoly on armed force is often presented as a question of national identity. In the current debate on PMSCs, there is a strong sense that France represents a peculiar exception in this regard. Some claim that the privatization of 'royal functions' is contrary to French sovereignty and the country's constitution, and regard it as threatening the specificity of the military sector (Saint-Quentin 1998; Renou 2006). Others argue that France's exceptional status is untenable because of the costs it entails and the need to 'make both ends meet' in a context of economic crisis (Chapleau 2011). According to this line of reasoning, too strict an observance of the monopoly on the use of force could mean that France's armed forces would end up having to contract with an American PMSC in the event of an international crisis, which would threaten the very sovereignty the monopoly was supposed to guarantee. Accordingly, the disagreement is not over the centrality of national sovereignty and international standing, but only how to achieve these things. Moreover, both sides seem to agree that current French practice is exceptional in a world that seems to have embraced the 'Anglo-Saxon' version of defence contracting (Irondelle and Olsson 2011).

The issue of PMSCs remains highly controversial in France. Controversies concern the terminology to be used, the definitions of the particular terms chosen and the purview of legitimate contracting practices. What is interesting, though, is that everyone seems to know what is being discussed when reference is made to PMSCs. The debate turns only on the choice of terminology, not on the actual domain covered by that terminology. Obviously, however, once one starts to look at definitions, difficult questions soon arise. If 'military contracting' is the defining feature of PMSCs, then Sodexo's serving food at French military bases in Afghanistan would make it a PMSC. This, of course, is not the case (except in the context of the company's UK branch, Sodexo Defence), and this example thus highlights the need to distinguish the question of PMSCs from military contracting understood as the outsourcing (*externalization*) of functions, generally ancillary ones, previously performed by the armed forces themselves. There is significant overlap between the two, but they should nonetheless be seen as distinct.

However, if a PMSC is to be defined by the fact that its personnel are bearing arms in conflict-ridden areas, companies advising armed forces on a raging battlefield would not be PMSCs, which leads to an equally problematic situation. To reduce PMSCs – or even PMCs[2] – to companies whose personnel are authorized to engage in direct combat or to carry a weapon on a battlefield is too simplistic. Such an approach would mean that there were no French PMSCs at all, since, by virtue of a decree of 6 May 1995,[3] it is in principle not permissible for private agents to carry firearms. There are exceptions to this rule, however – for example, in the case of the security guards of armoured vans used to transport money. Moreover, the principle can be circumvented abroad through the granting of diplomatic status to security personnel, through subcontracting, through the signing of offshore contracts or through the creation of company branches in third countries. For example, Gallice Security provides armed protection teams for merchant vessels on the high seas through a branch based in Ireland (Assemblée nationale 2012: 26), while Secopex trains part of its personnel in the Czech Republic. It ought lastly to be mentioned that the rules preventing private agents from carrying weapons are increasingly coming under criticism and viewed as being out of date.

What we will here refer to as PMSCs are companies that pretend to 'sell security' and have a 'military perspective' on security. Whether the latter is the case can often be ascertained by looking at the sociological composition of a company's staff, employees, clients or networks (former soldiers?), its long-term business strategy (does it want to 'militarize' its services in the future?) or the nature of the services it offers: peace operations, strategic transport including assault landing, C3I,[4] etc. While this might seem to give us a rather vague definition, in practice the approach proves sufficiently concrete in terms of identifying what is intersubjectively perceived as a particular, albeit fragmented and weak, business sector. Indeed, it seems to be more or less clear to a range of different actors – proponents and critics alike – what companies are being discussed, which makes the question of formal definitions somewhat abstract. In France, a PMSC is currently understood to be a company that either profiles itself as being actively interested in the question of defence outsourcing and the selling of military services or is considered to be so by commentators and analysts. Another difficult question, however, concerns what a 'French' company is. Indeed, some of the relevant companies are registered abroad (e.g. Aspic Ltd. in the Seychelles, Earthwind Holding Corporation/EHC in the US). Here, too, there exists relative consensus on which companies are French, which is decided on the basis of their social networks of employers, employees and clients.

In spite – or perhaps because of – the vagueness of the very object under discussion, the issue of PMSCs has led to a profusion of more or less Orwellian terms and acronyms, sponsored by a range of different bureaucracies and/or defence analysts. The expression *sociétés militaires privées* (PMCs) has negative connotations because of its evocation of 'private armies' and hence mercenarism. It is also associated with the 'Anglo-Saxon model' and therefore considered to be unsuited to French know-how, traditions and needs. This is paradoxical, since in the UK the expression 'private military companies' is equally shunned (Percy 2007). Moreover, although they reject the aforementioned 'model', French defence analysts and PMSCs have never defined the alternative French 'model' they often call for. Only Secopex and the mainly French company EHC consider themselves to be small-scale PMCs. Secopex's future as a company, however, is currently in limbo: the company's CEO, Pierre Marzali, was killed in Benghazi, Libya, on the night of 12–13 May 2011 while purportedly prospecting the future PMSC market in rebel-held territory – an event that highlighted the discrepancy between Secopex's claim to be a 'French PMC', on the one hand, and the fact that it could not protect its own CEO, on the other.

Alternative expressions have been suggested as ways of avoiding and circumventing the social stigma attached to the notion of PMC: 'private companies of military interest' (SPIMs)[5] is one of the terms sponsored by the French defence ministry; the term 'external security companies' (SSEs)[6] has also been suggested, but was rapidly abandoned as being too similar to DGSE the acronym of the Directorate-General for External Security, France's counter-espionage service; for its part, the SGDSN, France's interministerial national security and defence secretariat,[7] has been developing the notion of 'safety and defence security companies' (SSSDs).[8] Numerous other terms and acronyms (e.g. SAS, SASO, SPSM, ESOA, SSI, ESSD) have been suggested by defence analysts and politicians, and are frequently used by the companies themselves. The question of which companies fall under which different terms is equally embattled. The profusion of terms bears testimony to the bureaucratic struggles that unfold in a context in which military contracting is increasingly seen as both inevitable and rewarding in terms of institutional profile and prerogative. At the same time, it highlights differing attempts at defining, circumscribing and legitimizing the purview of future contracting activities (Olsson 2003).

In fact, the public debate in France tends to revolve around the question of the scope of legitimate military contracting rather than around the nature and legitimacy of the companies themselves. Hence, the confusion created by the profusion of acronyms is partly mitigated by the fact that the still-circumscribed debate is focused on the less controversial 'outsourcing in the field of defence' (*externalisation dans le domaine de la défense*). In the realm of privatization, the concept of 'outsourcing' (*externalization*) is currently understood as different from 'subcontracting' (*sous-traitance*), since it usually entails a higher degree of control of the relevant private contractor (Hubac and Viellard 2009).

Another potentially controversial issue concerns the outer limits of the concepts of 'PMSC' and 'mercenary'. Two examples are of particular interest here. First, the company Défense Conseil International (DCI), along with its many joint ventures and branches, has since 1972 been involved in training foreign armed forces using French military equipment and know-how. Since the turn of the millennium, it has also entered into contractual agreements with the French Armed Forces – for example, contributing to the training of some army pilots. DCI is a private firm (the state owns 49 per cent of the company's shares); however, it is under the tutelage of the Ministry of Defence and is closely integrated with France's armed forces, on which it depends for its workforce of about 600–800 individuals, mainly seconded and retired military personnel. It is even allowed to use the official label '*armées*', which is in principle reserved for the state's armed forces. The various private companies that own the rest of the shares in DCI either have the same type of ambiguous status as DCI itself (e.g. ODAS) or are part of the defence industry. DCI representatives sometimes attend meetings at which the abrogation of the 2003 law on 'the suppression of mercenary activity' is discussed. In informal French parlance, DCI is para-public, *para-étatique*. It is clearly not considered to be a PMSC. Rather, it might be termed a *public military company* – a hybrid of a PMC and a state bureaucracy. DCI offers an interesting example of the interpenetration of the public and private spheres that can also be observed, albeit in a different form, in US or British PMCs (Leander 2005, 2006).

The second example concerns the status of the *Légion étrangère*, the French Foreign Legion. While virtually nobody in France would claim that this is a mercenary organization, it is worth noting that one of the main reasons why the French government has never signed the UN Mercenary Convention of 1989 is its fear of seeing the Foreign Legion labelled a mercenary force (Lechervy 2003).

Global market or local artisanship?

Given the long-term macro-sociological trends of French state formation, it may be worth asking to what extent the emergence of a relatively small PMSC sector in France is illustrative of a specifically French trajectory or whether it is rather the effect of a general convergence on the 'Anglo-American model' and hence a product of globalization. In order to answer this question, it will be necessary to analyze the main features of the sector.

First, the sector is an unstable microcosm of small firms. In general, France's PMSCs, thought to be around 30–40 in number, are small companies whose average annual turnover has been estimated to be in the region of €3 million. Geos Group, with a turnover of €38 million in 2010, and Risk & Co. (€28 million in 2011) are among the largest (Assemblée nationale 2012). Secopex, one of the more famous PMSCs, is much more modest in size, with a turnover of around half a million euros in 2006. As an example of the small size of the French PMSCs, we might mention that although a handful are or have been present in Iraq (Gallice Security, EHC, AICS, KAIS International, Anticip, Risk & Co.), both the French oil company Total and a French delegation of CEOs (in October 2010) have subcontracted their security to the US firm Triple Canopy rather than to French PMSCs when working in the country. Indeed, the limited size of the French companies does not permit them to escort large delegations.[9] Some French PMSCs have been dissolved in recent years (Groupe Barril Sécurité) or are currently in judicial liquidation (Vitruve Defence & Security). The instability of the sector has led many companies to focus on 'non-military' security services, while ostensibly waiting for a change in legislation or public demand to militarize their services (e.g. Geos Group, Epée). However, the sector's perception of itself as being 'underdeveloped' is at least partly linked to the fact that the companies often compare themselves with their British and American 'counterparts'. In relation to the other Continental European countries considered in this volume, such a self-perception is unjustified.

Second, there is a high level of fragmentation within the 'sector' (to such a degree that one might ask whether it really is a 'sector'), which has sought to compartmentalize itself into various niches, with specialization being seen as providing a degree of defence against global competition. French PMSCs tend to focus on strategic advising, consultancy and prevention (PHL Consultants, Kargus Sea Interconnection), crisis management (Aspic, SAS), economic intelligence (Atlantic Intelligence, Geos Group),[10] humanitarian demining (Pretory Technologie), and static or mobile protection (OGS, SIA). Nevertheless, in spite of efforts to compartmentalize the 'sector', competition is fierce and accusations of conflicts of interest or of not respecting workers' rights seem to be frequent.[11] In spring 2011, however, a group of French companies (Thales, Geodis, Sodexo and GIE Access) together established a new company, Global [X], with the aim of providing support services to peacekeeping operations.

Third, the business thrives on political networks and is linked to influential individuals who straddle the boundaries between the private and public sectors, on the one hand, and between the fields of security professionals and politics, on the other (Olsson 2003). The best example here is probably that of Lieutenant-Colonel Frédéric Gallois, the commander of the renowned special intervention unit of the Gendarmerie Nationale (GIGN)[12] between 2002 and 2007. Gallois created the PMSC Gallice Security and is also known for his many high-profile political contacts. The fact that many of the CEOs of French PMSCs have held important positions within the country's security forces and services facilitates the interpenetration of the public and private spheres (Olsson 2003; Wasinski 2008). For example, Marc de Rodellec, CEO of Concord Risks ('corporate and maritime security') and formerly a member of the navy's special forces (*commando marine*), worked between 2002 and 2005 for the public company DCNS (*Direction of Naval Constructions*), and was subsequently employed by the Geos Group in 2006 and Kargus Sea International in 2007. He has also been a 'security officer' for the UN Mission in Haiti. Interested in the fight against maritime piracy, he established political contacts through Louis Petiet, a right-wing (UMP)[13] politician active in the department of l'Eure and close to former president Nicolas Sarkozy, whom he has also accompanied in travels abroad. Louis Petiet is also director of Bernard Krief Consulting (KBC), which owns a part of Concord Risks through one of its affiliates, Francom.[14] Interestingly, while generally on the right-wing side of the political spectrum, these political contacts are not necessarily at high levels. For example, Stéphane Malvoisin, director of Crisis Consulting, was parliamentary assistant to right-wing (UDF)[15] members of the lower house, one of whom was the vice president of the foreign affairs commission. Accordingly, the phenomenon seems more comparable to the idea of the 'strength of weak ties' (Granovetter 1973) than to the type of widespread collusion at high levels associated with Wright Mills (1956) or the concept of a military–industrial complex.

Several elements might be stressed concerning the ramifications of these political networks. They sometimes involve extreme right-wing undercurrents of the political scene (Chapleau 2005). Moreover, the asset represented by these political contacts has less to do with their leverage on the public administration than with the privileged access that politicians have to other private interests, as well as to third countries. Furthermore, there is much continuity with the traditional networks of the '*Françafrique*' in sub-Saharan Africa. There is hence significant overlap between the 'old' business of mercenarism and the 'new' one of PMSCs. Lastly, these political networks raise the question of the extent to which one can speak of a 'privatization of the state' itself. Indeed, as shown by Béatrice Hibou (1999), privatization never amounts to a unilateral retreat of the state. Rather, it extends, furthers and transforms the networks of patronage though which a state's political elites govern populations (Hibou 1999). Yet, however seductive, this line of argumentation is nevertheless to a certain extent inapplicable to the French 'PMSC sector'. Indeed, as we shall see, the world of PMSCs and the realm of military contracting are still very much disconnected from each other.

Fourth, the politicization of the French sector is paradoxical because its clients are largely private companies or, more rarely, NGOs. There is no quasi-monopsony of public administrations, as in the US. In France, it is mainly the private sector that allows for the few PMSCs to survive. The oil consortium Groupe Total is one of the most important clients of the sector and has worked, for example, with the French PMSCs Amarante (in Yemen) and Risk & Co. Essentially pragmatic, however, it opted for British Control Risks in Nigeria.[16] The successive heads of 'general security' of Groupe Total – Hervé Madéo, Jean-Philippe Magnan and Jérôme Ferrier – have played a pivotal role in the French PMSC business, and each 'succession' has led to a thorough re-examination of the company's security contracts.[17] All information currently available indicates that there are very few French PMSCs working for the public sector. There are some exceptions to the general trend, however. For example, Amarante protects some of the more sensitive parts of the Ariane rocket programme for the National Centre of Space Studies (CNES).[18] The same company provides an explosives expert to the Ministry of Foreign Affairs for security auditing of diplomatic posts, but otherwise remains relatively marginal (Assemblée nationale 2012: 14). As a consequence, French PMSCs either have turned towards domestic private demand or have tried to 'go international' – generally both.

'Internationalization' is limited, however, and while some French 'private contractors' work in sub-Saharan Africa, most of these firms are formally based in Africa. A few companies work for foreign companies and states. Secopex, for example, signed a contract with the Somali government in June 2008 to provide maritime security. In 2010, Gallice Security claimed to have a contract with the Iraqi Ministry of Foreign Affairs to protect its premises. It is currently training the armed forces of Gabon, and about 45 per cent of its turnover comes from states (Assemblée nationale 2012: 39). Employees of the French company Galea were accredited by the Libyan National Transitional Council to sell security services in the country, and the European Union's mission in Libya has admittedly been protected by Argus, a company registered in Hungary but led by Frenchmen (Assemblée nationale 2012: 11). Many companies have delocalized part of their activities. More rarely, some have delocalized all of their activities. In the latter case, EHC is one of the more militarized companies, having sent personnel to Iraq as subcontractor to an American PMC. It is registered in Delaware and based in London, but its staff and personnel are French. It even used to be part of the International Peace Operations Association (IPOA),[19] the American PMC lobby, but left in 2005 allegedly giving two reasons: high membership costs and their impression that they were mistrusted by other IPOA members because of their French nationality.[20]

Fifth, French companies tend to prioritize potential recruits from among the elite units of France's various security services: GIGN for the gendarmerie,[21] marine infantry[22] or the foreign legion[23] for the French army, marine commandos for the French navy,[24] along with the 'action service' of French counterintelligence unit the DGSE,[25] and more rarely special units of the national police such as the BRI 'anti-gang' unit or the RAID counterterrorist unit.[26] Retired but high-ranking generals also represent an important asset for the companies. For example, General Jean Heinrich, former head of the DGSE's Service Action and first head of the Directorate of Military Intelligence (DRM), is currently at the head of Geos Group. What explains the attraction exerted by this business on the personnel of the very units that are presented as the spearhead of the state's monopoly on legitimate violence?

A Bourdieu-inspired approach to the question might give us some clues (Bourdieu 1990; Bigo 2008). It would be an error to consider the PMSC microcosm to be mainly populated by 'amateurs' or adventurers rather than by 'professionals'. For the time being, however, the sector's professionalism seems to centre on action-oriented and operational know-how, rather than on the capacity to produce expert knowledge on threats and risks other than to very limited referent objects (particular firms, persons, etc.). Arguably it is the latter capacity, in a context where the state and society as a whole are taken as the relevant referent objects, which constitutes the main asset structuring the field of security professionals (Bigo 2008). From this point of view, the PMSC sector is undeniably marginal within the security field. Moreover, the French 'sector' is characterized more by 'artisanship' than by 'industry', at least in comparison with the international PMSC market within which most of these companies want to compete. Hence, we can hypothesize that 'going private' is a strategy of economic accumulation for highly trained and skilled elite operatives who, because of the 'operational' focus of their training, are both excluded from the centre of the field of security professionals (yet clearly part of the privileged few within the margins) and increasingly disadvantaged as their age advances and operational missions become out of reach in the public sector. The values that are linked to their *habitus*, and centred on the operational and action-centred dimension of security (Olsson 2009), can hence be revived in the private sector. Leaving the public sphere is, however, a permanent move. Indeed, other than for a very few exceptions – such as Alain Juillet, a businessman[27] who became director of intelligence at the DGSE in 2002, a high official at the SGDN[28] and then returned to the private sector in 2009 – there is no 'revolving door' through which capital accumulated in the private sector can be reinvested in the public one. Or, rather, the 'revolving door' is in general unidirectional, from the public to the private sector.

To some extent, the first four features could be considered as highlighting the specificity of the French 'sector' in comparison with the Anglo-Saxon private military companies that are generally seen as 'setting the tone' for the business. Indeed, the fragmented nature of the French sector, which is made up of an unstable microcosm of small firms whose clients are overwhelmingly private firms, could be said to distinguish it. The importance played by political networks, even though it is not a French peculiarity, also accentuates the French sector's relative 'insulation', since these networks are tightly linked to the French state. It is only the last element, the role played by former soldiers from elite units, that could point towards international convergence. On the whole, the transnational security market postulated by Deborah D. Avant (2005) remains pretty remote.

The politics of military contracting in international operations and beyond: standpoints, practices, institutionalizations

Rather than starting with the institutional framework of military contracting and then moving on to analyze actual contracting practices, here we will do the reverse. Practices often precede institutionalization (Balzacq *et al.* 2010). This is especially the case in international operations in which the practices of other troop-contributing countries play a determining role.

French contracting practices in the context of NATO/ISAF

Relative to US or British practice, military contracting plays a limited role within French contributions to international operations. There have, however, been a few noticeable examples outside of the Afghan theatre. In Kosovo, for example, the 'management' of a military base was contracted out by the French army, including responsibility for food, fire protection, energy, water and waste services, as well as maintenance of the security fence (Chapleau 2011: 140). In the context of European Union Force Tchad (EUFOR Tchad) between 2007 and 2009, elements of the logistical transport services between Douala and N'Djamena were contracted out, as well as demining activities around Faya-Largeau in the north of the country.

In many regards, the French contribution to ISAF with no less than 3,600 military personnel is different from France's contributions to EUFOR Tchad or the Kosovo Force. Indeed, the mission is taking place in the context of a deadly conflict and, unlike in Chad, the French contingent is part of a NATO force. These troops are mostly based in Afghanistan, although there is an air-transport detachment in Tajikistan and a naval force in the Indian Ocean (Task Force 150). Within Afghanistan, since 2009 most of the French troops have either been based in Kapisa province (Regional Command – East) or in Surobi valley (Regional Command – Capital) in the northeast of Kabul province. Although placed under different regional commands, both components are part of Task Force Lafayette. Furthermore, there are about 200 gendarmes training the Afghan police, mainly in Kapisa province. In contrast to the situation for most of the other NATO members, no Provincial Reconstruction Team is under French command, and the level of integration of civil and military missions is minimal compared to that for France's European partners. The Ministry of Foreign Affairs has, however, established a 'stability pole' of civilian experts embedded in Task Force Lafayette.

As mentioned earlier, there is a certain 'Afghan paradox' involved in French military contracting. While 'experimental' contracting is encouraged by NATO norms, there are only a few French PMSCs in Afghanistan. Geos Group, which has about a hundred telecommunications engineers in the country, is one of these (Assemblée nationale 2012: 39). If we limit ourselves to official sources, we find that most of the French companies working for the French armed forces are from France's defence industry. Furthermore, there seem to be very few French PMSCs working for private companies or French people working for non-French PMSCs in Afghanistan. EHC claims to have worked in Afghanistan, most likely as a subcontractor to an American PMC, as in Iraq. Risk & Co. makes a similar claim, probably in relation to a contract with a French firm or NGO. The 'Afghan paradox' is all the more noticeable given that even in the Iraq war, in which the French government has ostensibly refused to engage, some French companies have been able to operate, as we have already seen. The paradox can be largely explained by the specificities of the 'Afghan market' itself, controlled as it is by Afghan companies close to the Karzai regime (Forsberg and Kagan 2010). This situation, however, has been justified as a way of defusing tensions by 'Afghanizing' the mission's outlook and giving jobs to impoverished Afghans. This is what French troops usually describe as the 'French touch' – their purported ability to interact with 'indigenous' people and to adapt to foreign cultures. The resort to Afghan companies for interpreters or transport, however, has less to do with any such 'French touch' than with the Afghan private security market, the extremely low cost of local labour and the 'imperative' of keeping French casualty figures as low as possible.

Let us here rapidly give a general overview of what is known about the purportedly 'experimental' contracting taking place in the context of the French contribution to NATO/ISAF. We will start with so-called ancillary activities, before moving closer and closer to 'core military functions' (*le coeur du métier militaire*). The bulk of French experimentation with military contracting in Afghanistan concerns logistics, support and transport. Indeed, under the 'Additional Capacities for Support – France' contract,[29] private contractors manage Camp Warehouse's (Kabul) dining facility, telephone and internet networks, and part of the camp's military logistics. Contract supervision and coordination is under the responsibility of the Economat des Armées (EDA), the joint logistics and supply agency that is itself partly privatized at Camp Warehouse. At Forward Operating Base Tora/Surobi, the dining facility has been contracted out to Sodexo. In the case of the outsourcing of support to the French Air Force Detachment (DETAIR) in Kandahar, supervision, integration and coordination are under the responsibility of the NATO Maintenance and Supply Agency (NAMSA). This clearly shows the role played by NATO norms and standards in French 'experimentation'. Both in Kabul and in Kandahar, the personnel involved are generally local. Some aerial transportation supporting French ISAF troops has been contracted out to Volga–Dnepr Airlines and Antonov Airlines under the Strategic Airlift Interim Solution (SALIS).

Humanitarian demining in the Shamali plain, north of Kabul province, has also been outsourced. It is doubtful, though, whether this can be considered a specifically French contracting practice, although it has been described as being such (Ecole Militaire 2010: 30). In fact, the demining activities are being carried out under UN responsibility, though the region is under French operational control and the French authorities have approved of the demining activity.

Another important dimension of French military contracting in Afghanistan concerns technical support and maintenance of sophisticated military equipment such as drones or airplanes. In the case of US armed forces, these functions have been openly privatized through the resort to PMCs. In the French case, however, outsourcing is more discrete. Maintenance of Harfang drones, airplanes and other technology-intensive systems is carried out by employees of EADS (Harfang), Dassault (Rafale jets, etc.) or Thalès (management of strategic telecommunications). However, since these are often the very companies that designed and produced the equipment in the first place, it is doubtful whether they can be regarded as PMSCs. Moreover, to ensure that such arrangements do not look like rampant outsourcing, these contractors are granted a temporary operational reservist status – a status they usually do not enjoy on a permanent basis prior to deployment. This makeshift and hybrid status – partly inspired by the British *sponsored reserves* – is the result of an attempt on the part of France's defence ministry to reconcile outsourcing, on the one hand, and the operational need to integrate the relevant personnel within the military apparatus, on the other. More concretely, the operational reservist status enables the civilian employees concerned to benefit from military logistics, transport, support, insurance, social security and military hospitals (Chapleau 2011). Protection is also an important aspect in this context, since the operational reservist status does not permit the carrying of weapons.

In the context of providing support for imagery intelligence, we note that French firm Spot Images, a subsidiary of EADS Astrium, is the commercial operator for the SPOT Earth Observation satellites. As such, it provides French troops in Afghanistan with satellite images. And, in terms of support for human intelligence, according to some anecdotal sources, the British branch of the French Geos Group, known as Geos International Consulting Ltd., has about 100 'private soldiers' in Afghanistan, some of whom are allegedly active in intelligence activities (Alonso 2011). While this does not seem unlikely, it is very difficult to verify. On the other hand, it seems to be common practice that French private security contractors working in war-affected countries transmit intelligence to French services through informal channels. This has been the case, for example, for the French contractors working in Iraq after the 2003 invasion, even when they were hired by American or British companies working for the US or Iraqi authorities.[30] However, what is often referred to as the 'privatization of intelligence' is a very different matter, as that expression refers to contracts with firms for the performance of activities involving the purposeful extraction, treatment and analysis of secret information. To our knowledge, no reliable source indicates that the French military or intelligence services have engaged in the latter type of activities in Afghanistan.

According to one quasi-official source, security and protection services (*gardes d'emprise*) for a French base have been partly outsourced (Ecole Militaire 2010: 30). If true, this would be noteworthy, because such a situation would be the closest the French military has ever come to the contracting out of a military 'core function'. What exactly has been contracted out, and to whom, is difficult to ascertain. However, given common NATO practices in Afghanistan, it can be assumed that it would be the protection of external perimeters, and that responsibility for this has been contracted out to an Afghan company or a local group of people.

On the whole, externalization of tasks previously performed by French Armed Forces in Afghanistan is far more limited than is the case for US Armed Forces, concerns 'non-core tasks', and involves many Afghan contractors. French 'experimentation' in the context of ISAF can be seen as a reflection of the specificities of the overall PMSC business in Afghanistan. Companies are over-whelmingly Afghan and usually very close to ruling factions, and the money spent fuels state corruption and political infighting. It is no longer any secret that, rather than contributing to a de-escalation of the conflict, the massive resort to private security by NATO has allowed for diverse strongmen to maintain their militias. Moreover, a substantial share of the money spent on the protection of military bases or strategic transport has ended up in Taliban hands and thus fuels the ongoing 'insurgency' (Forsberg and Kagan 2010; US House of Representatives 2010). Finally, augmenting the number of NATO-friendly armed groups in Afghan society – whether by encouraging local PMSCs or by promoting 'tribal' militias – may prove detrimental to the ongoing negotiations with the Taliban. Indeed, it casts doubt on the coalition's ability to exert effective control over its own allies. Should there one day be an agreement between the international forces and the current Afghan government, on the one hand, and the Taliban, on the other, this will be all the more difficult to enforce (Dorronsoro 2010: 25).

French institutions and debates: the coming of age of defence contracting?

The institutional framework, procedures and norms under which current defence outsourcing is taking place are extremely heterogeneous. Moreover, to give a more or less complete picture, there are many aspects that need to be accounted for.

First, existing legislation is relatively neutral. The 2003 French law on 'the suppression of mercenary activity' has the same pitfalls as the Additional Protocols to the Geneva Conventions or the 1989 UN Mercenary Convention (Kinsey 2008). The law was passed in part to appease international tensions following an attempt by mercenaries to instigate a coup d'état in the Comoros in 2001 (Lechervy 2003). It is difficult to enforce, very permissive and excludes in advance any individual working for the French armed forces or any corporate entity from the definition of 'mercenarism' (Assemblée nationale 2012). The 1983 law 'regulating private security activities' introduces important limitations to private security, but is generally understood to apply exclusively to private security companies (PSCs) operating domestically. Its terms are on the whole not seen as applying either to PMSCs or to PSCs working abroad.[31] Despite this, there is a sense within the 'industry' that legislation is undermining military contracting. However, the reason there does not exist a 'big' PMSC market in France is that all markets need some form of institutionalization in order to exist as markets (Polanyi 1944). Often it is the state that provides this. In the UK and the US, for example, the private military sector has been fuelled and institutionalized by the existence, among other things, of a state demand for PMSCs. This pull effect of state demand is not present in France.

However, public policy over the last 20 years seems to be progressively creating an environment more favourable to the existence of such a market in France. First of all, the abolition of conscription in 1996, the reduction in personnel levels since the end of the Cold War, the increasing costs and sophistication of military specialization, and the number of soldiers involved in international operations all converge – as for most NATO countries – to make the PMSC option increasingly seductive for policymakers, military staff and former soldiers. Second, the rationale of the market is becoming increasingly pervasive in military contexts. The 'organic law pertaining to the financial law' of 2001 requires the armed forces to undergo similar types of annual evaluations and efficiency assessments as their civilian counterparts. The 'general revision of public policies' launched in 2007 goes in a similar direction. It promotes 'New Public Management' and structural reforms within public administrations. More specifically, it is bent on reducing the size and cost of the latter, including the armed forces. Third, the most recent White Paper on Defence and National Security,[32] from 2008, opens up for the outsourcing of 'non-core military functions' through so-called public–private partnerships (PPPs), directly inspired by the UK's 'private finance initiatives'. One of the first PPP in the field of military contracting was signed in 2008 with Héli-Dax, a joint venture between DCI and Inaer Hélicopter France, and concerned the loan of 36 EC-120 Colibri helicopters to the French army's light aviation training application school (EA-ALAT). The authors of the white paper, however, were opposed to any privatization of armed activities – activities involving the use of weapons – although even that disposition is increasingly being questioned (Assemblée nationale 2012). Actually, this progressive acceptance of military outsourcing already started around 2000 and is merely confirmed by the white paper. Finally, several administrations and organizations are trying to spur and orient the debate on military contracting. Let us look more closely at this last point.

Among political professionals, PMSCs and military contracting are increasingly seen as inevitable – and hence increasingly framed in terms of regulation rather than prohibition. Former President Sarkozy and his government were clearly favourable to a 'controlled opening' of the PMSC market: in the summer of 2010, the president's special military staff asked the SGDSN to study under what conditions such a sector could develop in France. A complementary mandate on maritime security contracting was also issued. The conclusions of both studies remain confidential. However, on 1 January 2012, a National Council on Private Security Activities (CNAPS)[33] was established by the government. This public and administrative establishment is tasked with controlling and regulating the domestic security market, and although it does not officially have anything to do with PMSCs, its creation signals a positive stance towards security contracting in general. On 14 February 2012, a bipartisan report on 'Private Military Companies' presented by MPs Christian Ménard (UMP) and Jean-Claude Viollet (PS: Socialist Party) was submitted to the lower house's defence commission. The report unequivocally calls for the state to support the sector, claiming that this is an urgent issue of strategic interest (Assemblée nationale 2012).

Within the defence community, there is a wide array of conflicting standpoints. The defence ministry's General Secretariat for Administration (SGA),[34] in charge of the reform both of the ministry's administration and of a large share of its relations with service providers, has not shown any significant interest. The Delegation for Strategic Affairs (DAS)[35] seems to be more positively inclined – if not to PMSCs then at least to the 'opening' of the debate on private contracting. In 2008, it initiated a thorough reassessment of the issue of military outsourcing of logistical and combat-support missions. The intelligence service in charge of military infrastructure protection, the DPSD,[36] has initiated similar studies (Hubac and Vieillard 2009). The Joint Staff (EMA) are also reputed to favour a more open debate on defence outsourcing. The difference between the SGA, on the one hand, and the DAS and the EMA, on the other, can largely be explained in terms of the different temporalities of these services' activities. The SGA is in charge of everyday practices, while the two others are involved in long-term planning (Hubac and Viellard 2009). The IHEDN,[37] an institute responsible for spurring interest in defence matters throughout French society, also appears to be positively inclined towards the ongoing debate: part of its sixty-second session (2009–10) was dedicated to the issue. Straddling the boundary between military and civilian sectors, the stance adopted by the IHEDN can be explained in terms of its interest in civil–military networks and the integration of former soldiers in the civilian sector. Lastly, the regular officer corps is still very much opposed to PMCs. The idea that the state and its armed forces 'made France' is very explicitly present in the dominant discourse. However, more and more young officers are beginning to see the state's resort to PMSCs as inevitable and think it may make it possible to refocus the military profession on its 'core functions'. Lately, the French navy's military staff, previously staunchly opposed to private security on the high seas, adopted a 'pragmatic' approach towards the role of PMSCs in providing maritime security to commercial vessels (Kouar 2010; Guibert 2012).

What is important to note here is that 'opening the debate' on military security contracting and being favourable to PMSCs tend to become *de facto* synonymous. Indeed, the debate on PMSCs plays an active role in creating a demand for their services. The very knowledge of the possibilities that an 'open and free' PMSC market would create plays into the hands of such a market by shedding new light on tragic incidents that would previously have been viewed with fatalism and resignation. For example, the shock following the 2002 suicide bombing in Karachi, Pakistan, in which 11 employees of the Direction des Constructions Navales (DCNS) died, led to a popularization of the argument that if French security forces cannot protect French employees, than private contractors must do so. This reasoning highlighted the fact that awareness of the possibility of privatizing security was already in everybody's minds at the time of the event. The controversy surrounding the privatization of security was relaunched by acts of piracy off the coast of Somalia that saw the development of French PMSCs specializing in the 'fight against piracy' (Kouar 2010): Kargus Sea Interconnection (KSI), Gallice Security and Securymind signed a contract with Crisis Consulting and Ineo Defense (a branch of GDF Suez) to cooperate on the protection of merchant and military vessels from piracy.[38]

On 16 September 2010, five employees of the French nuclear energy group Areva were kidnapped in Arlit, Niger, by an armed group. At that time, Areva's personnel were under the protection of the French PMSC Epée, a company that was created by Colonel Jacques Hogard, a former Foreign Legion paratrooper, and counted among its employees the former French defence attaché in Niamey, Colonel Gilles Denamur. Epée was immediately accused of amateurism, particularly since its personnel were unarmed at the time of the attack – which would not have been the case, it was argued, with a real professional PMC. The very knowledge of the various possibilities offered by the private option thus seems to create a demand for such companies. The above two examples show that, as some scholars have highlighted, PMCs do exert epistemic and structural power (Leander 2005; Krahman 2008): mere cognition of the possibilities offered by PMCs creates a demand; the very existence of privatized security practices construes an event such as the Karachi bombing as a 'risk to be countered' rather than a 'foreordained tragedy'. Consequently, the very act of 'opening the debate' is often in itself a way of advancing the point of view of which one is in favour in the debate.

The question that needs to be asked is how far the French administration is prepared to go in contracting out military functions, since once the decision to privatize has been taken, it will undoubtedly prove very difficult to undo. Officially, when we look only at the existing legislation and commonly held views and norms, French defence contracting concerns only 'non-core tasks'. For the time being, it officially excludes direct participation in combat, the guarding of prisoners of war, intelligence gathering, military planning, mobile protection for state officials, training of French troops in 'sensitive' fields and civil–military cooperation (CIMIC) (Ecole Militaire 2010: 30). Yet, some of these restrictions are increasingly being questioned by French politicians and security professionals alike.

Conclusion: have the two ends met?

'To make both ends meet' – both in the sense of matching costs and revenues, on the one hand, and in the sense of bringing together the world of defence outsourcing and that of PMSCs, on the other – sums up the increasingly pervasive narrative in France today. Indeed, although the subject is rife with controversies, arguments related to budgetary necessities and the supposed (but unproven) cost-effectiveness of 'military outsourcing' are gaining ground in political discourse. Promoters and detractors seem nevertheless to agree that, for the time being, the microcosms of PMSCs, on the one hand, and of 'experimental military contracting' on the part of the military authorities, on the other, are still very distinct from each other: contracting does not concern 'military and security' issues, and French PMSCs do not work for the defence establishment. Accordingly, the 'statist model' seems to have remained unscathed in the historical cradle of the Weberian state. But, given what we have seen, is this actually the case?

To answer that question, it may be useful to disentangle the different conceptual dimensions of the state–market continuum in matters of coercion (Thompson 1994). There are at least three dimensions here: the question of ownership of the means of military might (private or public ownership of weapons, training assets, etc.); the question of who has the authority to decide over the use of armed force (state or non-state); and the mode of allocation of the means of coercion (market allocation or allocation by the appropriate authorities). These three dimensions do not necessarily overlap: there can be a market allocation of weapons owned by the state (e.g., to a certain extent, the 'lend–lease' programme during the Second World War), or weapons can be privately owned, while the authority to decide over their use is vested in state representatives (which is often the case with state-controlled militias). The monopolistic state ideal-type of Weber (1946) would then simultaneously involve all three criteria: public ownership, the state's monopoly in decision making, and an authoritative allocation of the means of coercion. Does this ideal-type correspond to the reality in France today?

Concerning the first criterion, in general French PMSCs operating abroad cannot 'legitimately' own weapons. However, as we have seen, there are ways of circumventing this general principle and there exist various legal loopholes and exceptions. Moreover, the general principle is unlikely to remain unchanged in the coming years (Guibert 2012). Concerning the second criterion, decision-making authority, as far as we know this is in principle monopolized by public administrations. If the latter contract or work with armed security contractors at home or abroad, as the French embassy and business centre in Baghdad do when accrediting French PMSCs, it is under very strict supervision on the part of state security services. At the very least, the use of force is limited to legitimate defence. There may be some exceptions of which we are unaware, but these would not necessarily make a great difference since an ideal-type never exists in its 'pure' form in social reality.

The third criterion sheds light on French security practices in an unexpected way. As we saw earlier, Défense Conseil International (DCI) uses public resources in terms of both personnel (seconded military personnel), logistics (military infrastructure) and symbolic resources (the label '*armées*') to train foreign military forces. Yet, resource allocation is here very much done through the market, although there is of course some level of public control. The question of whether DCI is a PMSC is immaterial. Its activities remain a case of partial marketization as defined by Janice E. Thompson (1994). We have also seen that similar types of marketized training assets also are used by the French military to an increasing degree.

Although the PMSC microcosm and public outsourcing remain largely separate in the French case, market allocation of military training and the appearance of armed contractors in relative proximity to the French embassies of various countries seem to indicate that the line between both ends is increasingly becoming a grey zone. More fundamentally, as we have also seen, the tables have lately seemed to be turning in favour of an alignment with the 'siren song' of military outsourcing – in spite of all the known pitfalls of such an approach (Olsson 2003, 2007).

Notes

1 Which is not the case in the US, for example.
2 Private military companies (PMCs) are supposed to be more militarized (in terms of the services they offer or the clients with whom they contract) than PMSCs or private security companies (PSCs).

3 Décret du 6 mai 1995 fixant le régime des matériels de guerre, armes et munitions [Degree of 6 May 1995 defining the legal regime of war materiel, weapons and munitions].
4 Communications, command, control, intelligence.
5 Sociétés privees d'interet militaire.
6 Société de sécurité extérieure.
7 Secretariat Général de la Défense et de la Sécurité Nationale (formerly SGDN).
8 Société de Surete et de Securite de Defense.
9 Telephone interview with Georges-Henri Bricet des Vallons, defence analyst, Paris, June 2011.
10 In 2002, a Geos employee working for Renault in Algeria was accused by the car manufacturer of spying on the firm.
11 *Intelligence Online (IOL)* no. 606, 26 November 2009, p. 7; see also Alonso (2011).
12 Groupe d'Intervention de la Gendarmerie Nationale.
13 Union pour un Mouvement Populaire/Union for a Popular Movement.
14 *IOL* no. 597, 2 July 2009, p. 5.
15 Union pour la Démocratie Française/Union for French Democracy (now defunct).
16 IOL no. 588, 19 February–4 March 2009, p. 7.
17 IOL no. 586, 22 January–4 February 2009, p. 6.
18 IOL no. 606, 26 November 2009, p. 7.
19 Since 2010 known as the International Stability Operations Association (ISOA).
20 Telephone interview with Georges-Henri Bricet des Vallons, defence analyst, Paris, June 2011.
21 For example, F. Gallois of Gallice Security and Ph. Legorjus of PHL Consultants are former gendarmes.
22 For instance, P. Marzali of Secopex is a former marine infantryman.
23 For example, the companies Epée and Vitruve Defence & Security draw heavily on recruits from the foreign legion.
24 For instance, L. Allouin of Securymind is originally from the marine commandos.
25 For example, G. Sacaze and G. Maréchal of Gallice Security.
26 Respectively, Brigade de Recherche et d'Intervention and Recherche–Assistance–Intervention–Dissuasion. L. Combalbert, who was formerly at Geos Group, has also worked for the RAID.
27 Among many things, CEO of Marks & Spencer France.
28 He was responsible for economic intelligence at the SGDN (Secretariat Général de la Defense Nationale), the precursor of the SGDSN.
29 Capacités additionnelles pour le soutien – France (CAPES–France).
30 Telephone interview with Georges-Henri Bricet des Vallons, defence analyst, Paris, June 2011.
31 Loi no. 83–629 du 12 juillet 1983 réglementant les activités privées de sécurité [Law no. 83–629 from 12 July 1983 regulating private security activities].
32 Livre blanc sur la défense et la sécurité nationale.
33 Conseil National des Activités Privées de Sécurité.
34 Secrétariat Général pour l'Administration.
35 Délégation des Affaires Stratégiques.
36 Direction de la Protection et de la Sécurité de la Défense.
37 Institut des Hautes Etudes de Défense Nationale.
38 IOL no. 596, 18 June–1 July 2009, p. 7.

References

Alonso, Pierre. 2011. 'Les mercenaires files à l'anglaise', *OWNI*, 13 June, http://owni.fr/2011/06/13/les-mercenaires-filent-a-langlaise/ (accessed 15 July 2011).

Assemblée nationale. 2012. 'Rapport d'information n°4350 déposé par la commission de la défense nationale et des forces armées sur les sociétés militaires privées' [Information Report no. 4350 handed in by the defence commission on private military companies], 14 February.

Avant, Deborah D. 2005. *The Market for force: the consequences of privatising security*, Cambridge: Cambridge University Press.

Balzacq, Thierry, Tugba Basaran, Didier Bigo, Emmanuel-Pierre Guittet and Christian Olsson. 2010. 'Security Practices' in Robert A. Denemark (ed.) International Studies Encyclopedia Online. Oxford: Blackwell Publishing. Blackwell Reference Online, www. blackwellreference.com/public/book.html?id=g9781444336597_9781444336597 (accessed 18 March 2010).

Bigo, Didier. 2008. 'Globalized (In)security: the Field and the Banopticon' in Didier Bigo and Anastassia Tsoukala (eds). *Terror, Insecurity and Liberty. Illiberal practices of liberal regimes after 9/11*. New York: Routledge.

Bourdieu, Pierre. 1990. *In Other Words : Essays towards a Reflexive Sociology*, Stanford, CA: Stanford University Press.

Chapleau, Philippe. 2011. *Les nouveaux entrepreneurs de la guerre. Des mercenaires aux sociétés militaires privées* [The new Entrepreneurs of War. From Mercenaries to Private Military Companies], Paris: Vuibert.

——2005. *Sociétés militaires privées, enquête sur les soldats sans armées* [PMCs, an inquiry on soldiers without armies], Paris: Editions du Rocher.

De Tocqueville, Alexis. 1955. *The Old Regime and the Revolution*. New York: Anchor Books.

Dorronsoro, Gilles. 2010. *Afghanistan: searching for political agreement*, Washington, DC: Carnegie Endowment for International Peace.

Ecole Militaire. 2010. *Cahiers de l'enseignement militaire supérieur*. April.

Elias, Norbert. 2000. *The Civilizing process: Sociogenetic and Psychogenetic Investigations*, Oxford: Blackwell.

Forsberg, Carl and Kimberley Kagan. 2010. 'Consolidating Private Security Companies in Afghanistan', 28 May, Washington, DC: Institute for the Study of War, www.under standingwar.org/sites/default/files/BackgrounderPSC_0.pdf (accessed 16 March 2012).

Granovetter, Marc S. 1973. 'The strength of weak ties', *American Journal of Sociology*, 78 (6): 1360–1380.

Guibert, Nathalie. 2012. 'Vers un rôle accru du privé dans la défense française' [towards a more important role of the private sector in French defence], *Le Monde*, 15 February.

Hibou, Béatrice. 1999. *La privatisation des Etats*, Paris: Karthala.

Hubac, Olivier and Luc Viellard. 2009. 'Politique d'externalisation: l'enjeu des société d'appui stratégique' [The policy of outsourcing: what is at stake with the strategic support firms], *Sécurité Globale*, 8 : 17–33.

Irondelle, Bastien and Christian Olsson. 2011. 'La privatisation de la guerre: le cas anglo-américain' [The Privatization of War : the Anglo-American Example], in Christian Malis, Didier Danet and Hew Strachan (eds), La Guerre irrégulière [Irregular War], Paris : Economica.

Kinsey, Christopher. 2008. 'International Law and the Control of Mercenaries and Private Military Companies', Cultures & Conflits, http://conflits.revues.org/index11502.html (accessed 10 of March 2012).

Kouar, Mehdi. 2010. 'La sûreté est-elle privatisable?', *Outre-Terre*, 2: 49–74.

Krahman, Elke. 2008. 'The Commodification of Security in the Risk Society', University of Bristol CGIA Working Paper no. 06–08, www.bristol.ac.uk/spais/research/work ingpapers/wpspaisfiles/krahmann0608.pdf (accessed 13 August 2012).

Leander, Anna. 2005. 'The Power to Construct International Security: On the significance of Private Military Companies', *Millenium*, 33 (3): 803–826.

——2006. 'Private agency and the definition of Public Security Concerns: The Role of Private Military Companies' in Jef Huysmans, Andrew Dobson and Raia Prokhovnik (eds) *The Politics of Protection*, London: Routledge.

Lechervy, Christian. 2003. 'Définir le mercenaire puis lutter contre le mercenariat "entrepreneurial": un projet de gouvernement' [to define the mercenary and to fight against entrepreneurial mercenarism: a government programme], *Cultures & Conflits*, 52: 67–90.

Musah, Abdel-Fatau and Kayode Fayemi. (ed.) 2000. *Mercenaries : An African Security Dilemma*. London: Pluto Press.

Olsson, Christian. 2003. 'Vrai procès et faux débats: perspectives critiques sur les entreprises de coercition para-privées' [True trials and false debates: critical perspectives on the para-private companies of coercion], *Cultures et Conflits*, 52: 11–48.

—— 2007. 'The Politics of the Apolitical, PMCs, humanitarians and the quest for (anti-) politics in post-intervention environments', *Journal of International Relations and Development*, 10(4): 332–61.

—— 2009. 'Les relations houleuses entre Sociétés Militaires Privées (SMP) et tenants de la contre – insurrection' [The tumultuous relations between Private Military Companies (PMCs) and counterinsurgency theoreticians], *Sécurité Globale*, 8: 65–84.

Percy, Sarah. 2007. *Mercenaries: the History of a Norm in International Relations*, Oxford: Oxford University Press.

Polanyi, Karl. 1944. *The Great Transformation*, Boston: Beacon Hill.

Renou, Xavier. 2006. *La privatisation de la violence* [The privatization of violence], Paris: Agone.

Saint-Quentin, Grégoire. 1998. 'Mercenariat et mutations stratégiques' [Mercenarism and strategic mutations], *Défense Nationale*, 597: 34–44.

Thompson, Janice E. 1994. '*Mercenaries, Pirates and Sovereigns: State-building and Extraterritorial Violence in Early Modern Europe*', Princeton, NJ: Princeton University Press.

Tilly, Charles. 1975. 'Reflections on the History of European State-Making', in Charles Tilly (ed.) *The Formation of National States in Western Europe*. Princeton, NJ: Princeton University Press.

——1992. 'Coercion, Capital *and European States: AD 990 – 1992*', Cambridge, MA: Blackwell.

US House of Representatives. 2010. *Warlord inc., Extortion and Corruption along the Supply Chain in Afghanistan*, Report of the Majority Staff, Committee on oversight and government reform, subcommittee on national security and foreign affairs, June.

Wasinski, Christophe. 2008. 'Recruteurs et recrutés au sein des sociétés militaires et de sécurité privées' in Frederik Naert (ed.) *Private Security Companies in Situations of Disturbances or Armed Conflicts*. Brussels: Defense Printing House.

Weber, Max. 1946. 'Politics as a Vocation' in H. H. Garth and C. Wright Mills (eds) *Essays in Sociology*. New York: Macmillian.

Wright Mills, Charles. 1956. *The Power Elite*, Oxford: Oxford Press.

9 Germany

Civilian power revisited

Elke Krahmann

Introduction

Germany's role in international peace and reconciliation operations has changed radically over the past decades. During the Cold War, German contributions to international conflict resolution were confined to civilian missions, based on the ideal of a 'civilian power' that had been developed after 1945 in an explicit break with the expansionist and militarized regime of the Nazis (Maull 1990). Following the end of the Cold War, German reunification and sovereignty gave rise to a new self-perception as a 'normal' major power with related international responsibilities and ambitions (Hellmann 1996). Germany's closest allies in NATO and the European Union have fostered this transition, demanding that Germany carry its full weight in international peace and reconciliation missions, including military interventions. Since Germany's armed forces had been designed purely for territorial defence, these demands have necessitated major and costly reforms. The German government has identified the privatization and outsourcing of military services as one way of funding the restructuring of its military into an expeditionary force. In the meantime, private military and security companies (PMSCs) have helped Germany address urgent personnel and capability gaps that would otherwise have limited its ability to participate in multilateral operations. This chapter examines the development of Germany's policies and practices in relation to the use of PMSCs in international operations, focusing on the recent intervention in Afghanistan. It proceeds by discussing the impacts on German peace and reconciliation strategies, ranging from a growing focus on military operations to the challenges for parliamentary control. The chapter concludes that the German government urgently needs to engage in a public debate about these implications and how they may be addressed, since military and security contracting is expected to further expand following the 2010 decision to suspend conscription and transform the German armed forces into a professional military (Ministry of Defence 2011: 16).

German national context

In order to understand the evolution of German military and security contracting in international operations, it is useful to examine the national context that has shaped Germany's changing approach. Three interrelated developments appear particularly relevant. The first relates to the German Constitution, the Basic Law, and how it has been (re)interpreted in the light of recent history, particularly in Germany's shift from a 'civilian' to a 'normal' power in international relations. The second applies to military and security contracting in the armed forces, including the progressive delimitation of military core functions. The third concerns the divergent public and governmental views on the use of PMSCs in international interventions.

The Basic Law and Germany's approach to conflict resolution

Germany's security and defence policy has strong roots in the reconstitution of the country after the end of the Second World War. The traumatic experience of a lost war of aggression and the exposure of the atrocities committed by the Nazi regime created desire for a radical historical break among the German population. In West Germany, this desire met with the aims of the three occupying powers – the US, the UK and France – to turn Germany into a stable democracy and prevent its resurgence as a global military power. The (West) German Basic Law, which came into force in 1949 and became the constitution of the reunited Germany in 1990, was a central measure designed to achieve these objectives.[1] It still forms the basis of Germany's security and defence policy, but the reinterpretation of key articles has been central to Germany's changing self-perception and approach to international conflict resolution.

A key characteristic of the Basic Law is its acknowledgement of 'inviolable and inalienable human rights as the basis of every community, of peace and of justice in the world' in Article 1. This Article was a result of Germany's own experience with ethnic cleansing under the Nazi regime and has often been perceived to imply a moral commitment towards the international defence of human rights.

A second feature is the anti-militarism of the Basic Law, specifically its objective to prevent Germany from becoming engaged in offensive or expeditionary wars ever again. It includes the explicit prohibition of wars of aggression in Article 26, which states that 'acts tending to and undertaken with intent to disturb the peaceful relations between nations, especially to prepare for a war of aggression, shall be unconstitutional'. Article 87(a) accordingly limits the purposes of the armed forces, by declaring that 'apart from defence, the Armed Forces may be employed only to the extent expressly permitted by this Basic Law'. What is 'expressly permitted' by the Basic Law, however, has been subject to considerable debate and redefinition. Much discussion has revolved around the question of what is entailed in Article 24 of the Constitution, which permits Germany to 'enter into a system of mutual collective security'. Originally, Article 24 was intended to prevent Germany's remilitarization and re-establishment as independent military power by containing its security and defence policy within systems of collective security, such as those of NATO and the Western European Union. As Lord Ismay has been credited with saying, the aim of NATO was to 'keep the Americans in, the Russians out, and the Germans down'. However, as will be discussed below, in 1994 Article 24 became the foundation for a reinterpretation of the Basic Law's restrictions on the international use of armed force.

The third feature of the Constitution is its preference for conscripted citizen-soldiers as a way of civilizing and safeguarding the democratic control of the German armed forces. Article 12(a) of the Basic Law thus establishes the government's right to conscript males above 18 years of age to serve in the armed forces or in civilian security functions. In this way, the creators of the Basic Law sought to ensure democratic control over the military and prevent its reversal into a 'state within the state', as happened during the Weimar Republic, or its abuse by nationalist and fascist forces like the Nazis. They also hoped that conscription would thwart the use of the German armed forces in expansionary wars. Compulsory military service was, as Germany's first federal president Theodor Heuss argued, the 'legitimate child of democracy' (cited in Dinter 2004: 112).[2]

Finally, the Constitution has been read as prohibiting unlimited privatization of the military (Krahmann 2010: 159; Richter 2007: 170). This interpretation has built on two articles. Article 87(a) of the Basic Law prescribes the federal government's monopoly on the right to establish armed forces, stating that 'the Federation shall establish Armed Forces' (see Portugall 2007: 147–8). Article 87(b) entails a functional and institutional separation between the military organization of the armed forces and a civilian, federally owned armed forces administration, which has the 'jurisdiction for personnel matters and direct responsibility for satisfaction of the procurement needs of the Armed Forces' (see Richter 2007: 170).

On the basis of these particular interpretations of the Basic Law, Germany developed a unique self-perception as a 'civilian power' that influenced its international security strategies and policies until the end of the Cold War (Maull 1990, 2000; Hyde-Price 2001). At the centre of Germany's civilian-power approach were two principles: multilateralism and anti-militarism (Maull 1990: 92; Duffield 1999: 780–3). Multilateralism included a strong commitment to international institution building, supranational integration and the constraint of the use of force through international norms (Maull 2000: 56; Hyde-Price 2001: 19). Anti-militarism took the shape of an 'aversion, or at least profound scepticism, vis-a-vis any use of military force' and a preference for civilian conflict resolution (Maull 2000: 56). In practice, both principles determined that Germany defined and pursued its security interests and policies through international organizations such as the UN, NATO and the EU (Hellmann 1996: 3). Placed within the context of the confrontation between NATO and the Warsaw Pact, the German military, the 'Bundeswehr', was created exclusively for the continental defence of Western Europe. Moreover, Germany's defence posture and policies were an integral part of NATO strategy, including the stationing of US nuclear weapons on German territory. Rather than being forcibly contained, Germany embraced multilateralism with fervour, believing that increased integration was the key to conflict prevention. Beyond Europe, the German government followed a policy of civilian conflict management through multilateral operations.

After the end of the Cold War, the conditions and context of German conflict resolution policy changed radically. Reunification and full sovereignty created the largest economic and military power in Western Europe. In addition, the changing security environment put into question the German military's focus on national defence. While some foreign observers feared a military resurgence of Germany, the government remained initially true to the principles of multilateralism and anti-militarism. In fact, Germany's continued refusal to engage in international military operations exasperated its allies. The government's decision to support the first Gulf War in 1990–91 only financially led to accusations of 'chequebook diplomacy' and severely damaged Germany's international reputation (Hyde-Price 2001: 20; Maull 2000: 57). In the following years, Germany was torn between multilateralism and anti-militarism, and between international and domestic opinion. Its allies demanded a greater German contribution to international peacekeeping and peacemaking, including the deployment of soldiers out of area. Conversely, the German population remained strictly opposed to military operations abroad, citing the Basic Law and the lessons learnt from a history of military expansion.

When civil war erupted in Yugoslavia, two factors combined to challenge Germany's civilian-power approach to international conflict resolution. First, reports of ethnic cleansing in the former Yugoslav republics reminded many politicians and large sections of the population of the Holocaust and Germany's special responsibility to prevent similar atrocities elsewhere. Historical sensibility combined with Germany's perceived constitutional and moral obligation to uphold international human rights. Second, the international humanitarian interventions in the region were legitimized by UN Security Council resolutions and conducted under the auspices of collective security systems of which Germany was a member. Germany's dedication to multilateral conflict management and its integration into NATO's defence strategy thus seemed to demand its participation. A case in point was the German soldiers who were an integral part of NATO's Airborne Warning and Control System (AWACS) planes, which had been requested to monitor and enforce the no-fly zone over Bosnia and Herzegovina (Maull 2000: 58). Asked to clarify whether the decision of the government to permit the participation of German soldiers in international military operations was constitutional, the Federal Constitutional Court ruled in 1994 that such missions were legal as long as they were conducted under the auspices of a collective security organization such as NATO or the UN.

This reinterpretation of the Basic Law by the Federal Constitutional Court marked a major turning point in Germany's security and conflict resolution policy, as it permitted the government to consider a new – military – role in international operations. Since then, Germany has progressively expanded its military contribution to international missions, including the EU's maritime operation ATALANTA, the United Nations Interim Force in Lebanon (UNIFIL), the European Union Force (EUFOR) in Bosnia and Herzegovina, NATO's Kosovo Force (KFOR) and the International Security Assistance Force (ISAF) in Afghanistan. Although the German government has maintained its commitment to multilateralism, anti-militarism has increasingly been viewed as outdated and inappropriate for the contemporary security environment. The keywords of Germany's new approach to conflict resolution have been 'responsibility' and 'normalization' (Hellmann 1996: 6, 10). The German government has argued specifically that reunification and sovereignty have placed on it an increased 'international responsibility for peace and freedom' (Ministry of Defence 2011: 3). It has justified the use of armed force as an element of German conflict resolution strategy by pointing to the policies of other 'normal' powers, such as the US, the UK and France. In addition, the government has defended the normalization of Germany's foreign and security policy in terms of fairer burden sharing within NATO and its ambitions to gain a permanent seat within the UN Security Council, arguing that Germany's international influence depends on making 'an adequate political and military contribution in accordance with its size' (Ministry of Defence 2011: 9).

On the basis of these new imperatives, the German government has gradually stepped up its emphasis on multilateral military operations within a comprehensive approach that has included 'political and diplomatic initiatives as well as economic, development policy, police, humanitarian, social and military measures' (Ministry of Defence 2011: 5). 'Military instruments' have become an explicit part of Germany's crisis-prevention strategy (Federal Government 2004: 1). A key focus of the government has been on strengthening international systems of conflict resolution by providing appropriate resources, including military capabilities, to international organizations such as the UN, NATO and the EU (Ministry of Defence 2011; Federal Government 2004).

The growing importance of military operations has been reflected more in Germany's policies and budget allocations than in government publications. In Afghanistan, Germany has deployed up to 5,350 soldiers as part of ISAF since 2002 (Armed Forces 2011). Their tasks have included the running of two Provincial Reconstruction Teams in Kunduz and Faisabad, training and support for the Afghan National Army, and, since 2008, functions within ISAF's Quick Reaction Force (Armed Forces 2011). By comparison, Germany only sent 260 police and civilian experts for the development of the Afghan National Police for which it had taken lead responsibility (Federal Government 2011: 7, 10). The unwillingness or inability of Germany to speed up its police training mission even led to the US taking over large parts, most of them implemented through PMSCs such as DynCorp and MPRI (Inspectors General *et al.* 2006). In 2011, Germany spent €430 million for its civilian missions, compared to €980 million for its military operation in Afghanistan (Federal Government 2011: 14; Parliament 2011a: 4). In the following, this chapter will therefore focus on the growing role of PMSCs in military operations and its consequences for Germany's peace and reconciliation strategy.

Armed forces reform and military contracting

The preceding changes in the German approach to international conflict resolution have necessitated significant internal reforms. Foremost, they have required a major restructuring of the armed forces. Neither the German military's capabilities nor its system of universal conscription has been considered appropriate for the growing number of military operations abroad. The prolonged cost of reunification has also meant that financial resources for armed-forces reform have been scarce. Following the examples of the US and the UK, the German government identified defence privatization and military contracting as a possible means for turning the German military into an expeditionary force. The Kohl government (1982–98) took the first step with the introduction of market testing as a mechanism for establishing whether public or private provision of particular military services was more cost-efficient (Portugall 2007: 148–9). However, as late as 1998, the German Ministry of Defence excluded a wide range of military 'core functions' from market testing, including defence-political tasks, military leadership, military intelligence, combat and local combat support, local support in crisis and conflict environments, military services related to operational and combat capabilities, military leadership and combat education, logistics and medical services in international operations, military minimum capabilities, planning, personnel management, organization and administration (Keller 2007: 56).

The Gerhard Schröder government (1998–2005) took a more favourable view of defence privatization and military contracting as a tool for armed-forces reform. In the 'Framework Agreement on Innovation, Investment and Efficiency in the Bundeswehr', signed with representatives of German industry in 1999, the government committed itself to expanding the role of private firms in military service provision through 14 pilot projects (Ministry of Defence 2001). To implement these projects, the government used two approaches: the development of hybrid public–private companies and the outsourcing of military services to the private sector. The first approach involved the creation of hybrid public–private joint ventures – that is, legally private companies that are owned in part by the state – including Bw FuhrparkServices for the management of the 'white fleet' of civilian vehicles used by the armed forces, LHBw Bekleidungsgesellschaft for the comprehensive supply of clothing for the armed forces and Heeresinstandsetzungslogistic for the supply of army maintenance material, followed in 2006 by BWI Informationstechnik for major information-technology projects within the military (see Table 9.1). The second approach has been the contracting of PMSCs for military services in select areas and locations, including central depot management, the running of the army's Combat Training Centre in Altmark, logistic supply, simulator training and air-force maintenance and repair (Ministry of Defence 2001). Since the government distrusted the ability and willingness of civil servants in the Ministry of Defence to manage the collaboration with industry, it created another legally private company, this time fully government owned, the Company for Development, Supply and Management (Gesellschaft für Entwicklung, Beschaffung und Betrieb, GEBB) exclusively for the purpose of managing large-scale privatization and outsourcing projects (R. H. 2003: 2; Bittner and Niejahr 2004; Heinen 2003). GEBB was given responsibility for the overall direction of the 14 pilot projects and the identification of future possibilities for major commercial contracts with the armed forces, while the Federal

Table 9.1 Hybrid public–private joint ventures in Germany

Name of public–private company (service area)	Contract duration	Estimated cost (billion)*	Ownership
Bw Fuhrpark Service (white fleet)	2002–09 2009–	€2.8	75.1% state-owned, 24.9% owned by the state-owned Deutsche Bahn
LHBw Bekleidungsgesellschaft (clothing supplies)	2002–14	€1.7	25.1% state-owned, 74.9% owned by a consortium of Lion Apparel and Hellmann Worldwide Logistics
Heeresinstandsetzungslogistik GmbH (army maintenance)	2005–13	€1.77	49% state-owned, 51% owned by a consortium of Krauss-Maffei Wegmann, Rheinmetall Landsysteme and Industriewerke Saar
BWI Informationstechnik GmbH (information technology)	2006–16	€7.1	49.9% state-owned, 50.1% owned by a consortium of Siemens Business Services and IBM Deutschland

* Estimates based on data in Ministry of Defence (2006: 16).

Office for Defence Technology and Procurement (Bundesamt für Wehrtechnik und Beschaffung) remained in charge of contracting for the remaining material and service requirements of the Bundeswehr (Ministry of Defence 2000). Although the Schröder government took a more narrow view of the military's 'core functions', the formation of hybrid public–private companies was considered to safeguard government and armed-forces control over the supply of major service areas.

Under Chancellor Angela Merkel (2005–), the German government has further expanded military contracting, including both hybrid companies and direct outsourcing. It even passed specific legislation to ease the formation of hybrid public–private companies (*Bundesgesetzblatt* 2005: 2676). At the same time, the first defence minister of the Merkel administration, Franz Josef Jung, was critical of GEBB's independence and decided to transfer the co-ownership and co-management of hybrid public–private companies to the Ministry of Defence (Kersting 2006). The decision suggested a weakening of GEBB's pro-business approach, and in the following years internal optimization and efficiency measures within the armed forces were given greater consideration over contracting with the private sector. Nevertheless, the German government has expanded its cooperation with commercial suppliers where suitable (GEBB 2008). New projects have included a public–private partnership for the refurbishment of the Fürst Wrede Garrison in Munich, the outsourcing of logistics and supply-chain management, and contracting for information-technology training (GEBB 2011a).

The armed forces have also significantly expanded their use of PMSCs in international operations. In Kosovo, the German military hired private firms for transport, to build field camps, to manage sanitation systems, and for maintenance and repair; in Bosnia and Herzegovina, it outsourced, for the first time, catering services in a theatre of operations; in the former Yugoslavian Republic of Macedonia, it contracted local businesses for vehicle support (Parliament 2007: 7; Petersohn 2006: 18–9; Reimann and Weiland 2006; GEBB 2007: 25; Armed Forces 2002). In Afghanistan, where Germany has been engaged in ISAF, the European Union Police (EUPOL) mission and the bilateral German–Afghan Police Project, contracting has so far reached its most extensive scope, including transport, logistics, catering, maintenance, repair, laundry, sewage, waste disposal, fuel supplies and protective services (Parliament 2010a, 2010b). While some of these contracts have served to counteract the personnel shortages and fill capability gaps and urgent operational requirements caused by Germany's growing contribution to multilateral peacekeeping and peacemaking missions, the preceding analysis shows that outsourcing in international operations is part of a long-term strategy to expand the commercial provision of services to the armed forces (Federal Accounting Office 2006: 178).

Competing discourses on military and security contracting

Despite the consistent progression towards increased armed forces–industry collaboration in contexts ranging from national defence to international operations, discussions on military contracting have been and continue to be marked by a significant degree of controversy in Germany. In fact, there appear to be two divergent and largely disconnected discourses, each with its own own language and ideals. On the one hand, there is the parliamentary and media discourse that has been shaped strongly by the view that the use of PMSCs in international operations may undermine their legal and democratic control as well as, ultimately, the state monopoly on violence. On the other hand, there is the internal discourse within the government, the Ministry of Defence, GEBB and the armed forces that has been characterized by the neoliberal language of cost-efficiency and modernization through increased military contracting.

In the light of the government's expansion of contracting for military services since the late 1990s and parliamentary policies and legislation that have enabled this development, the lack of knowledge about and opposition to the growing role of PMSCs in German international peace and reconciliation operations expressed in the parliamentary and media discourse is puzzling. Characteristic of the ignorance of parliamentarians and the public news media is the persistent belief that military and security contracting is not a common practice in Germany's international missions and that it can and should be contained. As late as 2011, Roderich Kiesewetter (2011: 9528) argued that 'if one examines the large extent to which US armed forces currently rely on PMSCs, it is obvious that Germany is still far away from such conditions … For us, the premise is: Act before it is too late!'

The fear that military and security contracting may subvert the state's monopoly on or control over the use of armed force, enshrined in the Basic Law, forms the basis for a broad consensus among parliamentarians from the main German parties, including the CDU/CSU, the SPD, the Green Party and the LINKE. A joint application by the CDU/CSU and SPD government factions in 2008 warned explicitly that 'the privatization of military functions may in the long term lead to a fundamental change in the relationship between the armed forces and the nation-state. The state monopoly on violence could be put into question, possibly renounced completely' (Parliament 2008a: 1). Another parliamentary concern has been that 'the international laws of war that have been developed with much effort over centuries are now at risk of being undermined by PMSCs' (Parliament 2008a: 2). As a consequence, no less than three proposals have been submitted by various parliamentary parties between 2008 and 2011 calling for the prohibition or improved regulation of the industry in Germany (Parliament 2008a, 2010f, 2011b).

Leading German newspapers and TV stations share these concerns and have published critical reports on the use of PMSCs in international interventions. An op-ed in the national weekly paper, *Die Zeit*, for instance, has argued that PMSCs

> are hired by Western governments that want to deploy more troops than are available through national armed forces; they are called when Western governments seek to remove the use of military force from parliamentary control; when they plan to intervene where international humanitarian law does not permit them to do so; when they want to support allied regimes or groups in their fights against internal enemies; or when they seek to protect economic interests through military means without officially deploying national armed forces.
>
> (Speckmann 2010)

The most-watched TV news programme, *Die Tagesschau* (2010), has strongly criticized the government for failing to regulate German PMSCs operating abroad. The media typically call private military contractors 'mercenaries' and have described their actions as 'between illegality and immunity' (Leyendecker 2010; Rüb 2007). As the *Süddeutsche Zeitung*, one of Germany's two national newspapers, has written, 'in the age of the outsourcing of war, also the responsibility for law and order has been delegated. Simultaneously, private intervention forces undermine the monopoly on violence of the states that hire them' (Leyendecker 2010).

In contrast to the German parliament and media, the government and its agencies have shown little concern that military contracting in international operations may be problematic. For one thing, the government has argued that the Basic Law does not allow, and the armed forces have not permitted, the transfer of 'military' functions to private companies, irrespective of whether they are executed within or outside German territory, thus giving no cause for apprehension about the use of PMSCs (Parliament 2005: 5). However, the range of services that the government considers 'military' functions has decreased considerably over the years. In 2005, the government asserted that maintenance and repair belonged to the 'essential military core capabilities of Bundeswehr logistics' that, particularly in international operations, are as a matter of principle excluded from commercial contracting (Parliament 2005: 19). Yet, in Afghanistan both services were regularly supplied by private companies (Parliament 2010b: 4–6; Fasse 2010). A discussion of how 'military' functions should be defined has been conducted outside the public view, if it has occurred at all (Krahmann 2010: 161–5). GEBB (2006: 2) has interpreted its responsibility to 'relieve the Bundeswehr of all possible functions that are not core military capabilities' very broadly. According to GEBB (2006: 2), the 'operational support of the Bundeswehr with so-called service functions should be transferred largely to GEBB and private partners'.

The official discourse of the Ministry of Defence, the armed forces and GEBB has focused on the notions of 'cost reduction', the 'mobilization of private sector capital', increased effectiveness and efficiency, and the 'modernization' of the military (GEBB 2004: Summary). Business strategies have been praised as superior models for the supply of services in the armed forces (GEBB 2004: 2, 2006: 3). Performance has been measured in terms of cost reductions, not as the effective provision of national and international security (GEBB 2006: 3). The expansion of military service contracting in international operations has been considered a success rather than a potential threat to the state monopoly on violence. GEBB (2004: 24) enthused: 'In outsourcing the entire responsibility for catering for troops in deployment, the German Bundeswehr is breaking new ground'. It also celebrated the expansion of the Bw FuhrparkService contract to partially militarized vehicles and support for the EUFOR mission in Bosnia and Herzegovina, although the privatization of the armed forces' white fleet in the form of a hybrid public–private company was originally legitimized through the argument that the privatization entailed only services provided on German territory and not in international interventions (GEBB 2006: 6–7).

The existence and persistence of these two distinct national discourses has been possible because the German government has given ambiguous information about its contracting in international operations. Foremost, the government has claimed that the German armed forces have not hired 'private security companies' (PSCs) (*private Sicherheitsunternehmen*) in Afghanistan, although the military has employed corporate and individual contractors for a wide range of military and security services in the country (Parliament 2010d: 1). The government has been able to make this statement without being outright dishonest because it has, by its own admission, no generally accepted definition of private security companies or private military companies (Parliament 2010d: 2). On the same basis of lack of an agreed definition, the government has argued that it does not outsource any 'military' functions to private firms (Parliament 2005: 5). Fundamental to this claim seems the implicit but widespread notion there is a difference between the offensive use of armed force and functions where violence plays no or only a defensive role (cf. Kiesewetter 2011). The German government has thus been able to admit that private firms supply static security services for its Police Training Centres in Mazar-e-Sharif and Faisabad, as well as for the Germany embassy in Kabul, without having to agree that it has outsourced 'military' or 'security' tasks (Parliament 2010d: 2). Finally, the government appears to distinguish between the hire of contractors and that of individual guards, excluding the 264 Afghan security guards employed directly by the German armed forces from parliamentary information about the 'German use of private security contractors in Afghanistan' (Parliament 2010a: 7, 2010d: 1).

The differentiation between civilian, security and military functions has also been central to the government's assertion that improved national regulation of PMSCs is unnecessary (Parliament 2005: 4). According to the government's interpretation of the Basic Law, only 'military' functions within Germany and abroad may not be contracted out to private firms (Parliament 2005: 5). Moreover, as one of the supporters and initial signatories of the Montreux Document,[3] the German government has claimed that existing European and international laws are sufficient to control companies with 'military intentions' (Parliament 2010e: 9–10). Since PMSCs are legal companies and distinct from mercenaries in the view of the German government, it has also seen no need to prioritize the ratification of the UN Mercenary Convention (Parliament 2010e: 9). Insofar as additional controls have been considered beneficial, the German government has supported industry self-regulation (Parliament 2005: 18).

German contracting in Afghanistan

Despite the government's protestations and the public and parliamentary scepticism towards military contracting, the intervention in Afghanistan illustrates the extensive use of PMSCs in Germany's international operations. Already the buildup of the German ISAF deployment and bases in Afghanistan relied heavily on private contractors. To support the expansion of their contingent, the armed forces used STUTE Verkehrs GmbH, a subsidiary of Kühne + Nagel, to transport field-camp infrastructure overland to the three German bases in Mazar-e-Sharif, Kunduz and Faisabad. According to STUTE (2007), the company transported over 500 train-wagon loads of logistic supplies to German bases in Afghanistan between 2005 and 2007. The chosen supply route went by train via Poland, Belarus, Russia, Kazakhstan and Uzbekistan to the northern Afghan city of Hairaton, where the material had to be loaded onto the trucks of an Afghan subcontractor for further delivery by road to its ultimate destinations. Additional ground transport and airlift have been supplied by Müller & Partner, Schenker, Uzbekistan Airways, Kühne + Nagel Airlift, Transa Spedition, UZ Aeronavigation, JP-International Air, Shell Niederlande and Sara Spa (Parliament 2010b: 5–6). Notably, transport and logistics companies and their subcontractors have generally not been protected by the military. According to the German Ministry of Defence, the security of contractors in Afghanistan has been their own responsibility (Hötte *et al.* 2010).

PMSCs have also provided a broad range of services on German bases in Afghanistan. The German company Kraus-Maffei Wegmann (KMW), a major producer of tanks and armoured vehicles, already supported the military with maintenance and repair services in former Yugoslavia. Since 2003, KMW has had up to seven technicians in Kabul, and since 2004 it has also had a team at the base in Kunduz, where it maintains primarily KMW vehicles. The personnel working at these so-called Sixt-Stations were typically former Bundeswehr soldiers, employed by KMW at higher salaries (Fasse 2010). In 2011, KMW (2011) further signed a cooperation contract with Daimler AG for the repair and maintenance of Mercedes-Benz trucks and G-model vehicles for international missions of the German military, NATO, the EU and the UN. Another German company, Rheinmetall Services, has maintained and repaired the armed forces' three HERON 1 unmanned aerial systems (UAS), including two ground-control stations in Mazar-e-Sharif (*Handelsblatt* 2010). As the government has pointed out, however, the operation of the UAS remained in the hands of military personnel (Rheinmetall 2010).

Civilian services such as laundry, sewage, waste disposal and fuel supplies have been provided by a range of German and international companies, including sewage and containers by Ecolog; laundry services by AK Company; construction services by Abrown Fayzabad and BAL Construction Company; waste disposal by Sani and Tiofor; energy supplies and systems maintenance by ABY Henstedt-Ulzburg; and aviation and ground fuel by Nordic Camp Supply (NCS Fuel) and Badakhshan Pump Station (Parliament 2010b: 4–5).

From 2005, catering and the provision and management of the associated facilities at the German base in Mazar-e-Sharif were outsourced to Supreme. In 2011, the follow-up contract went to competitor LOG (Logistik-System-betreuungs-Gesellschaft mbH) (2011), with subcontractors ES-KO, a food supply and catering firm, and National Air Cargo responsible for the transport of foodstuffs to Afghanistan. The catering contract in Afghanistan has been surprising, since the internal optimization of armed-forces catering for EUFOR and KFOR had been considered major successes (GEBB 2011b). Moreover, according to GEBB (2011b), catering for international operations is a military core function.

Finally, German government agencies have hired security guards in Afghanistan. Although the information provided by the German government has been contradictory on this issue, one government answer to Parliament states that, as of December 2009, the armed forces employed directly 264 Afghan security guards, including 61 in Faisabad, 77 in Mazar-e-Sharif, 79 in Kunduz and 47 in Taloquan (Parliament 2010a: 7). In addition, the German Police Project Team has hired Saladin Security Afghanistan, a local subsidiary of Saladin Security (UK), to secure its training centres in Mazar-e-Sharif and Faisabad. Pre-mission training for German police personnel about to be deployed in Afghanistan has been executed by Testudo Security Consultants, a company registered in the tax haven Isle of Man, with offices in Berlin and Amman (Parliament 2008b: 3). However, no private firm has been involved in the development and conceptualization of the pre-deployment training programme, according to the German government (Parliament 2008b: 3). Lastly, Germany's foreign ministry has relied on PMSCs for the protection of 170 of its 230 embassies and consular representations abroad, including static security services for the German embassy in Kabul (Parliament 2005: 9).

In addition to direct contracts, the German missions in Afghanistan have benefitted from the indirect contracting of military and security services by other contingents or organizations. As part of ISAF, for instance, German soldiers have received catering from Supreme Foodservices AG, and EUPOL's headquarters in Kabul are protected by about 150 guards from Hart (Parliament 2010e: 6, 2010c: 3). The organizations implementing development and stabilization programmes for the German foreign ministry have used the services of four local and international PMSCs to protect their facilities in Afghanistan: Kabora (Afghanistan), LANTdefence (Germany), Asia Security Group (Afghanistan) and Servcor (US) (Parliament 2010d: 3). Altogether, the framework contract for these services has involved 319 Afghan and seven international security guards. Projects in Kandahar and Oruzgan have been protected by 48 local guards.

Laws and regulations

Germany's particular national context has had considerable implications for the government's approach towards the legal control and regulation of PMSCs. Presumably owing to the widespread public and parliamentary scepticism towards PMSCs, the government has persistently downplayed its reliance on military and security contractors in international operations. Simultaneously, it has argued against the need for new laws and regulations on PMSCs registered in or used by Germany that may restrict its own use of these firms abroad. Several motions for improved legislative control from both government and opposition factions have so far been ignored (Parliament 2008a, 2010f, 2011b).

However, existing national laws that could be used to control PMSCs are severely limited (Krahmann and Abzhaparova 2010; Krahmann and Friesendorf 2011). The Security Guarding Act includes extensive licensing and training criteria for commercial security providers,[4] but only applies to companies registered and working in Germany. Article 109(h) of the Criminal Code prohibits recruitment for foreign military service, but not for foreign security companies.[5] Germany's Export Control Act requires export licenses for a few select services, such as armaments brokering, transhipment, intangible transfers of software and technology, and the provision of technical assistance required for the development, production, operation, installation, maintenance, repair, overhaul and refurbishing of some items specified in the EU Common Military List, but not security or military services in general.[6] Germany also applies EU sanctions that increasingly include controls on the export of military services, such as 'the provision of any assistance, advice or training related to military activities' (European Union 2011). However, 'military activities' are not defined clearly by the EU, leaving considerable scope for interpretation by national authorities, and Germany has failed to include prohibitions or licensing requirements for such services in its own national sanctions. Finally, Germany has been among the signatories of the UN Convention on Mercenarism and the Montreux Document, but has so far failed to ratify the former and systematically implement the non-binding 'good practices' of the latter.

Implications for peace and reconciliation

The direct and indirect implications of Germany's use of PMSCs in international operations for its national peace and reconciliation strategy can be analyzed in terms of three questions. First, how has the proliferation of PMSCs influenced the German government's approach to international peace and reconciliation? Second, what impact has the expansion of military and security contracting had on the political decision-making process in Germany with regard to these missions? Third, how has the growing role of PMSCs in German operations impacted on the implementation of its peace and reconciliation policies?

Military and security contracting has played an important role in the transformation of Germany's policies on 'civilian crisis prevention, conflict resolution and post-conflict peace building' in the post-Cold War era (Federal Government 2004: 1). At the core is the shift from a 'civilian power' strategy to a 'comprehensive approach' that has increasingly focused on military interventions as a means of conflict resolution and as a way of meeting the international interests, ambitions and responsibilities of the reunited Germany. Defence privatization and military contracting have contributed directly and indirectly to this development. According to the government, military privatizations have allowed the transition of surplus soldiers into civilian employment through the creation of public–private joint ventures in the defence sector. Contracting with industry has also freed funds for the reform of the armed forces through increased cost-efficiency and the mobilization of private-sector capital (GEBB 2004). As this chapter has illustrated, military contracting has even contributed to changing the internal discourse – and arguably self-perception – within the German armed forces from that of a national defence force into that of a service provider, which measures performance also in terms of cost-efficiency and not purely in the achievement of military objectives (GEBB 2006: 3). The new self-perception of the Bundeswehr has paved the way for the professionalization of the armed forces, since general conscription has been viewed not only as too costly, but also as an impediment to Germany's participation in international military operations. Finally, the availability of commercial services has allowed Germany to expand its contribution to international missions quickly and decisively before the completion of armed-forces reform. In particular, PMSCs have provided the logistic capabilities necessary for the deployment of German soldiers abroad and sustained the small expeditionary force of 6,000 soldiers by taking over non-core functions. Indirectly, the above developments have helped harmonize the German approach to peace and reconciliation and military contracting with those of other leading powers and international organizations such as the UN, NATO and the EU. They have allowed Germany to use its historical commitment to multilateralism and integration to justify its new self-image as a 'normal' power with military responsibilities for international peace and stability.

The consequences for political decision making on peace and reconciliation missions have stemmed partially from the government's reluctance to acknowledge the growing scope of military and security contracting in international operations. Presumably because of a wish to avoid a public and prospectively divisive debate over the question to what extent contractors may legitimately become involved in German military operations, the government has chosen to argue that the armed forces do not employ 'private security companies' abroad (Parliament 2010d: 1). By so doing, it has deprived itself of the opportunity to improve the accountability of PMSCs and its own changed peace and reconciliation strategy by creating appropriate legal and institutional checks and balances, including a greater role for the German parliament in decisions on whether and how to use these firms.

The implications have become apparent in the increasingly close and unsupervised relationships between government agencies and industry. The Federal Accounting Office (2003: 165) has accused GEBB of taking decisions in favour of public–private partnerships on the basis of incorrect projections or foregone conclusions. Moreover, in Afghanistan, Müller & Partners received an armed-forces logistics contract in return for a €25,000 bribe (Leersch 2000; Spilcker 2005; Schmalenberg 2005). Although the responsible official was taken to court and convicted, the military did nothing to address the danger of corruption among its contracting staff (Parliament 2006: 31). The contract with Müller & Partners was re-awarded until at least 2009 (Parliament 2010b: 5–6). Repeated and long-term contracting has contributed to the development of close relationships with, and possibly dependencies on, a small number of German firms. The same companies that supply particular services within Germany are usually also able to gain contracts for operations abroad, such as two of the co-owners of the hybrid public–private company Heeresinstandsetzungslogistik, KMW and Rheinmetall, who have provided maintenance for Bundeswehr vehicles in Afghanistan (*Handelsblatt* 2010).

Moreover, PMSCs can shape Germany's peace and reconciliation strategies through the identification, development and provision of new military technologies. The 'synthetic training' supported and coordinated by Rheinmetall at the army's Combat Training Centre in Altmark since 2008, for example, could have a potentially significant impact (Oelschlägel 2009). All army contingents have to complete a two-week training course at Altmark immediately before deployment abroad. Although military personnel remain responsible for the training, the growing role of simulations illustrates the incursion of (cost-)efficiency rationales into the sphere of military exercises. That such rationales may impact on the learning of soldiers has been suggested by academic research (Vogel-Walcutt *et al.* 2010).

The hiring of PMSCs also has the potential to undermine the 2005 Parliamentary Participation Act, which requires annual approval for international missions by Parliament, including its permission for the maximum numbers of soldiers to be deployed. Even leading armed forces officers such as Brigadier General Dieter Warnecke (2010; see also Fasse 2010) have noted that the political advantage of circumventing nationally or internationally agreed troop limitations has been one factor in contracting decisions. Decision-making power has thus shifted to the executive, allowing the government to factually expand military operations and limit the possible negative publicity of military casualties by replacing soldiers with contractors.

Lastly, the failure of the German government to establish clear operational and legal foundations for the employment of PMSCs has also affected the implementation of Germany's peace and reconciliation policies. These policies have changed as a result of government decisions that have progressively narrowed the definition of the core functions of the armed forces in favour of a greater role for contractors. However, neither Parliament nor the German public, which appear to have very different conceptions of what tasks are inherent in the state's monopoly on the legitimate use of violence in international affairs, have been involved in these decisions. For the implementation of Germany's peace and reconciliation strategy, this has meant that PMSCs and local guards have been involved in providing potentially controversial services such as security guarding and protection (Parliament 2010a: 7, 2010d: 3). And, it is not only members of the German parliament that harbour doubts about the legitimacy of outsourcing such functions; local populations share these views. In Afghanistan, focus groups told Swisspeace that private security guards had at best little positive impact on their own security, at worst decreased it because they 'are armed, block the road, are badly behaved and seem to attract trouble' (Schmeidl 2008: 27). Moreover, contract security personnel were believed to be 'sending a strong message that security is not a public good, but a commodity of foreigners and wealthy Afghans' (Schmeidl 2008: 26). The real or perceived impunity of security contractors in Afghanistan and the unwillingness of states such as Germany to accept legal responsibility for them can thus contribute to undermining the ability of foreign armed forces and police to 'win the hearts and minds' of ordinary civilians (Mojumdar 2009).

Conclusion

Military and security contracting has played a major role in the post-Cold War transformation of Germany's approach to peace and reconciliation. However, the German government has so far refused to analyze and discuss the implications of this transformation. The resulting discrepancy between the public discourse and parliamentary institutions in Germany that have their foundations in the increasingly outdated model of a 'civilian power', on the one hand, and the government's policies and practices, on the other, has serious implications. The consequences include the lack of public and parliamentary support for Germany's growing military engagement and increased use of PMSCs in international operations, as well as the government's reluctance to address concerns regarding the legitimacy and perceived impunity of security contractors because this could be understood as an admission of the extent to which PMSCs have become integral to German missions abroad.

Following the passing of the Defence Reform Act (*Wehrrechtsänderungsgesetz*) on 1 July 2011, an open debate about the use of PMSCs in Germany's military and civilian operations is more important than ever. In particular, the planned reduction in the number of active soldiers to 185,000 as part of the suspension of conscription and the professionalization of the Bundeswehr will have serious consequences for Germany's ability to participate in multiple operations without contractor support. How is Germany to meet its international responsibilities outlined in the latest Defence Policy Guidelines, including the provision of military capabilities for peacekeeping and peacemaking? Experts, politicians and military representatives, such as Ulrich Kirch of the Bundeswehr Union, have already argued that the projected size of the new professional armed forces is 'politically irresponsible' if the aim is to sustain Germany's contribution to multilateral interventions, not least increase it, as the government has been suggesting. The government seems to assume that possible shortfalls will be met by the private sector. As the Defence Policy Guidelines state, 'industrial capabilities will be especially important where the Bundeswehr contributes significant and recognized capabilities to national tasks and tasks within alliances' (Ministry of Defence 2011: 16). Only by publicly acknowledging its growing use of PMSCs and engaging in an open debate will the German government be able to deal with the possible consequences for Germany's peace and reconciliation strategy at home and abroad.

Notes

1 In the following, 'Germany' refers to West Germany between 1945 and 1990 and the reunited Germany thereafter. Quotations from the Basic Law are taken from the official English translation as of October 2010, available at www.btg-bestellservice.de/pdf/ 80201000.pdf (accessed 15 December 2011).
2 All quotes from German-language publications have been translated by the author.
3 See www.icrc.org/eng/resources/documents/misc/montreux-document-170908.htm (accessed 15 December 2011).
4 See www.gesetze-im-internet.de/bewachv_1996/index.html (accessed 19 December 2011).
5 See www.gesetze-im-internet.de/stgb/index.html (accessed 19 December 2011).
6 See www.gesetze-im-internet.de/awv_1986/ (accessed 19 December 2011).

References

Armed Forces (Bundeswehr). 2002. 'Bundeswehr als Arbeitgeber für Kfz-Betriebe im Kosovo und Mazedonien', press release, 22 July.
——2011. 'Hintergrundinformationen zu ISAF und Afghanistan', version of 21 November, available at www.einsatz.bundeswehr.de (accessed 20 December 2011).
Bittner, Jochen and Elisabeth Niejahr. 2004. 'Die Berater-Republik', *Die Zeit*, 5 February.
Bundesgesetzblatt. 2005. *Gesetz zur Beschleunigung der Umsetzung von Öffentliche Privaten Partnerschaften und zur Verbesserung gesetzlicher Rahmenbedingungen für Öffentlich Private Partnerschaften*, 1 September, Teil I, Nr. 56, 2676.
Dinter, Henrik. 2004. 'Wehrpflicht, Freiwilligenarmee und allgemeine Dienstpflict: Aktuelle Argumentationslinien', in Ines-Jacqueline Werkner, ed., *Die Wehrpflicht und ihre*

Hintergründe. Sozialwissenschaftliche Beiträge zur aktuellen Debatte. Wiesbaden: VS Verlag für Sozialwissenschaft, pp. 109–29.

Duffield, John S. 1999. 'Political Culture and State Behavior: Why Germany Confounds Neorealism', *International Organization* 53(4): 780–3.

European Union. 2011. *Restrictive Measures (Sanctions) in Force,* 6 October, available at http://ec.europa.eu/external_relations/cfsp/sanctions/docs/measures_en.pdf (accessed 15 December 2011).

Fasse, Markus. 2010. 'Panzerhersteller liefern nicht rasch genug', *Handelsblatt,* 16 April.

Federal Accounting Office (Bundesrechnungshof). 2003. *Bemerkungen 2003 zur Haushalts-und Wirtschaftsführung des Bundes.* Bonn: Bundesrechungshof.

—— 2006. *Bemerkungen 2006 zur Haushalts-und Wirtschaftsführung des Bundes.* Bonn: Bundesrechnungshof.

Federal Government (Bundesregierung). 2004. 'Action Plan "Civilian Crisis Prevention, Conflict Resolution and Post-Conflict Peacebuilding"', Berlin, 12 May.

—— 2011. *Fortschrittsbericht Afghanistan zur Unterrichtung des Deutschen Bundestages,* Berlin, July.

GEBB. 2004. *100% Service: Annual Report 2004.* Cologne: GEBB.

GEBB. 2006. *Leistung ist messbar.* Cologne: GEBB.

GEBB. 2007. *Teamarbeiter.* Cologne: GEBB.

GEBB. 2008. *Das passt perfekt: Die Bundeswehr und die g.e.b.b. – gemeinsam erfolgreich.* Cologne: GEBB.

GEBB. 2011a. 'Projekte', available at www.gebb.de/de/projekte.html (accessed 15 December 2011).

GEBB. 2011b. 'Verpflegung im Einsatz', available at: www.gebb.de/Projekte/Verpfle gung/Einsatzverpflegung.html (accessed 15 April 2011).

Handelsblatt. 2010. 'Gute Geschäfte an der Front', 8 December.

Heinen, Guido. 2003. 'Auch Struck gab Aufträge an Berger', *Die Welt,* 19 December.

Hellmann, Gunther. 1996. 'Goodbye Bismarck? The Foreign Policy of Contemporary Germany', *Mershon International Studies Review* 40(1): 1–39.

Hötte, Ralph, Jochen Leufgens and Nikolaus Steiner. 2010. 'Afghanistan: Steuergelder für Warlords und Taliban?', TV report transcript, *Monitor,* 8 July, available at www.wdr. de/tv/monitor//sendungen/2010/0708/pdf/afghanistan.pdf (accessed 15 December 2011).

Hyde-Price, Adrian. 2001. 'Germany and the Kosovo War: Still a Civilian Power?', *German Politics* 10(1): 19–34.

Inspectors General, US Department of State and US Department of Defense. 2006. *Interagency Assessment of Afghanistan Police Training and Readiness.* Washington, DC, November.

Keller, Jörg. 2007. 'Streitkräfte und ökonomisches Kalkül: Top oder Flop? Grundsätzliche Überlegungen zu einer Ökonomisierung der Bundeswehr', in Gregor Richter, ed., *Die ökonomische Modernisierung der Bundeswehr: Sachstand, Konzeptionen und Perspektiven.* Wiesbaden: VS Verlag für Sozialwissenschaften, pp. 51–64.

Kersting, Silke. 2006. 'Jung bremst Privatisierer. Bundeswehr wird wieder Staatsangelegenheit', *Handelsblatt,* 7 July.

Kiesewetter, Roderich (CDU/CSU). 2011. *Deutscher Bundestag,* Debatte, 17. Wahlperiode, 84. Sitzung, 20 January, Anlage 4, p. 9528.

KMW. 2011. 'KMW und Daimler AG unterzeichnen Service-vertrag für Einsatzgebiete', press release, 21 February.

Krahmann, Elke. 2010. *States, Citizens and the Privatization of Security.* Cambridge: Cambridge University Press.

Krahmann, Elke and Aida Abzhaparova. 2010. 'The Regulation of Private Military and Security Services in the European Union: Current Policies and Future Options', EUI Working Paper 2010/8. Florence: European University Institute.

Krahmann, Elke and Cornelius Friesendorf. 2011. 'Debatte vertagt? Militär-und Sicherheitsfirmen in deutschen Auslandseinsätzen', HSFK Report. Frankfurt am Main: HSFK.

Leersch, Hans-Jürgen. 2000. 'Kritik an Scharpings Privatisierungsplänen', *Die Welt*, 4 July.

Leyendecker, Hans. 2010. 'Private Militärfirmen Krieg als Geschäft', *Süddeutsche Zeitung*, 13 January.

LOG. 2011. 'LOG betreibt seit dem 01.01.2011 in MAZAR-E-SHARIF im CAMP MARMAL das Wirtschaftsgebäude und verpflegt Soldaten und zivile Mitarbeiter', press release, 9 March.

Maull, Hanns W. 1990. 'Germany and Japan: The New Civilian Powers', *Foreign Affairs* 69(5): 91–106.

——2000. 'Germany and the Use of Force: Still a Civilian Power?', *Survival* 42(2): 56–80.

Ministry of Defence (Bundesministerium der Verteidigung). 2000. *Neuausrichtung der Bundeswehr: Grobausplanung, Ergebnisse und Entscheidungen*. Berlin.

——2001. *Die Bundeswehr der Zukunft. Sachstand der Reform*. Berlin, 15 June.

——2006. *Bundeswehr Plan 2007*. Berlin: Ministry of Defence.

——2011. *Defence Policy Guidelines*. Berlin, 27 May.

Mojumdar, Aunohita. 2009. 'Afghanistan: Private Security Contractors Become a Source of Public Scorn', 7 August, available at www.unhcr.org/refworld/docid/4a8414f52d. html (accessed 20 December 2011).

Oelschlägel, Thomas. 2009. 'Rheinmetall Defence sorgt in der Altmark für reibungslosen Betrieb des Gefechtsübungszentrums des Heeres', September, available at: www.rhein metall-defence.com (accessed 15 December 2011).

Parliament (Deutscher Bundestag). 2005. *Antwort der Bundesregierung, 'Auslagerung spezifischer Sicherheits-und Militäraufgaben an nichtstaatliche Stellen'*. 15. Wahlperiode, Drucksache 15/5824, 24 June.

——2006. *Unterrichtung durch den Bundesrechungshof, 'Bemerkungen des Bundesrechungshofes 2006 zur Haushalts-und Wirtschaftsführung des Bundes'*. 16. Wahlperiode, Drucksache 16/3200, 13 November.

——2007. *Unterrichtung durch den Wehrbeauftragten*. Jahresbericht 2006, Drucksache 16/4700, 20 March.

——2008a. *Antrag der Abgeordneten Dr. Karl-Theodor Freiherr zu Guttenberg, et al. un der Fraktion der CDU/CSU sowie der Abgeordneten Dr Rolf Mützenich et al. und der Fraktion der SPD, 'Nicht-staatliche militärische Sicherheitsunternehmen kontrollieren'*. 16. Wahlperiode, Drucksache 16/10846, 12 November.

——2008b. *Antwort der Bundesregierung, 'Besserer Schutz für Polizisten bei ihrem Auslandseinsatz in Afghanistan'*. 16. Wahlperiode, Drucksache 16/8644, 20 March.

——2010a. *Antwort der Bundesregierung, 'Bewaffnete Gruppen in Afghanistan'*. 17. Wahlperiode, Drucksache 17/492, 20 January.

——2010b. *Antwort der Bundesregierung, 'Kosten der militärischen Intervention in Afghanistan'*. 17. Wahlperiode, Drucksache 17/2026, 9 June.

——2010c. *Antwort der Bundesregierung, 'Deutsche Polizeiarbeit in Afghanistan'*. 17. Wahlperiode, Drucksache 17/2878, 8 September.

——2010d. *Antwort der Bundesregierung, 'Deutsche Zusammenarbeit mit privaten Sicherheitsdienstleistern in Afghanistan'*. 17. Wahlperiode, Drucksache 17/3559, 26 October.

180   Elke Krahmann

———2010e. *Antwort der Bundesregierung, 'Deutsche Staatsbürger in Sicherheitsdienstleistungsunternehmen und der Fremdenlegion im Auslandseinsatz'*. 17. Wahlperiode, Drucksache 17/4012, 1 November.

———2010f. *Antrag der Fraktion der SPD, 'Nichtstaatliche militärische Sicherheitsunternehmen registrieren und kontrollieren'*. 17. Wahlperiode, Drucksache 17/4198, 15 December.

———2011a. *Antrag der Bundesregierung, Fortsetzung der Beteiligung bewaffneter deutscher Streitkräfte an dem Einsatz der Internationalen Sicherheitsunterstützungstruppe in Afghanistan (International Security Assistance Force, ISAF) unter Führung der NATO auf Grundlage der Resolutionen 1386 (2001) und folgender Resolutionen, zuletzt Resolution 1943 (2010) des Sicherheitsrates der Vereinten Nationen*. 17. Wahlperiode, Drucksache 17/4402, 13 January.

———2011b. *Antrag der Abgeordneten Paul Schäfer et al. und der Fraktion DIE LINKE, 'Internationale Ächtung des Söldnerwesens und Verbot privater militärischer Dienstleistungen aus Deutschland'*. 17. Wahlperiode, Drucksache 17/4673, 8 February.

Petersohn, Ulrich. 2006. *Die Nutzung privater Militärfirmen durch US-Streitkräfte und Bundeswehr*. Berlin: Stiftung Wissenschaft und Politik.

Portugall, Gerd. 2007. 'Die Bundeswehr und das Privatisierungsmodell der "Öffentlich-Privaten-Partnershaft" (ÖPP)', in Gregor Richter, ed., *Die ökonomische Modernisierung der Bundeswehr: Sachstand, Konzeptionen und Perspektiven*. Wiesbaden: VS Verlag für Sozialwissenschaften, pp. 141–58.

Reimann, Anna and Severin Weiland. 2006. 'Bundeswehr Mandat überdenken', *Der Spiegel*, 7 June.

R.H. 2003. 'Das Neueste zum Neuen Flottenmanagement der Bundeswehr', *Bundeswehrkurier* 1: 2.

Rheinmetall. 2010. 'Rheinmetall gewinnt Folgeaufträge über Fuchs-Fahrzeuge und Heron-Flugsysteme für die Bundeswehr', press release, 17 September.

Richter, Gregor. 2007. 'Privatization in the German Armed Forces', in Thomas Jäger and Gerhard Kümmel, eds, *Private Military and Security Companies: Chances, Problems, Pitfalls and Prospects*. Wiesbaden: VS Verlag für Sozialwissenschaften, pp. 165–76.

Rüb, Matthias. 2007. 'Erst schießen, dann fragen', *Frankfurter Allgemeine Zeitung*, 19 September.

Schmalenberg, Detlev. 2005. 'Ein Lehrstück aus dem Kabul-Einsatz', *Kölner Stadtanzeiger*, 21 March.

Schmeidl, Susanne. 2008. 'Afghanistan', in Ulrike Joras and Adrian Schuster, eds, *Private Security Companies and Local Populations: An Exploratory Study of Afghanistan and Angola*. Bern: Swisspeace, pp. 9–37.

Speckmann, Thomas. 2010. 'Söldner in Afghanistan Schmarotzer des Krieges', *Die Zeit*, 2 June.

Spilcker, Axel. 2005. 'Korruptionsaffäre "Überweisen Sie 25 000 E"', *Focus*, 21 March.

STUTE. 2007. 'STUTE unterstützt Bundeswehr mit kompetenter Transportlogistik', press release, 15 June.

Tagesschau. 2010. 'Der selbst verschuldete "Sündenfall"', 24 May, available at www.tagesschau.de/inland/asgaard104.html (accessed 15 April 2011).

Vogel-Walcutt, Jennifer, Teresa Marino Carper, Clint Bowers and Denise Nicholson. 2010. 'Increasing Efficiency in Military Learning: Theoretical Considerations and Pratical Applications', *Military Psychology* 22(3): 311–39.

Warnecke, Dieter, Brigadier General. 2010. 'Modernisierung vom Einsatz her denken', *Symposium 10 Jahre g.e.b.b.*, 13 September, available at www.gebb.de/Downloads/10_09_13 – Vortrag_Warnecke.pdf (accessed 15 April 2011).

10 Italy

Keeping or selling stocks?

Stefano Ruzza

Introduction

While Italy is often regarded as having little to do with security commercialization – especially by Italians – several pieces of evidence prove that assumption wrong. However, it is true that the phenomenon is developing quite slowly, sometimes informally, and is seldom related to armed PMSCs. For these reasons, Italian security commercialization is hard to track, which makes it possible to maintain a tight public discourse on the limited role granted to private actors. Appearances notwithstanding, the room of manoeuvre progressively gained by commercial practices is not irrelevant, as their impact on the engagement in Afghanistan shows. This chapter aims to shed some light on the often under-recognized process of Italian security commercialization and its implications.

As a first step, the Italian national context – including the relevant lexicon regarding the use of force and the role allowed private actors in this context – is examined. Normative elements – both formal and informal, from national law to public ethos – present Italy as an environment deeply entrenched in the republican conception of the state, and thus quite hostile to commercialization. Yet, following the end of the Cold War, a need for defence reform, coupled with ideological shifts, has slowly but continually changed this picture, with little-to-no public awareness. This first section is complemented by information about the Italian market for private security providers, showing how national peculiarities have influenced this market in terms of its dimension, the range of services offered and the degree of institutionalization.

The section that follows considers the Italian engagement in Afghanistan. Along with many other countries, Italy has adopted what is known as a 'comprehensive approach' to its operations in Afghanistan, and for this reason the roles of both civilian and military actors are taken into account. Particular attention is devoted to the Italian-led Provincial Reconstruction Team (PRT) in Herat.

Then, Italian security-related commercial practices in Afghanistan are analyzed. The primary focus here is on military contracting, but civil–military cooperation (CIMIC) activities developed through the help of a civilian component and addressed to non-strictly military needs are also included in the picture. The practices considered are not limited to the formal hiring of PMSCs – whether that is done directly or indirectly – but also include informal actors and economic arrangements. Implications are evaluated contextually. A core argument is that while the Italian engagement in Afghanistan is presented as being particularly concerned with economic development and capacity building, the involvement of commercial actors often works against this overall policy.

The last section is devoted to tracing some general conclusions, drawing from the Afghan case and relating back to the national context. All in all, it could be argued that while Italy still presents itself as a comparatively strict environment in relation to commercialization (especially when contrasted with Anglo-Saxon countries), it has begun to sell some stocks on the issue of security, often without real awareness among either policymakers or the general public.

The Italian national context: a tight space for commercialization?

General background

Modern Italy is a country of recent creation, with a history of fragmentation and foreign interference dating up to the middle of the nineteenth century. Wars for Italian unification started in 1848 and formally achieved their goal in 1861, but the country in its current geographic sense was not formed up until the end of the First World War. The nation-building process lasted even further, moving through fascism and the current republican period, one of its core tools being universal military service.

The need to build a reliable military instrument in the hands of the state and keep it under the latter's control (see Leander 2006), to shape a cohesive national identity, and – more broadly – to generate unity out of fragmentation are factors that can help us understand how the Italian context was formed during the country's recent history and account for the centrality of the state in security-related matters. The relationship between citizenship and military service – the latter considered simultaneously both a privilege and an obligation – is also very central and has been coupled with the explicit prohibition on citizens providing similar kinds of services to foreign countries on a private basis (Ruzza 2011: 23–24).[1] In addition to various contingencies, customs inherited from other Continental traditions – and particularly from France (Barberis 1988) – played a role. Italy clearly situated itself closer to the republican ideal type of state than to its liberal counterpart (Krahmann 2010: 36–41), and thus the legitimate room for manoeuvre granted to private actors has been limited to the more conventional small-scale and well-regulated security services generally available to private customers (protection of premises, bodyguarding, etc.). Given such a background, it is not hard to understand why Italy is a party to the UN Convention Against Mercenarism, was one of its first signatories (February 1990), and also recently became a signatory to the Montreux Document (June 2009).

Apologia for the use of force typical of the fascist period – along with the devastation, internecine conflict, and substantial defeat of the Second World

War – established another fundamental trait of the national context, making Italy a country basically distrustful of war and the use of military means in general. This is reflected both on the institutional level – the rejection of war is explicitly declared in the Italian Constitution[2] – and within the public discourse, where the decision to present a military operation as being somewhat 'war-related' means delegitimizing it. This does not mean that significant military assets are lacking, nor that their use is always neglected: rather, they are usually employed in cooperation with other countries and within the framework of multilateral agreements, and presented as a means of maintaining or re-establishing peace, reducing human suffering and sustaining development. All of this also applies to the current engagement in Afghanistan (Coralluzzo 2000; Bonvicini and Colombo 2010, 2011; Osservatorio di Politica Internazionale 2010).

On the internal front, post-Second World War republican Italy had to face serious challenges to its capacity to monopolize violence and provide security, from powerful criminal organizations and terrorist groups. While the most serious threats were ultimately defeated by state and society, Italy has had to endure an uneasy co-existence with private armed actors for some considerable time, a challenge that is not completely over even now (Dalla Porta 1984, 1990; Ginsborg 1989; Lupo 2004; Santarelli 1996; Sciarrone 2009). The effect of this has been a further strengthening of the distrust for private force and privately held resources of violence.

Post-Cold War military reforms and openings toward commercialization

The end of the Cold War triggered processes that gradually changed this picture, because of demands for structural changes and ideological shifts. This is most evident in the reform process that interested the Italian Armed Forces and the Ministry of Defence.

In 2000, the Italian Parliament approved a law (L. 14/11/2000, n. 331) that called for the full professionalization of the military career, replacing conscripts with personnel in permanent service or with fixed-term volunteers. The draft became a complementary resource to be used only in emergencies and was suspended in 2005 (L. 23/08/2004, n. 226). The military apparatus was downsized to 190,000 men and women serving within the army, navy, and air force. This was not the only figure that was shrinking: military expenditures went from 2.1 per cent of GDP in 1990 to 1.8 per cent in 2009, in a clear and steady trend of progressive reduction.[3] On the other hand, the pressure on the armed forces was increasing, mostly in relation to involvement in international operations and consequent adaptations from a mainly defensive apparatus to a projectable force.

These transformations generated a demand for professional skills not present or scarce among personnel in active service: country advisors, engineers and medics with peculiar specializations, public relations experts, and so on. In accordance with Italy's republican background, a way of obtaining the needed capabilities without resorting to the market was devised: the 'Selected Reserve' (*Riserva Selezionata*, RS), a pool of voluntary part-time officers with specific qualifications.[4] Citizens accepted into the RS as specialists are granted a proper military status, which ensures that they fall completely within the boundaries of military laws and regulations, thus avoiding normative 'grey areas' often attached to the use of civilian contractors, especially when employed abroad.

However, Italian military institutions have not been totally impenetrable to the market's charms. In 2002, the Ministry of Defence published a white paper (*libro bianco*) setting out the path for reform (Ministero della Difesa 2002). The first openings to commercialization – revealing small ideological shifts toward a neo-liberal approach – appear in this document. The loss of readily available and cheap (even if underqualified) manpower caused by the end of compulsory service, coupled with cuts to the numbers of civil servants, were used as main elements in favour of the outsourcing of services, mostly menial (like cleaning or canteen management) but eventually also of a more advanced nature (like IT and engineering). Interestingly enough, economic effectiveness is taken into account, but is not considered as being as central as the need to fulfil the armed forces' institutional mandate.

A further shift in favour of commercialization is the recent establishment of 'Difesa Servizi spa', a commercial venture fully owned by the Ministry of Defence. The stated rationale for its creation was to optimize the income from assets owned by the armed forces. This covers revenue from sources stretching from renting estates to requesting fees for services previously delivered for free (e.g. weather forecasts) or claiming royalties for the use of armed forces logos on clothes. More controversial is the possibility of securing revenue for promotional services in favour of the defence industry – that is, a percentage commission on every order of military hardware obtained with the help of the armed forces. No matter the source, all income earned by Difesa Servizi is in turn to be used to facilitate the fulfilment of the institutional mandate of the defence administration by paying for needed goods and services (with the exclusion of armaments) in times of shrinking budgets.[5]

The idea of a private venture linked to the Ministry of Defence was met with suspicion by Italy's Parliament. For this reason – and after several failed attempts since 2008 – Difesa Servizi was finally created through a few paragraphs inserted in the 2010 budgetary law (L. 23/12/2009, n. 191, Art. 2, paras 27–36) on which a vote of confidence was requested by the government. Further political resistance to the adoption of the implementing decrees did not allow Difesa Servizi to become a working reality until February 2011 (Ministero della Difesa 2011).[6]

Difesa Servizi can buy services from other entities, both public and private. While hiring armed contractors seems to contravene the terms of the relevant legislation – which states that Difesa Servizi is excluded from acting in connection with the 'operational needs of the armed forces'[7] – it is not a foregone conclusion that the organization will not be used as a way of acquiring technical services (in accordance with the directions set out in the Ministry of Defence white paper).

Difesa Servizi also generates an overlap between the public interests of the national defence apparatus and the private interests of the defence industry, introducing financial incentives for the armed forces in relation to the effective promotion of military hardware.

The history of Difesa Servizi is also revealing of Italian attitudes toward security commercialization. On the one hand, detractors of the project were afraid of the potential implications of coupling defence with private logics. On the other hand, its advocates (from the undersecretary for defence to high-ranking military officers) were very firm in stating that the new private venture was just a way of gathering more resources to benefit the armed forces of the state. There have been shifts in the arguments used by both parties, but the core point remains the same: the use of force is something that can be rightfully handled only by the state.

The Italian market for private security

In Italy, in addition to the provision of mundane security services, there is a functioning market for services delivered abroad, even if this is relatively underdeveloped. In this section, this market will be considered in terms of its supply side, with the analysis moving from the more informal actors (individuals and unofficial networks) toward the more institutionalized (companies). Some considerations regarding the Italian state as a customer will be added in conclusion.

The risk of legal implications (owing to existing legislation) and a general distrust for private force account for the absence of large Italian entities devoted to recruiting and deploying armed personnel abroad or to providing services closer to the tip of Singer's (2003) spear. This does not mean that Italian citizens do not get involved in this line of work: in some cases, military personnel deployed in the field come into contact with foreign PMSCs and decide to change employer; in others, Italian citizens establish contact through informal networks. These latter are quite elusive and are often run through training centres for bodyguards or private investigative agencies.

The case of Fabrizio Quattrocchi – kidnapped and killed in Iraq in April 2004 – is illustrative both of these recruiting methods and of national feelings toward this kind of profession. Quattrocchi and his colleagues were deployed in Iraq through a shady mix of informal circles in Italy and small Italian-run firms located outside of the country's borders. Both Salvatore Stefio and Giampiero Spinelli – the first was kidnapped with Quattrocchi, while both were involved with his deployment in Iraq – were put under trial for potential violation of Article 288 of the Penal Code in 2008, but subsequently acquitted.[8] Feelings of sympathy for an Italian citizen murdered in an unpopular conflict were, of course, present in public opinion, although Quattrocchi's work was publicly perceived as controversial.[9]

Moving into the field of more formal realities, the Security Consulting Group (SCG, formerly known as 'Start Sicurezza') is probably the best-known Italian company owing to the frequent media appearances of its director, Carlo Biffani, a former paratrooper colonel. Based in Rome, SCG is not a huge company (in 2008, it had around 30 employees). It is most active in the field of security advising and crisis management, and also operates abroad, where it sometimes employs armed personnel. The firm has been very vocal in its support for allowing armed guards to carry out anti-piracy functions aboard Italian ships,[10] an option forbidden by law until very recently.

The piracy debate itself is revealing of the changes afoot with regards to private actors of security. During the period of the final Berlusconi government, several bills to allow private guards on Italian ships were proposed and rejected. The navy chief of staff has repeatedly expressed his scepticism towards such a development, advocating instead the creation of *ad hoc* military teams, while the minister of defence has stated his preference for the private solution. Maritime organizations were divided on the issue, but two of the largest – the Italian Federation of Shipowners (Confitarma) and the Italian Federation of Fishing Enterprises (Federpesca) – ultimately leaned in favour of the private option. The possibility of carrying private armed guards was finally granted in summer 2011 with bipartisan consensus (D.L. 07/07/2011, CdM n. 145; L. 02/08/2011, n. 130), though coupled with the option of choosing military teams instead.[11]

Italian companies are active in the provision of support services to armed forces abroad, two good examples being Ciano and Essegi Forniture Militari. The first started in the 1990s as a small firm, and is now a relatively large reality with offices in Egypt, India, Peru, the US, and Switzerland. Ciano is currently operating in Afghanistan, Albania, Bosnia and Herzegovina, Iraq, Kosovo, and Lebanon with a range of military contingents (not just Italians). Its core services are food and supply delivery, catering, telecommunications, welfare activities, and construction management.[12] Essegi Forniture Militari was born in 1964 as a small company furnishing goods to military shops in national bases, but evolved during the 1990s and is currently providing a range of services similar to those offered by Ciano.[13] The defence industry has developed in a similar fashion as well. Iveco has responsibility for the maintenance cycles of its armoured vehicles in use among the Italian Armed Forces (e.g. the 'Lince' and the 'Freccia'), both within national borders and abroad. Similar arrangements are in place with the manufacturers of military aircraft.[14]

Moving on from the supply side of security-related services, it is interesting to check how Italy has acted as a customer. Unsurprisingly, the country has made use of support firms like Ciano and Essegi in the course of several international operations, from the 1990s onwards. However, services purchased were mainly meant for the welfare of troops (e.g. management of small shops and restaurants) and have enlarged only recently to include more substantial activities, such as the renting of materials, delivery of goods, construction services, maintenance of materiel, etc.

Italy also hired a PMSC for the provision of armed services in at least one case. Military withdrawal from Iraq in 2006 left the Italian civilians working in the Dhi Qar Provincial Reconstruction Team (PRT) without protection, and the British company Aegis Defence Services was hired to fill the void.[15] This may be explained in terms of a political bargain in the domestic arena: even if private armed contractors are not appreciated by the Italian public, keeping Italy's armed forces deployed was probably considered worse (both candidates to premiership promised withdrawal during the 2006 electoral campaign). The option of hiring a PMSC may have been perceived as a convenient way of reducing political costs (see Avant and Sigelman 2010; Krahmann 2010; Ruzza 2008, 2010, 2011; Singer 2003), especially given the very limited awareness of such organizations among the Italian public.[16] Few parliamentary questions were raised on the issue, and the use of Aegis was presented by the government as being necessary for supporting reconstruction efforts in Iraq, and thus perfectly legitimate.[17] This case suggests that the refusal for private force apparent in the public discourse may be just a facade, and would perhaps be better defined as a lack of public awareness.

The Italian engagement in Afghanistan

Owing to certain characteristics of the national context, while it does not totally reject the use of military tools, Italy prefers to present itself as a civil power concerned with human rights and humanitarian issues. International operations are thus structured as multilateral joint military–civilian efforts aimed at maintaining or re-establishing peace and reducing human suffering, even if highly kinetic activities of a purely military nature – while often little reported – are not completely out of the picture.[18]

Like many other countries, Italy has adopted the whole-of-government 'comprehensive approach' (*approccio nazionale multidimensionale*) in its deployed operations.[19] On the military side, one of the tools devised to implement this concept in the field is 'civil–military cooperation' (CIMIC), defined as the management of interactions between the military and the civilian components present in a particular area of operation. Thus, CIMIC may be described as the tool used by the armed forces to achieve objectives that lie outside their own institutional boundaries but that can help them to fulfil their mission.[20]

On the civilian side, besides the normal diplomatic functions performed by the Ministry of Foreign Affairs, another relevant actor is the development cooperation agency (*Cooperazione Italiana*), which is formally a part of the Ministry of Foreign Affairs itself. As with the military budget, the financing for development cooperation has been steadily reduced over time,[21] and appropriations allocated to this purpose cannot be used – either directly or indirectly – to finance military activities (L. 26/02/1987, n. 49, Art. 1), a fact that influences the sourcing of funds for deployed operations (e.g. the PRT budget is almost entirely covered by the Ministry of Defence for this reason).

Moving onto the specific engagement in Afghanistan, Italy claims that it is pursuing – not unlike the rest of the intervening countries – the 'rebirth of a free and democratic Afghan state' through its active support of the reconstruction and stabilization efforts in the country, providing both military and civilian assistance and thus applying the comprehensive approach in the field. More specifically, the stated strategy:

> is a twofold one: on the one hand, to strengthen local capacities and improve the management of projects and funds by the Afghan authorities within the framework of the government's growing role as partner and creator of aid and development programmes. … [O]n the other, a ready response to emergencies on behalf of local populations, with special attention to their weaker and more vulnerable segments.
>
> (Ministero degli Affari Esteri 2009)

On the civilian side, Cooperazione Italiana is the most relevant actor for long-term programmes and – being an emanation of Ministry of Foreign Affairs – is acting in synergy with the diplomatic mission in many governance- and capacity-building projects. NGOs complying with specific standards and active in relevant sectors can, in turn, secure support or financing from Cooperazione Italiana.[22] Infrastructure development (roads, bridges, schools, hospitals) and humanitarian aid have been key priorities for the Italian development agency in Afghanistan.[23] Links between Cooperazione and Italy's armed forces are not incidental: Cooperazione guidelines for the years 2011–13 call for continuity in the geographical concentration of activities in the western part of the country, where Italian armed forces are also deployed and where Cooperazione is working within the framework of the Herat PRT. The same guidelines also call for further efforts in interlinking Ministry of Foreign Affairs–Cooperazione Italiana activities with military CIMIC actions financed by the Ministry of Defence (Ministero degli Affari Esteri 2010).

Moving on to the military side, Italy is active in Afghanistan with about 4,000 troops (as of January 2012), which makes it about the fourth- or fifth-largest in terms of deployed military personnel,[24] a ranking that has been stable over time. Most of these troops are employed within the framework of the ISAF mission, but a small portion of them are part of the EU's police-training programmes (EUPOL Afghanistan). The stated goals of the Italian Armed Forces in Afghanistan are 'supporting the local government in carrying out development activities; strengthening the local institutions, in order to make Afghanistan a stable and secure environment, and no longer a safe haven for international terrorism, as well as providing humanitarian assistance to the population'.[25] In the field, Italy's armed forces are involved in the full spectrum of operations, from kinetic and counterinsurgency actions to providing support in stabilization and reconstruction efforts, passing through training and mentoring activities for the Afghan national security forces, both police and military.

Within the ISAF framework, a small number of personnel have been allocated to the Regional Command Capital and to ISAF HQ (both in Kabul), but the bulk of the force is deployed in the western part of the country, where Italy is in charge of Regional Command West (RC-W). Troops and assets are mainly concentrated in the base at Herat (Camp Arena) and in the two forward support bases in Bala Murghab (Badghis province) and Bala Baluk (Farah province).[26]

In the field of police training, Italy is operating in a twofold fashion. On one side, EUPOL Afghanistan is employing small numbers of Carabinieri (gendarmerie) and Guardia di Finanza (financial police) to train personnel from both the Afghan National Police and the Afghan Border Police. On the other, Italian forces are involved in a bilateral initiative with the US Combined Security Transition Command-Afghanistan (CSTC-A) in relation to the formation of the Afghan National Civil Order Police (ANCOP) in Adraskan, Herat province.[27]

Italy is in charge of the Provincial Reconstruction Team (PRT) located in Herat, which has been active since 2005. Officially, the goal of the PRT is to 'assist the Islamic Republic of Afghanistan to extend its authority, in order to facilitate the development of a stable and secure environment in the identified area of operations, and enable security sector reform and reconstruction efforts'.[28] It is commanded by a full colonel from the Italian Army, and its civilian component – made up predominantly of personnel from Cooperazione Italiana – is led by a mid-ranking diplomat.[29] The military CIMIC component implements the so-called quick impact projects (QUIPs) that are meant to deliver rapidly perceivable results and thus promptly generate an acceptable level of trust among the local population, while the civilian component takes care of long-term projects.[30]

Appearances notwithstanding, the PRT is basically a military structure. For one thing, uniformed personnel number close to 200, while the number of civilian technicians is around half a dozen (Senato della Repubblica 2006). For another, since the end of 2009, the civilian component no longer lives side by side with the military (in Camp Vianini), but has instead moved to a structure located outside of the camp. The transfer was justified in terms of alleged 'logistical reasons',[31] but as a matter of fact is due to specific preferences expressed by NGOs seeking to avoid becoming too closely linked to the armed forces – for ideological, security, and public image reasons.[32] In short, the PRT is basically a CIMIC task force, with small injections of civilian personnel from the Ministry of Foreign Affairs and Cooperazione Italiana.[33]

The PRT in Herat had a budget of €5 million for 2011, a figure that has been relatively stable over time (though the initial budget when the PRT began its operations in 2005 was just €2 million).[34] PRT activities are mostly financed with Ministry of Defence money, but small amounts of funding (which are managed through the military administration) are provided by public and private donors and by the Ministry of Foreign Affairs–Cooperazione Italiana complex. As previously noted, funding from the latter cannot be used for projects with potential military implications, which explains why the largest part of the budget is provided by the Ministry of Defence.

Specific objectives notwithstanding, the contracting of local firms and individuals by the PRT is often presented as a good way of building capacities, enhancing Afghan ownership, improving the economy in the region, and more broadly generating conditions for growth and stability. This overall policy seems to be coherent with the opinions of the US and NATO that the insurgency in the western part of Afghanistan consists mainly of disgruntled individuals rather than truly ideologically motivated groups (Osservatorio di Politica Internazionale 2010: 71–80).

Security commercialization and its implications

In compliance with national attitudes toward private force, Italian contracting of security-related tasks in Afghanistan is concentrated around non-core functions. Armed tasks are regularly assigned to uniformed troops, and PMSCs are not hired for the provision of security training. As far as it was possible to investigate, there is no trace of substantial use of armed PMSCs (direct or indirect) for personal or site protection by the Ministry of Foreign Affairs, Cooperazione Italiana, or the Italian Armed Forces. Cases in which Italian troops have received protection from armed contractors are short term, incidental and related to previous agreements made by a different country (mostly the US). One relevant example concerns the defence of ISAF HQ, as the US hired private personnel to carry out that task alongside regular troops. These arrangements remained in place during the brief period of Italian command.[35]

To account for Italian contracting practices and their implications (summarized in Table 10.1), it will be necessary here to introduce the actor in charge of military administration (including logistics, CIMIC, and PRT needs): the Administrative Superintendency Centre (*Centro Amministrativo d'Intendenza Interforze*, CAI-I).[36] This organization's formal contracting procedure is burdensome in terms of time and bureaucratic requirements; for that reason, the full procedure is rarely used in the field, and then only for the largest and longer-term expenses, such as base construction. In its everyday activities, the CAI-I mostly employs a simplified contracting procedure (*acquisizione in economia*: D.M. Difesa 16/03/2006, D.Lgs. 12/04/2006, no. 163), applicable for contracts up to €130,000.[37] This simplified procedure formally requires that no less than five firms be contacted, and that at least three different cost estimates be obtained, but exceptions to the general rule exist (e.g. in situations of urgency or if five competitors for the bid are not available). While such flexibility may be perfectly justifiable in terms of military and contingency needs, it does generate a space that is open to informal – and potentially arbitrary – practices. On one hand, the CAI-I takes centre stage in terms of formulating needs and ways of addressing them, while the reliance on commercial actors – who may choose not to cooperate simply by not submitting their bid for a specific project – also influences the means of implementation available to the armed forces. Also, the autonomous nature of the CAI-I pushes the need for a comprehensive rethinking of contracting practices off the political agenda, with the focus shifting solely to contracts over the €130,000 threshold.

As noted earlier, Italy regards providing local people with jobs as a good way of strengthening stabilization, enhancing local ownership and building capacities.[38] Accordingly, Italian direct contracting (handled through the CAI-I) often

Table 10.1 Summary of main Italian contracting practices in Afghanistan and their impact

---

CAI-I direct contingency contracting (includes contingency maintenance and technical services)
Room for informal practices; relevance of CAI-I in terms of policy formulation and implementation; relevance of commercial actors in terms of implementation.

Local direct contracting (mostly transport services)
Impact on implementation (indirect bribing); consequences on coordination.

Contracted support (mostly direct)
Impact on implementation (efficiency as a criterion for selection; hiring of third-country nationals).

Contracting of armed services by US ally in area under Italian responsibility
Subcontracting of local militias hampers stabilization efforts and Italian credibility; coordination issues.

Contracted security training (indirect): ANCOP programme
Dysfunctional effects on training; possible shifting of priorities by the commercial actor; coordination issues between partner countries.

---

involves Afghan individuals and firms. The former – labelled 'local employed persons' (LEP) – are generic workers, cleaners, or translators employed in military bases. Local personnel are also hired for unarmed guard duty and access control on the most external belt of Italian bases.[39]

Moving one step up in terms of the complexity of tasks, contracts central to civilian-oriented efforts (the building of schools, bridges, wells, etc.) are often assigned to Afghan firms,[40] regardless of whether a given initiative and/or the resources behind it come from the Ministry of Defence, the Ministry of Foreign Affairs or Cooperazione Italiana. Another kind of task often contracted to local commercial actors is transport.[41] Subcontracting is officially regulated and limited (D.Lgs. 12/04/2006, n. 163),[42] but there is another practice that actually makes these externalizations potentially disruptive: bribery. It is well known that civilian contractors, regardless of the tasks they are hired to carry out, will face security problems in performing their jobs, and it is informally accepted that they will have to pay bribes to armed groups or local criminal gangs in order to be able to deliver their services. The general policy is thus to pay a contractor enough to get the service delivered and then to ignore whatever the contracted party would have to do in order to achieve the specified objectives.[43]

This kind of bribery is different from the type exposed by WikiLeaks and frowned upon by the US government – that is, directly paying off hostile forces in order to contain attacks and casualties (Di Feo and Maurizi 2011) – since it is *indirect* and thus not under immediate Italian control. By lengthening the chain of agency and thus reducing the possibility of exercising control, the involvement of commercial actors changes the means available for policy implementation, making accessible means that would otherwise be barred – such as bribery. And, while direct bribery officially ended in 2009, the same ultimately cannot be said for the indirect practice.[44] The potential negative effects are quite obvious, as the receivers of the bribes may be basically anyone, but are probably not actors of good governance. Such practices may also be disruptive in terms of coordination, as contractors may end up paying bribes in areas where other states or agencies are operating.

A number of corporations have been directly contracted by the Italian Armed Forces to provide support services of various kinds. Outsourced tasks include construction and related enhancements (e.g. passive force protection), catering, welfare activities (restaurant and shop management), telecommunications, food shipping, renting of various materials and demining activities. Large firms involved in these tasks are Ciano (Italy), the TN Group (US), and Rais Shipping (UAE).

The Italian firm, Ciano, is mostly praised for its ability to deliver goods in a timely fashion.[45] Besides Italy, the firm has been contracted in Afghanistan by France and the US.[46] The TN Group of Companies is another large commercial reality operating in Afghanistan on behalf of Italian military institutions and several other customers, including the US Department of the Army, ISAF, the Spanish Army, and the NATO Maintenance and Supply Agency (NAMSA). The firm obtained Italian contracts both directly and via a subcontract from Recon International.[47] The Rais Shipping Agency is employed for the rapid supply of groceries, as it can deliver in Kabul within three–five days of receiving an order.[48]

Italy's armed forces do not appear to have shown a preference for contracting Italian firms in Afghanistan, as in some case the role of the latter has been gradually marginalized (e.g. Essegi Forniture Militari). Rais Shipping (a UAE company), on the other hand, has been favoured over Italian alternatives because it is deemed quicker and cheaper and delivers excellent goods. Efficiency seems to be the criterion of selection behind military contracting practices, and while this is perfectly understandable, it also generates a tendency to exclude Afghan firms, which may be cheaper but are unable to keep up with the quality standards of foreign companies.[49] Further, many non-Afghan firms claim to make the largest possible use of local manpower, but it is known that in several cases they prefer to hire cheaper and more reliable Pakistani workers instead.[50] All of this contradicts the core tenets of Italy's stated policy and hampers their implementation by negating chances for improvement of local businesses, capacities, and skills. Similar issues also apply in relation to the indirect externalization of military support (e.g. Italian reliance on Supreme via NAMSA contracting for long-range delivery of goods from Pakistan to Afghanistan).

The defence industry plays a central role in the upkeep of military vehicles and aircraft deployed in Afghanistan. While menial maintenance is handled by uniformed personnel, only civilian staff approved by the manufacturers are allowed to perform more advanced routines and repairs. To carry out these functions, technical teams are regularly sent to Camp Arena.[51] Other contracting practices related to the upkeep of vehicles and materiel are dependent upon the requests made by the military unit in charge of field maintenance (*Gruppo Logistico d'Aderenza*, GSA) to the CAI-I, and thus fall under the set of practices – and their implications – already considered.

Hiring of PMSCs closer to the tip of the spear on the part of Italy's partner countries in Afghanistan is a well-known fact and basically a tolerated practice, even if it could negatively affect coordination. In 2007, the US Air Force Center on Energy and Environment (AFCEE) hired the Environmental Chemical Corporation (ECC) to carry out the construction of the Afghan Air Corps base in Shindand (Herat province), and ECC subcontracted ArmorGroup for site security. This latter company, in turn, decided to rely on local warlords to find the needed personnel (US Senate 2010).

Hiring enemies as guards definitely does not sound like a great idea, and it is certainly dysfunctional in terms of stabilization efforts. The approach was, of course, also contrary to the wishes of the prime principal (the US Air Force), but since it proved difficult for that actor to discover what was taking place quickly enough to take action in response, we might assume that it was even more difficult for the Italian ally – basically just a third party in the matter – to address the issue adequately. Since Italy is in charge of the RC-W and particularly active in the Herat province (where it also leads the PRT), it may have been seen by locals as somewhat responsible for giving jobs, status, and opportunities to militiamen and thus depriving honest Afghans of the same. The paradoxical nature of these developments becomes even clearer when we note that Italy is supporting the multilateral fund for the Disbandment of Illegally Armed Groups (DIAG) and the Counter Narcotics Trust Fund (CNTF).

A similar case – with analogous implications in terms of coordination – concerns the Afghan National Civil Order Police (ANCOP) training programme, jointly run by Italy and the US and meant to strengthen Afghan state police capabilities. In 2008, the US Combined Security Transition Command-Afghanistan (CSTC-A) awarded the contract for guarding the ANCOP training centre just built in Adraskan (around 80 kilometres south of Herat) to EOD Technology (EODT). Like ArmorGroup in Shindand, EODT decided to turn to local strongmen for its personnel needs (US Senate 2010).

Once again, Italy was practically ignorant of the policy of subcontracting to militias enacted by the commercial actor. However, locals may have perceived Italian responsibilities as even deeper in this case, as Italy is an explicit partner of the US in the running of the ANCOP training programme. An analogy could be traced between the indirect bribery practice informally accepted by Italy in relation to its contractors and the militia-hiring policy enacted by ArmorGroup and EODT, as both strategies were seen as ways of buying off potential threats. However, while in the first case armed groups are kept at a distance by money, in the second they are actually hired, which puts them in a position that can enhance the level of danger they represent – even if simply by providing them with access to information about Coalition activities.

How Italy and the US share the burden in the ANCOP programme is also quite revealing of different national lexica. Half of the training cycle is run by the Carabinieri, a corps that lies close to the heart of the Italian state and is deeply involved in the fight against organized crime, while the other half is run by US-contracted private personnel (Ministero degli Affari Esteri 2009). The appropriateness of using private instructors as trainers for a job that may demand considerable self-sacrifice may be questioned, as their preference for immediate economic reward is obvious. Also, showing to recruits that a private security sector not only exists but is also an accepted and viable way of making a living may generate incentives for some of them to leave state service in favour of a private career. All of this can be – quite obviously – disruptive of efforts at police capacity building. In terms of implementation, the commercial actor may also have the chance to shift training priorities in a context were coordination between Italy and the US is complicated by the chain of agency on the US side.

Conclusions: keeping or selling stocks?

Italian commercialization practices in Afghanistan corroborate the thesis about shifts in the national lexicon: while the space allowed to commercial actors remains somewhat limited, it is growing; and even if Italian officers sometimes display a degree of mistrust toward PMSCs contracted by allied countries,[52] the practice is basically accepted.

As has been shown, the impact of commercialization may have a negative effect upon stabilization efforts in terms of their formulation, implementation, and coordination. Yet, the concentration of contracted tasks in areas not perceived as sensitive makes it possible to keep the involvement of commercial actors out of the public eye and away from national political debate, thus sheltering it from the automatic rejection typically associated with privatization of security-related services. However – as the Aegis case demonstrated – if the situation is thought to demand it and the level of public awareness is low, the role of commercial actors may be escalated to levels normally considered unacceptable. In Iraq, the hiring of Aegis provided Italian decision makers with a quick exit strategy, and while it is not a foregone conclusion that something similar will happen in Afghanistan (or anywhere else), such a possibility ultimately cannot be excluded.

Contracting in relation to military support, logistics, and material maintenance makes the Italian effort in Afghanistan easier to sustain, both on military (quantity of deployed assets, operational flexibility, welfare and morale of the troops, etc.) and on political grounds (smaller number of uniformed men mobilized, proportional reduction of casualties, etc.). These effects are amplified by the complementary practice of indirect bribing, something that shifts the responsibility to corrupt over to the contracted party, and yet lowers the need for deployed manpower and reduces the risks on the side of the principal. In other words, the recourse to formal or informal economic practices acts as a legitimizing strategy, especially when linked to efforts at reconstruction and local development, which are indispensable for maintaining an image of the engagement that is palatable to domestic public opinion.

Since most of these elements are off-radar in terms of national awareness, the stimulus for a comprehensive rethinking of the role that commercial actors and practices should play – and thus for the creation of a general and coherent policy (Leander 2007) – is substantially absent. In many ways, Italy's national lexicon is still standing its ground only formally, while being eroded by informal practices, changes pushed by contingencies, and a general '*ad hoc*' attitude. While this is understandable (and somewhat unavoidable) in the short term, might it not also express an Italian preference to sell security stocks instead of keeping them?

Notes

1 This is explicitly stated in Italian laws. See Article 52 of the Constitution of the Italian Republic and Articles 244 and 288 of the Italian Penal Code.
2 Constitution of the Italian Republic, Article 11.
3 Statistics from the SIPRI Military Expenditure Database. Figures for 2009 are estimates.
4 Based on a royal decree dated 1932 (R.D. 16/05/1932, n. 819) and refurbished in 1997 (D.Lgs. 30/12/1997, n. 490). Subsequent adaptations are D.M. Difesa 15/11/2004 and D.Lgs. 15/03/2010, n. 66.
5 See the speech by Undersecretary of Defence Guido Crosetto (2010) at Tor Vergata University, Rome. See also L. 23/12/2009, n. 191, Art. 2, paras 27–36.
6 The bulletins published from 2008 to 2011 by FLP Difesa, an organization for defence civil servants, provides a comprehensive report of the political struggle surrounding the establishment of Difesa Servizi (FLP Difesa 2008a, 2008b, 2008c, 2008d, 2009a, 2009b, 2009c, 2011a, 2011b, 2011c; see especially the 2008 bulletins numbers 137, 149, 152, and 167, the 2009 bulletins numbers 33, 39, and 136, and the 2011 bulletins numbers 22, 29, and 41). On the sensitivity of the topic, see Cadalanu (2010) and the TV debate 'L'inchiesta' (Torrealta 2010).
7 Vincenzo Camporini (at the time defence chief of staff) stated the same in a TV debate (see Torrealta 2010).
8 See *La Repubblica* (2008) and *Corriere del Mezzogiorno* (2010).
9 Before being shot, Quattrocchi said, 'I will show you how an Italian dies'. For this reason, he was awarded posthumously the Gold Medal for Civic Value (Medaglia d'Oro al Valore Civile), one of the highest honours for non-military personnel (Presidenza della Repubblica 2006). Huge controversy surrounded the award; see *Il Tempo* (2006) and *La Repubblica* (2006).
10 See the news section of the SCG website.
11 See ANSA (2011), Gaiani (2010), *Il Corriere della Sera* (2011), Senato della Repubblica (2011), and the websites of Confitarma, Federpesca and Sindacato dei Marittimi (Union of Maritime Workers). For a comprehensive overview of this process, see Ronzitti (2011).
12 See the Ciano Group website.
13 See the Essegi Forniture Militari website.
14 Interview with major, chief of logistics in Afghanistan, Turin, 25 January 2012.
15 The Italian Parliament approved an appropriation of about €3.5 million for this task.
16 At the time, the Italian government's hiring of Aegis received incredibly little media coverage, the exceptions being primarily the financial newspaper *Il Sole 24 Ore* and the left-wing *Il Manifesto*.
17 Five questions were raised in parliament: on 28 March, 16 April, 2 May, 4 June, and 13 June 2007 (Parliamentary interrogations 2007a, 2007b, 2007c, 2007d, and 2007e).
18 E.g. anti-insurgency activities conducted by Italian troops in Afghanistan, also reported by WikiLeaks (Di Feo and Maurizi 2010).
19 See Stato Maggiore della Difesa (2011). Similar definitions have been provided in the course of many public speeches by military officers (Fantastico 2011; Ruggiero 2010).
20 See Ruggiero (2010) and the websites of both the Ministry of Defence and the Italian Army.

21 See Viciani (2011). This is also evident in the figures from the Organization for Security and Co-operation in Europe (OCSE) provided on the Cooperazione Italiana website.
22 L. 26/02/1987, no. 49; D.P.R. 12/04/1988, no. 177; Senato della Repubblica (2006); Ministero degli Affari Esteri (2009); and the website of Cooperazione Italiana.
23 A complete list of the supported programmes is available at the website of Cooperazione Italiana. See in particular the page dedicated to Afghanistan.
24 The figures for Italian and French deployed troops are often very close, and the actual ranking depends on the inclusion or exclusion of non-ISAF activities in the count.
25 See the website of the Ministry of Defence website.
26 Ministero degli Affari Esteri (2009); see also the websites of ISAF and the Italian Ministry of Defence.
27 Bindi (2009); Ministero degli Affari Esteri (2009); Ministry of Defence website.
28 See the website of PRT Herat.
29 Similar definitions can be found in other sources. See, for example, Ministero degli Affari Esteri (2009); Fantastico (2011); and the websites of the Ministry of Defence, the Multinational CIMIC Group and the Italian PRT in Herat.
30 See the website of the Multinational CIMIC Group.
31 See the website of the Multinational CIMIC Group.
32 Interviews with captain, former ISAF counter-intelligence analyst in Afghanistan, Turin, June 2011–January 2012.
33 Interview with lieutenant, former chief of acquisitions in Afghanistan, Turin, 10 June 2011.
34 Sky News (2011); see also the websites of the Ministry of Defence and PRT Herat.
35 Interviews with captain, former ISAF counter-intelligence analyst in Afghanistan, Turin, June 2011–January 2012.
36 Information on the CAI (and its Herat incarnation) has mainly been gathered through interview (interview with a lieutenant, former chief of acquisitions in Afghanistan, Turin, 10 June 2011). Further information is available at the Ministry of Defence website.
37 The law also states that exceptions to the general rule are possible, and in specific circumstances expenses larger than €130,000 may also be contracted through the simplified procedure. However, this does require approval from a military authority above the CAI-I command.
38 This has been also officially confirmed by Italian officers in key positions: CAI-I commander (Col. Parrella) interview (Quaderno.it 2011) and PRT commander (Col. Pomella) interview (Sky News 2011). See also Avionews (2011).
39 Interviews with captain, former ISAF counter-intelligence analyst in Afghanistan, Turin, June 2011–January 2012; interview with lieutenant, former chief of acquisitions in Afghanistan, Turin, 10 June 2011.
40 Sky News (2011); see also websites of the Ministry of Defence and the Mountain Troops Command.
41 Interviews with captain, former ISAF counter-intelligence analyst in Afghanistan, Turin, June 2011–January 2012; see also Ministry of Defence website.
42 A PRT commander (Col. Pomella) explicitly recalled the importance of adhering to these limits and regulations during a public interview (Sky News 2011).
43 On the other hand, when civilian personnel from Cooperazione Italiana are deployed in the field, they are protected by Italian troops.
44 Interviews with captain, former ISAF counter-intelligence analyst in Afghanistan, Turin, June 2011–January 2012.
45 Interview with lieutenant, former chief of.acquisitions in Afghanistan, Turin, 10 June 2011.
46 See the Ciano Group website.
47 Interview with lieutenant, former chief of acquisitions in Afghanistan, Turin, 10 June 2011; see also TN Group website at http://tn-grp.com (accessed 15 September 2011).

48 Interview with lieutenant, former chief of acquisitions in Afghanistan, Turin, 10 June 2011.
49 Interview with lieutenant, former chief of acquisitions in Afghanistan, Turin, 10 June 2011.
50 Interviews with captain, former ISAF counter-intelligence analyst in Afghanistan, Turin, June 2011–January 2012.
51 Interview with major, chief of logistics in Afghanistan, Turin, 25 January 2012.
52 I have been able to personally observe this general attitude in the course of several lectures I have given in educational and training institutions of the Italian army since 2006.

References

Books, chapters, and journal articles

Avant, Deborah and Lee Sigelman. 2010. 'Private Security and Democracy: Lessons from the US in Iraq', *Security Studies* 19 (2): 230–265.
Barberis, Walter. 1988. *Le armi del principe: La tradizione militare sabauda*. Torino: Einaudi.
Bonvicini, Gianni and Alessandro Colombo. 2010. *La politica estera dell'Italia*. Bologna: Il Mulino.
——2011. *La politica estera dell'Italia*. Bologna: Il Mulino.
Coralluzzo, Valter. 2000. *La politica estera dell'Italia repubblicana, 1946–1992: Modello di analisi e studi di caso*. Milano: Franco Angeli.
Dalla Porta, Donatella, ed. 1984. *Terrorismi in Italia*. Bologna: Il Mulino.
——1990. *Il terrorismo di sinistra*. Bologna: Il Mulino.
Ginsborg, Paul. 1989. *Storia d'Italia dal dopoguerra a oggi: Società e politica 1943–1988*. Torino: Einaudi.
Krahmann, Elke. 2010. *States, Citizens and the Privatization of Security*. Cambridge and New York: Cambridge University Press.
Leander, Anna. 2006. *Eroding State Authority? Private Military Companies and the Legitimate Use of Force*. Roma: Centro Militare di Studi Strategici.
——2007. 'Regulating the Role of Private Military Companies in Shaping Security and Politics'. In *From Mercenaries to Market: The Rise and Regulation of Private Military Companies*, edited by Simon Chesterman and Chia Lehnardt, 49–64. Oxford and New York: Oxford University Press.
Lupo, Salvatore. 2004. *Storia della mafia, dalle origini ai giorni nostri*. Roma: Donzelli.
Ruzza, Stefano. 2008. 'Democrazia e privatizzazione della guerra: elementi per un'analisi'. in *Democrazie tra terrorismo e guerra*, edited by Valter Coralluzzo, 203–232. Milano: Guerini.
——2010. *Combattere: I dilemmi delle democrazie*. Roma and Acireale: Bonanno.
——2011. *Guerre conto terzi: Aziende di sicurezza e privatizzazione della funzione militare*. Bologna: Il Mulino.
Santarelli, Enzo. 1996. *Storia critica della Repubblica: L'Italia dal 1945 al 1994*. Milano: Feltrinelli.
Sciarrone, Rocco. 2009. *Mafie vecchie, mafie nuove: Radicamento ed espansione*. Roma: Donzelli.
Singer, Peter. 2003. *Corporate Warriors: The Rise of the Privatized Military Industry*. Ithaca, NY: Cornell University Press.

Laws and legislation

R.D. 16/05/1932, n. 819, Approvazione del testo unico delle disposizioni legislative riguardanti gli ufficiali di complemento della Regia Marina.

D.P.R. 14/02/1964, n. 237, Leva e reclutamento obbligatorio nell'Esercito, nella Marina e nell'Aeronautica.

L. 26/02/1987, n. 49, Nuova disciplina della cooperazione dell'Italia con i Paesi in Via di Sviluppo.

D.P.R. 12/04/1988, n. 177, Approvazione del regolamento di esecuzione della legge 26 febbraio 1987, n. 49, sulla disciplina della cooperazione dell'Italia con i Paesi in Via di Sviluppo.

D.Lgs. 30/12/1997, n. 490, Riordino del reclutamento, dello stato giuridico e dell'avanzamento degli ufficiali, a norma dell'articolo 1, comma 97, della legge 23 dicembre 1996, n. 662.

L. 14/11/2000, n. 331, Norme per l'istituzione del servizio militare professionale.

L. 23/08/2004, n. 226, Sospensione anticipate del servizio obbligatorio di leva e disciplina dei volontari di truppa in ferma prefissata, nonché delega al Governo per il conseguente coordinamento con la normativa di settore.

D.M. Difesa 15/11/2004, Ferme e requisiti fisici e attitudinali degli ufficiali delle Forze di Complemento e procedura per la nomina a ufficiale di complemento.

D.P.R. 21/02/2006 n. 167, Regolamento per l'amministrazione e la contabilità degli organismi della Difesa a norma dell'articolo 7, comma 1, della legge 14 novembre 2000, n. 331.

D.M. Difesa 16/03/2006, Modalità e procedure per l'acquisizione in economia di beni e servizi da parte di organismi dell'Amministrazione della Difesa.

D.Lgs. 12/04/2006, n. 163, Codice dei contratti pubblici relativi a lavori, servizi e forniture in attuazione delle direttive 2004/17/CE e 2004/18/CE.

L. 23/12/2009, n. 191, Disposizioni per la formazione del bilancio annuale e pluriennale dello Stato (legge finanziaria 2010).

D.Lgs. 15/03/2010, n. 66, Codice dell'ordinamento militare.

D.L. 07/07/2011, CdM n. 145, Proroga degli interventi di cooperazione allo sviluppo e a sostegno dei processi di pace e stabilizzazione, nonché delle missioni internazionali delle Forze armate e di polizia e disposizioni per l'attuazione delle Risoluzioni 1970 (2011) e 1973 (2011) adottate dal Consiglio di Sicurezza delle Nazioni Unite. Misure urgenti antipirateria.

L. 01/08/2011, n. 130, Cooperazione allo sviluppo e a sostegno dei processi di pace e di stabilizzazione, missioni internazionali e misure urgenti antipirateria.

Official statements and documents

Crosetto, Guido. 2010. 'La natura e le finalità di Difesa Servizi S.p.A'. Rome: Tor Vergata University [Speech by the Undersecretary of Defence on Difesa Servizi].

Fantastico, Antonio. 2011. 'Come cambia la funzione militare nei nuovi scenari di sicurezza'. Turin: Biennale Democrazia [Speech by an Army Colonel (Post-Conflict Operations Study Centre) on military transformation].

FLP Difesa. 2008a. 'Notiziario n. 137'. 29 October.
———2008b. 'Notiziario n. 149'. 19 November.
———2008c. 'Notiziario n. 152'. 24 November.
———2008d. 'Notiziario n. 167'. 19 December.
———2009a. 'Notiziario n. 33'. 9 March.
———2009b. 'Notiziario n. 39'. 19 March.
———2009c. 'Notiziario n. 136'. 2 November.
———2011a. 'Notiziario n. 22'. 18 February.
———2011b. 'Notiziario n. 29'. 4 March.

——2011c. 'Notiziario n. 41'. 31 March [Union of Defence civil servants bulletins].
Ministero degli Affari Esteri. 2009. 'Italia in Afghanistan'. Rome [Ministry of Foreign Affairs report: 'Italian activities in Afghanistan'].
——2010. 'La cooperazione italiana allo sviluppo nel triennio 2010–2013: Linee-guida e indirizzi di programmazione'. Rome [Ministry of Foreign Affairs report: 'Italian development cooperation 2010–2013'].
Ministero della Difesa. 2002. 'Libro Bianco'. Rome [Ministry of Defence White Paper].
——2011. 'Comunicato – Approvazione dello statuto della società "Difesa servizi SpA"'. Gazzetta Ufficiale (serie generale) n. 39, 17 February [Ministry of Defence Communiqué: 'Approval of Difesa Servizi statute'].
Osservatorio di Politica Internazionale (Senato della Repubblica, Camera dei deputati, Ministero degli Affari Esteri). 2010. 'Le missioni internazionali'. Rome [Parliament and Ministry of Foreign Affairs joint report: 'Italian International missions'].
Parliamentary interrogations. 2007a. 'Interrogazione a risposta scritta: 4/03113'. Elettra, Deiana. 28 March.
——2007b. 'Interrogazione a risposta scritta: 4/03280'. Galante, Severino. 16 April.
——2007c. 'Interrogazione a risposta scritta: 4/01810'. Bulgarelli, Mauro. 2 May.
——2007d. 'Interrogazione a risposta in commissione: 5/01095'. Mancuso, Gianni. 4 June.
——2007e. 'Interrogazione a risposta orale: 3/00738'. Martone, Francesco. 13 June.
Presidenza della Repubblica. 2006. 'Dettaglio decorato: Quattrocchi Sig. Fabrizio, Medaglia d'oro al valor civile'. 13 March [President of the Republic: 'Gold Medal for Civic Value to Fabrizio Quattrocchi'].
Ruggiero, Mario. 2010. 'Military support al 'Comprehensive approach'', Centre for Defense Innovation: Rome [Speech by an Army Brigadier General, Army (Defence Staff) on the comprehensive approach].
Senato della Repubblica, Servizio Studi. 2006. 'Afghanistan, un'economia di guerra'. Dossier n. 57. Rome [Senate report: 'Afghanistan: a war economy'].
——4ᵃ Commissione Permanente. 2011. 'Resoconto sommario n. 218'. 22 June. Rome [Summary of Senate activities].
Stato Maggiore della Difesa, III Reparto, Centro Innovazione della Difesa. 2011. 'La dottrina militare italiana'. PID/S-1. Rome [Italian military doctrine].
US Senate, Report together with additional views of the Committee on Armed Services. 2010. 'Inquiry on the Role and Oversight of Private Security Contractors in Afghanistan'. Washington, DC. 28 September.

News reports and op-eds

ANSA. 2011. 'Pirateria: La Russa, su navi no soldati ma vigilantes'. 8 February.
Avionews. 2011. 'Cambio al vertice del Centro Amministrativo di Herat: Intensa l'attività di stimolo allo sviluppo economico della regione'. 9 February. www.avionews.it/index. php?corpo=see_news_home.php&news_id=1125646&pagina_chiamante=index.php (accessed 15 September 2011).
Bindi, Federiga. 2009. 'L'Europa alla prova anche in Afghanistan'. *Affari Internazionali*, 18 May. www.affarinternazionali.it/articolo.asp?ID=1137 (accessed 15 September 2011).
Cadalanu, Giampaolo. 2010. 'Difesa spa, una nuova agenzia per il business delle spese militari'. *La Repubblica*, 1 February.
Corriere della Sera, 2011. 'Via libera all''affitto' di militari italiani su navi private in funzione antipirateria'. 13 July.
Corriere del Mezzogiorno. 2010. 'Ex ostaggi in Iraq, assolti Stefio e Spinelli'. 16 July.

Di Feo, Gianluca and Stefania Maurizi. 2010. 'Afghanistan, ecco la verità'. *L'Espresso*, 15 October.
——2011. 'Tangenti italiane ai talebani'. *L'Espresso*, 12 August.
Gaiani, Gianandrea. 2010. 'Guardie armate contro i pirati sui mercantili'. *Panorama*, 15 June.
Il Tempo. 2006. 'Medaglia d'oro a Quattrocchi. È polemica'. 21 March.
La Repubblica. 2006. 'Sgrena polemica su medaglia Quattrocchi: 'Non la meritava, era un mercenario''. 22 March.
——2008. 'Ostaggi italiani in Iraq. Stefio rinviato a giudizio'. 18 April.
Quaderno.it. 2011. 'Centro Amministrativo di Herat in Afghanistan: il sannita Parrella al comando'. 10 February. www.ilquaderno.it/centro-amministrativo-herat-afghanistan-sannita-parrella-comando-55543.html (accessed 15 September 2011).
Ronzitti, Natalino. 2011. 'Scorte armate contro la pirateria'. *Affari Internazionali*, 4 July. www.affarinternazionali.it/articolo.asp?ID=1804 (accessed 15 September 2011).
Sky News. 2011. 'Nel PRT di Herat, la 'casa' italiana colpita dai Talebani'. 30 May. http://tg24.sky.it/tg24/mondo/2011/05/30/afghanistan_herat_italiani_attentato_prt_attivita.html (accessed 15 September 2011).
Torrealta, Maurizio. 2010. 'Intervista a Difesa-Servizi Spa'. *L'inchiesta*, RaiNews24. 18 January. www.rainews24.rai.it/it/canale-tv.php?id=18051 (accessed 15 September 2011).
Viciani, Iacopo. 2011. 'La cooperazione italiana finisce 'fuori classe''. *Affari Internazionali*, 29 September. www.affarinternazionali.it/articolo.asp?ID=1869 (accessed 15 September 2011).

Websites

Ambasciata d'Italia a Kabul, www.ambkabul.esteri.it/Ambasciata_Kabul. (accessed 15 September 2011) [Italian embassy in Kabul].
Camera dei Deputati, www.camera.it. (accessed 15 September 2011) [House of Representatives].
——Banche dati professionali, http://banchedati.camera.it/testi/home_inter.htm. (accessed 15 September 2011) [House of Representatives databanks].
Ciano Group, www.cianogroup.it (accessed 15 September 2011).
Comando Truppe Alpine, www.truppealpine.eu (accessed 15 September 2011) [Mountain Troops Command].
Confitarma, www.confitarma.it (accessed 15 September 2011) [Federation of Shipowners].
Cooperazione Italiana, www.cooperazioneallosviluppo.esteri.it (accessed 15 September 2011) [Italian Development Cooperation Agency].
Esercito Italiano, http://esercito.difesa.it (accessed 15 September 2011) [Italian Army].
Essegi Forniture Militari srl, www.essegiit.com (accessed 15 September 2011).
EUPOL Afghanistan, www.eupol-afg.eu (accessed 15 September 2011).
Federpesca, www.federpesca.net (accessed 15 September 2011) [Federation of Fishing Enterprises].
International Security Assistance Force (ISAF), www.isaf.nato.int (accessed 15 September 2011).
Italian Provincial Reconstruction Team – Herat, www.prtherat.altervista.org (accessed 15 September 2011).
Ministero della Difesa, www.difesa.it (accessed 15 September 2011) [Ministry of Defence].
Multinational CIMIC Group, www.mncimicgroup.org (accessed 15 September 2011).
North Atlantic Treaty Organization (NATO), www.nato.int (accessed 15 September 2011).

Rais Shipping Agency, http://uae-shipping.net/Rais-Shipping-Agency.html (accessed 15 September 2011).

Security Consulting Group, www.securitycg.com (accessed 15 September 2011).

Sindacato dei Marittimi, www.sindacatomarittimi.eu (accessed 15 September 2011) [Union of Maritime Workers].

SIPRI Military Expenditure Database, http://milexdata.sipri.org (accessed 15 September 2011).

TN Group of Companies, http://tn-grp.com (accessed 15 September 2011).

United Nations Assistance Mission in Afghanistan (UNAMA), http://unama.unmissions.org (accessed 15 September 2011).

Wikileaks, www.wikileaks.org (accessed 15 September 2011).

11 Conclusion

Anna Leander and Christopher Spearin

Time has come to conclude this effort and to take stock of security commercialization in Europe. While the chapters have confirmed beyond a doubt the intuition from which this volume departed, namely that commercialization is not a distant future but an actual present in Europe, they do not depict *a* European model of security commercialization in the singular. Quite on the contrary, the approaches to commercialization and issues raised vary considerably across the chapters. These variations express the obvious, but too frequently neglected, fact that context really does matter and that there are profound differences between the countries covered in this volume; a core motivation indeed for undertaking this project. Nevertheless, having spent the entire volume making the plurality and variation of commercialization in Europe visible, we want to use these final pages to pull out some commonalities. We do this by putting words on the core characteristics of European security commercializations while hinting at the nuances that must be kept in mind. Since the common European features stand out most strongly when viewed from elsewhere, we sharpen the European characterization by contextualizing in relation to the US experience.

We organize this characterization/contextualization around the three pillars structuring the volume: national contexts, contracting practices and political consequences for military operations (see Figure 1.1 in the introduction). We therefore look first at the *national contexts*, suggesting that while the reliance on PMSCs points in the direction of a change, possibly Americanization, of the European 'ways of war', this is largely obfuscated by the persistent reluctance to openly discuss – let alone publicly embrace – security commercialization. Second, we underline that contrary to the US, where contracting practices frequently involve rather straightforward and well-documented contracting of companies by the public, European countries deemphasize and hesitate to document the private aspect of their *contracting practices*, which consequently often take complex hybrid (public/private) forms. Finally, we suggest that commercialization plays an important role shaping not only US but also European *operations* in international conflict zones as exemplified by Afghanistan. Commercialization refashions the politics of military operations by shifting priorities and ways of engaging with the local context while at the same time making accountability difficult to impose. However, by contrast to the US, Europeans do not analyze let alone debate these implications of commercialization; they are correspondingly less capable of

Table 11.1 Contrasting military contracting in Europe and in the US

	Europe	US
National context	Obfuscated	Publicly embraced and criticized
	No information provided	Ample information available
Contracting practices	Indirect and hybrid	Direct
	Technocractic, pragmatic justification	Political debate about justification
	Limited innovation and development of control and management mechanisms	Extensive adjustments and innovation to introduce new control and management mechanisms
Politics of military operations	Unacknowledged role of contractors	Acknowledged role of contracting
	Limited use in support of national policies	Extensive use in support of national policies
	Ambivalence about use of contracting for imprint	

ensuring that commercial arrangements are to their advantage. (These arguments are summarized in Table 11.1.) Since, as suggested at this chapter's close, security commercialization in Europe is likely to continue, more awareness and public debate about it is most warranted.

National contexts: obfuscating changes in the 'way of war'

With the onset of the Cold War and the decline of colonial engagement, European governments mostly took a restrained and reserved approach towards how and when they employed the military, an approach that reverberates still. Conscription/mandatory service requirements supported the training of personnel to serve immediate (i.e., territorial) national defense requirements rather than to be sent on expeditionary operations. Today, when European states do apply their militaries extraterritorially, they frequently insist on the benign characteristics of their intervention as currently reflected in the insistence on 'peace and reconciliation'.

As the chapters demonstrate, privatization in the European context has shaken these stances and facilitated change. With conscription ending or being very restrictively used, security commercialization allows both for force professionalization and for covering manpower gaps. This, in turn, reduces the territorial defense imperative and facilitates the move towards the more expansive mindset of expeditionary operations. Security commercialization, in other words, adds a sharper edge to the European approach to International Military Operations (IMO), bringing it closer to the American approach to IMO. However, this change is largely obfuscated as it sits uneasily in the national contexts.

Approaching the American way of war?

The US is much more prone to a ready and expansive application of military force and to behave as 'a zealous bearer of mankind's best intentions' (Rockman

2005: 33). Some tie this to the lack of foreign war on US soil since the War of 1812. Others link it to the reliance on voluntary professionals (except in the period 1948–72 and, even then, drafted personnel were used in a robust manner unlike in the European case). Finally, this approach to war is sometimes anchored in the American faith in technology (Hacker and Vining 2006). The overall outcome is what commentators dub the 'American Way of War' (e.g., Weigley 1973; Mahnken 2003; Boot 2003; Record 2002), which they contend, in its current form, features speed and focused firepower applied jointly by lighter and smaller forces that minimize casualties on all sides. The reliance on a more diversified range of forces – such as special and indigenous forces – is integral to this way of war.

This 'way of war' dovetails with the liberal traditions that have a strong hold on US political imaginaries and can be mobilized to give security commercialization positive connotations. Indeed, post-Second World War US presidencies drawn from both political parties have embraced privatization. Republican President Eisenhower introduced public–private competitions during the 1950s and in 1966, under Democratic President Lyndon Johnson, the US government codified this competition through the Office of Management and Budget Circular A-76. The presidencies of Ronald Reagan, Bill Clinton and George W. Bush gave further impetus to the A-76 process and its guiding assumptions that (i) 'in the process of governing, the Government should not compete with its citizens' and that (ii) market actors are more responsive and economically efficient than government actors (CRS 2007; Markusen 2003: 480; Carreau 2008).

The hold of these liberal assumptions is so strong that the current string of scandals and evidence of the economic waste linked to military contracting are interpreted as an indication that better public management is needed. Hence, in the 2010 Quadrennial Defense Review intended to introduce cautions regarding privatization, the role of companies in the 'total defense workforce' is nowhere questioned. Instead, the emphasis is on the need for increased and especially improved government oversight and management. The possibilities of either developing state competencies for activities done privately or for returning them to the state are not even raised (Ettinger 2011: 756–760). Similarly, while the 2011 Commission on Wartime Contracting recommends that some privately performed activities should be phased out – including convoy and static protection – military commanders may continue contracting if they deem that the risks they are exposed to make this warranted (CWC 2011: 61). What is more, just as the Defense Review, the CWC assesses that the United States is over-reliant on contractors, not with reference to what should be in state hands, but because 'the heavy reliance on contractors has overwhelmed the government's ability to conduct proper planning, management, and oversight of the contingency-contracting function' (CWC 2011: 3). Government must catch up with commercialization; it is not expected to (re)claim commercially performed tasks.

Obfuscating change

The chapters in this book show that Continental Europe is creating more space for commercial actors and in the process is moving closer not only to the more liberal, market-oriented approach of the US, but also to the more robust and expeditionary sides of the American way of war. The most striking aspect of this change is that it is passing largely unnoticed. If it is debated at all, it is as a question of efficiency and effectiveness, not as a change in the way the use of force is dealt with.

The silence has roots in the uneasy fit between security commercialization and existing European regulatory frameworks, historical practices and national lexica for dealing with the use of force; the friction between security commercialization and European national contexts. In her chapter on Germany for example, Krahmann shows the pivotal role of the notion of 'civilian power' in shaping self-understandings, practices and institutions since the Second World War. The chapter on Poland underscores the role of the military as a carrier of the national heritage combined with a reluctance to privatize core state functions nationalized under communism to highlight the hesitation to commercialize the military. In Norway, Østensen suggests that the intertwining of the nation-building role of the armed forces with domestic social policy and Norwegian military culture has created a dual approach to PMSCs: strict at home but hands-off abroad. Even if the reasons the national contexts militate against commercialization thus vary widely, they share one aspect: they make security commercialization seem suspect, illegitimate or verging on illegality.

The consequence is an obfuscation of the security commercialization process in all European countries. Obviously, insiders are well aware of the ongoing contracting processes as documented in the chapters above, but they are reluctant to provide information, let alone engage in public debate. The difficulty of gathering information both in the form of statistics and interviews shines through to an unexpected degree. Berndtsson and Stern describe how their requests for interviews and documentation are shuffled from one person and desk to the next as Swedish experts refuse to answer questions, let alone take responsibility for the policies. The silence is even more pronounced in the public sphere. As Olsson explains with regards to the French public position on military commercialization, 'there is no such stance'. In fact, this book amply documents that when policy makers and administrators are pushed to take a stance, they return to a 'safe space', underscoring that they do not allow outsourcing of military activities without specifying what is meant by this and/or how it relates to commercialization. As Pop shows for Romania, while the troops 'import into Afghanistan the kind of relationship that the army has with private suppliers in the domestic context', there is scarce documentation of – let alone debate about – the security commercialization entailed in this move. A generous interpretation is that it is unintended; that European military experts and policy makers fail to see that their own contracting (and not only contracting by the US) is a form of security commercialization. A less generous interpretation would be that the silence is a political strategy.

The obfuscation of security commercialization in Europe removes it from the political agenda. Thus, Mandrup's comments on the Danish case are germane to this book as a whole: there is 'very limited political debate' and this is in a context in which Mandrup suggests military experts are interested in 'not *if* but *how*' to increase the military reliance on markets. The absence of broader discussion is underpinned by permissive institutional regulations. As Varga explains, in Hungary the role of the Defence Committee of the National Assembly in approving military contracting has remained a formality. If and when commercialization does appear in public debate, it is usually for reasons other than the issues raised for the governance of the use of force. For example, in Italy as Ruzza shows, the creation of a state-owned commercial venture, Difesa Servizi, paves the way for a perfectly legal acquisition of 'technical services' entirely out of reach of parliamentary control. However, when this is publicly debated, it is not because of its implications for the governance of the use of force but because of the possibly corrupt practices this facilitates. This possibility is certainly a very real one. However, the exclusive focus on it deepens the misrecognition of the extent to which constructions, such as Difesa Serivizi, *also* signal a profound reorganization of the governance of the use of force.

Contracting practices: hybrid forms with long-term implications

The obfuscation of commercialization in Europe is directly related to the hybrid form of contracting practices. European security commercializations are organized in ways reproducing the illusion that the governance of the use of force is unaltered. The state usually remains present in the market as a token guarantee that the governance of the use of force remains unaltered. The resulting hybridity reproduces the impression that contracting is little more than a practical solution used by states to promote their interests. By the same token, hybridity distracts attention from the ways commercialization – even when hybrid – have long-term implications for governance of the use of force nationally and internationally. The overall consequence is that public debate appears unnecessary and demands for more information are seemingly unwarranted. This predominantly hybrid form of contracting contrasts with US contracting, which is mostly openly pursued, debated and about which considerable information is consequently publicly available. However, there can be little doubt that the US and European situations are similar in the sense that commercialization (hybrid or not) has long-term implications for the governance of the use of force.

US contracting in Afghanistan

US contracting has been openly declared and publicly debated. As a consequence, the security commercialization is relatively well documented. This is illustrated by the US contracting for its engagement in Afghanistan where the United States contracts unarmed and armed personnel across the multiple pillars that form the whole of government efforts in Afghanistan. We will give an idea of this strategy below by discussing contracting by the Department of Defense (DoD) and Department of State (DoS).

The DoD utilizes contractors in its multi-billion Euro 'Logistics Civil Augmentation Program (LOGCAP)' designed to supply US personnel with logistical support (e.g., maintenance, laundry, housing, food services, fuel services, water services, electrical services, waste management). From 2001 to 2007, KBR held the contract, but due to qualitative and billing criticism and the perceived need for greater competition, DoD recast LOGCAP by allowing two other firms – Fluor Corporation and DynCorp – to bid for LOGCAP contracts. Another prominent logistical contract is the €1.7 billion Host Nation Trucking (HNT) contract that facilitates the delivery of 90 percent of the supplies for US forces in Afghanistan. While the eight companies that service the contract are based either in Afghanistan, the United States or the Middle East, the bulk of the employees are Afghans. Finally, over the course of the Afghan mission, the DoD has employed smaller firms, like Presidential Airways, formerly owned by Blackwater, for the intra-theatre aerial transportation of personnel and supplies. As for armed PMSC personnel working for DoD clients, there are a number of examples. At times, firms provide close protection services for senior DoD personnel. As well, the security of Forward Operating Bases (FOBs) is contracted, so lower ranking officers and enlisted personnel rely upon PMSCs too. Additionally, for the HNT contract, the eight trucking firms subcontract their own security to Afghan PMSCs. The DoD also relies upon privately supplied training for Afghan operations. In some cases, this training is for US personnel. Cubic Applications, for example, train US advisors before they travel to Afghanistan to then train Afghan security forces.

Turning to the DoS, it has employed PMSCs in five prominent areas. First, while initially Afghan President Hamid Karzai relied upon US special forces personnel for his protection once he came to power, this task became the responsibility of DoS' Diplomatic Security Service in October 2002. DynCorp performed this task for the department, and it also provided security for the presidential compound, until Afghan guards took over in 2006. Second, PMSC personnel guard senior US diplomats when they venture outside the embassy in Kabul. The embassy itself has protection provided by the PMSC ArmorGroup North America. Third, DoS, with support from DoD, the US Drug Enforcement Administration and the Central Intelligence Agency, relies upon DynCorp to implement the US poppy eradication efforts in the hopes of preventing the drug trade from supporting insurgent forces. Fourth, but not least, perhaps the most prominent programme is DynCorp's efforts to train the Afghan National Police (ANP). From 2003–09, DynCorp held multiple ANP training contracts issued by the DoS and presently it holds the three-year €798 million training contract (now under the US Army's auspices). Finally, USAID (which operates under the foreign policy guidance of the Secretary of State, the President and the National Security Council) manages a €6.9 billion collection of projects implemented by a number of non-governmental and corporate partners in Afghanistan (Dilanian 2010). These projects range from electricity generation to business development to health initiatives. Some of these partners, in turn, hire PMSCs to protect their operations and personnel. For instance, the PMSC USPI provided security services for the Louis Berger Group, the USAID implementing partner responsible for constructing 1,500 kilometres of Afghan roads between 2002 and 2007.

Hybrid European contracting forms

Compared to the US case, while many European governments have increased the role of markets, they do not provide detailed information about their contracting practices (in Afghanistan or elsewhere), and especially not of contracting. The European countries discussed in this volume all have a three-tiered market. The first two tiers comprise the firms that unambiguously locate themselves as security firms (such as G4S) and firms belonging to the 'microcosm' (as Olsson terms it in the French context) of small companies and freelancers providing personal security details internationally. Even if both types of companies sometimes engage in military activities – as for example when G4S guards check points on the West Bank or when Norwegian 'freelancers'' French and Moland provide contracting out of Uganda – governments mostly deny that these activities mark any shift in their approach to governing the use of force: freelancers have always existed outside state reach and the line between security and military activities in conflict situations has always been difficult to draw. Denial is less plausible when the third tier of the market, in which firms specialize in activities that are directly 'military' in nature, is concerned and/or when the government itself pushes security companies to cross into the military tier of the market, as for example when they contract security companies for personal security in Kabul. While European states have not only allowed but encouraged the development of this third clearly military tier of the market, they do not and cannot publicly embrace it. Keeping the state involved ensures that the expansion of this third market tier appears to be under the public rubric.

Arrangements ensuring that the state is more or less formally placed in charge of the market – hybrid arrangements – therefore figure prominently in the chapters of this book. Consider, for instance, Krahmann's depiction of the German approach. Krahmann explains that the German state relies on two strategies: Public–Private–Partnerships and a fully government-owned private venture – the 'Company for Development Supply and Management' – which was (somewhat ironically) created because the government distrusted the civil servant side of the PPPs. Both are thoroughly hybrid in nature: they intertwine the state and the market. Similar formally hybrid constructions are common and are discussed in detail in the chapters focusing on Italy, France and Hungary. Even more striking is the extent to which state involvement is assumed and publicly insisted upon even when it is not formally enshrined. Hence, European contracting often involves longstanding 'national champions' that are brought in by the state with the clear and explicit intention of both supporting the company and creating markets (e.g., the shipping company DFDS that leases ships in the frame of the Danish sea-lift 'Sea Arc Project' discussed by Mandrup). Even less formally, hybridity is sometimes created through personal networks and mobility. In the

Romanian example, UTI, which provides security services internationally primarily for Romanians, was set up by the son of a retired army general Tiberiu Urdăreanu with ample connections to the national security community. This upholds the impression that even if the company is technically private, the doing is 'public'.

The implications for long-term governance

The hybrid form of contracting in Europe means that security commercialization appears banal; it is a 'practical approach' to solving problems. This impression is reproduced by the recurring references to pressing demands (efficiency drives, budgetary limitations, technology acquisitions, pressures from allies and/or strategic/tactical needs) to explain/justify security commercialization. While this distracts attention from the long-term implications, it does not make these implications disappear.

First and most obviously, the increased commercialization in Europe implies that companies become more central in carrying out military-related services with the rather straightforward consequence that the armed forces become locked into (at least in the short run) a dependence on their services. The fact that states are in charge of this process alters absolutely nothing to this rather trivial (and possibly to-be-welcomed) fact. However, Europeans behave as if this was a non-issue for them. While the US has had extensive, largely public, discussions about whether the right firms are contracted through the right kinds of processes (e.g. GAO 2010), nothing equivalent has taken place in Europe. While some European countries managed to nurture and create space for their own companies in various functions, others have come to rely mainly on contractors sometimes at the expense of, or perhaps even because of, their own industry. Ruzza, for instance, describes the market successes of the Italian Ciano Group contracted not only by Italian institutions in Afghanistan but also by a range of other agencies including US and Spanish Armed forces, ISAF and the NATO Maintenance and Supply Agency. By contrast, other European countries have not managed to create a space for their companies. Varga discusses how Orban's Hungary has opted for an 'in-sourcing' of services to rein in corruption and to force the recently privatized industry to provide more effective services. This is not merely an expression of Orban's statist nationalism or of his revenge on political predecessors. The privatized Hungarian companies could not deliver basic services such as the transportation of troops and equipment; they left the country dependent on allied contractors. These examples demonstrate the contextually informed and hence diverging choices of which companies to privilege and they underscore the profound implications for who is involved in governing the (national) use of force across Europe. Both deserve a more open and public reflection.

Second, contracting has implications for the relations among allies. Contracting is part and parcel of the struggle to influence the working of NATO. This is underscored particularly in the chapters on Hungary, Poland and Romania.

These three Central European countries consider contracting in the Afghan context mainly as a way of improving their status in the alliance. Inversely, reliance on contractors has been a way for the United States to loosen the ties to the alliance and of reducing dependence on allies seen as unwilling to carry their share of the burden. For instance, the chapters discuss the SALIS (Strategic Air Lift Interim Solution) as an example of how contracting can be used to knit a tighter alliance. However, from the US perspective, contracting is there because 'lift' at the operational and tactical levels in the Afghan theatre has often been wanting. European NATO countries have not sent sufficient numbers of smaller transport aircraft and helicopters to Afghanistan, in spite of pledges made. They have relied instead upon US air power. '[T]he U.S. extended its Aviation Bridging Force in Afghanistan in Kandahar because the mightiest and wealthiest military alliance in the history of the world was unable to produce 16 helicopters needed by the ISAF commander. Sixteen!' (Gates, US Secretary of Defense at the time, cited in Defense Industry Daily 2007). In lieu of aircraft provided by European NATO members, the US has shuffled its assets so that, increasingly, private firms are chartered to perform more routine cargo and personnel flights (Defense Industry Daily 2011).

The point here is not to adjudicate whether contracting ties the alliance closer together but to underscore the extent to which contracting and contractors are part and parcel of the struggle over who – which companies and which states – should matter and consequently how the alliance should function in the long run. The lack of European engagement (expert or public) with contracting, conveniently rendered banal by its hybrid form, thus not only contrasts markedly with the intense ongoing debate in the United States, it bars reflection about these long-term implications of security commercialization. By the same token, it also hampers an active approach to the short-term implications for ongoing military operations.

Impact on military operations: shifting initiatives, implementation and imprint

Security commercialization in Europe is having a far-reaching impact on international military operations. The chapters in the book show that this impact is not something that takes place against states and their national priorities. Contracting is encouraged and pursued by states and harnessed to bolster national interests. Contracting has an impact on military operations not because of what it does against states but because what it does in support of them. While this has been intensely debated in the US context (among many critical voices Minow 2003; Verkuil 2007; Rasor and Bauman 2007; Dickinson 2011), Europeans by and large still have to wake up to the fact that this is also happening in their milieu. As this book demonstrates, security commercialization shifts the kinds of initiatives that are involved in setting state priorities, how these priorities are pursued and how the interaction with the local context is shaped.

Shifting initiatives

Contractors are increasingly involved in setting priorities in Europe. They have become an 'integrated and needed part of the combined effort' that goes into a 'comprehensive strategy' wherein civilian actors play a core part to retake Mandrup's formulations in his account of the Danish contracting practices. This formulation is relevant beyond Denmark as epitomized by the weight placed on Civil–Military Co-operation in the Afghan context. To be an integrated and needed part implies being part of formulating priorities. Moreover, priorities are not only set in a national context of which contractors are part. Priorities are also set transnationally in the formal and informal networks of military/security professionals. Olsson's chapter, for example, brings up the informal channels through which French contractors working in Iraq bring back intelligence to France. In so doing the contractors obviously bring their ideas to the table. But it would be wrong to see this as a bilateral relationship between the French state and its contractors. Rather, the information that is brought back is generated in the web of transnational contracting relations where contractors (such as for the French para-public *Defense Conseil International*) train each other as well as armed forces. These processes are reinforced indirectly by countries (such as Poland, Romania and Hungary) that favour the development of contracting mainly to reinforce, to utilize the language in the Polish chapter, their 'position among allies'. By deciding to 'adapt rather to the strategies and plans of partners, than develop ... [their] own agenda' they are acquiescing to and reinforcing these strategies and plans as well as the processes behind them. In this context, as elsewhere, non-action is a form of action and power matters most when it is invisible and accepted.

As a consequence of not engaging seriously with the role of contractors in setting priorities, European policy makers and publics cannot seriously criticize or mobilize this role to their advantage. This contrasts markedly with the US where contractors are self-consciously used and (consequently) held responsible for transformations in the engagement strategies (Martin 2007). For instance, many European states are unsettled by US poppy eradication efforts. NATO member states, alongside the Afghan government, have pushed back against multiple US attempts to implement an aerial spraying programme similar to the work Dyn-Corp has performed as part of Plan Colombia for over a decade. They were fearful that eradication would unduly endanger all NATO troops and disaffect the Afghan population. However, they agreed to an intra-alliance compromise in 2008 such that individual military contingents could only participate in efforts 'against narcotics facilities and facilitators supporting the insurgency' under the authorization of their national capitals (NATO 2009). This made it possible for most NATO members to opt out of poppy eradication specifically. To compensate for their absence, the United States relied on contractors to fulfil its unilaterally decided priorities with implications for the alliance as a whole. While the Obama Administration's 2009 decision to phase out eradication efforts did not explicitly speak to intra-alliance tensions, it was informed by efficacy concerns similar to those raised by NATO allies. This example underlines again the importance of contracting in shifting priorities as well as the far greater US awareness of this.

Restructuring the implementation

Second and following directly from this, while commercialization does not contradict the way European states implement their policies, it has become part of this implementation that it has refashioned. One illustration in the present volume is provided by Berndtsson and Stern. The Swedish embassy has a 'security coordinator' (with diplomatic status) who is an employee of Vesper Group (a private company). The coordinator is responsible for determining and arranging security measures. Beyond the potential conflict of interest created by the coordinator being an employee of the company that provides the guards, the arrangement puts the company in charge of prioritizing who should have security when and on what terms. This is quite a step from the image of how the implementation of security policies is organized and worked out. An analogous situation occurs when a country is happy to take on the security arrangements provided by their allies including when the main motivation is 'to have the Hungarian flag figure on the ISAF placement' as Varga puts it. The implementation of security priorities is left to commercial actors in the field.

As indicated in the chapters, this practical influence is often viewed as insignificant since the public and private are indistinguishable, having the same background and coming from similar contexts. There are, however, important differences in terms of command structures, lines of responsibility and hence accountability and regulation. The involvement of contractors results in a complexity and fragmentation of command structures and responsibility and a related decentring/flattening of hierarchies that poses serious challenges to conventional military accountability and to military organizations. This is no small issue. Operations in Afghanistan and elsewhere have seen the emergence of 'strategic corporals,' and even 'strategic contractors', in what has become a 'captains' war' (Krulak 1999; Korteweg 2007; Shanker 2011 respectively). Tactical actions can have unwanted operational or even strategic effects. Moreover, they lead to an environment where non-state actors tend to take matters of law and justice into their own hands. Both because private actors are increasingly considered to be legitimate and because there is lack of clarity – not only among civilians but also among military actors – about who is who and hence entitled to do what, the extreme cannot be ruled out. Norwegian soldiers, as Østensen shows, ended up assisting an American contractor (Jack Idema) in arresting civilians without any mandate to do so. This underscores that European forces are not immune to this difficulty even when dealing with other foreigners. These differences are no minor matter. Yet Europeans do not deal with them.

In the US case, by contrast, these transformations have resulted not only in debate but in practical measures. For example, to deal with the complexity, the US created an Armed Contractor Oversight Directorate (ACOD) in Afghanistan.

This organization, amongst other things, tracks DoD-hired PMSCs, monitors the frequency that they deploy force and works to mitigate any negative effects stemming from the private use of force that could impact upon the military's mission. The ACOD became controversial when the US contracted a UK PMSC, Aegis, to run the operation worth €767,580 in January 2009. The DoD deemed Aegis' services crucial because of military manpower limitations, time constraints and a dearth of publicly held expertise. It also indicated that the PMSC' scope would remain limited; Aegis would not have 'direct input into daily operations, force protection, or combat operations' (Gates cited in Flaherty 2009). The Commission on Wartime Contracting, however, protested that Aegis was *primarily running* ACOD as the military was slow to provide leadership and support personnel to ACOD and that it consequently raised 'inherently governmental concerns'. Aegis, it suggested, was 'in a role of significant official responsibility in reviewing activities of other private security contractors' (CWC 2011: 74).

This controversy, as well as the creation of the ACOD itself, signals that the US has not only acknowledged the practical implications in terms of decentring decisions and responsibility, it has also taken measures to deal with it that are debated beyond the closed circles of military experts. There is a public focus on whether security commercialization grants contractors the operational space to both 'row' and 'steer' in US engagement in Afghanistan (Osborne and Gaebler 1993). In Europe, the equivalent is patently absent.

Transforming the imprint

The last way security commercialization fashions military operations breaks the general pattern of contrast between the US and Europe: both the US and the Europeans use and more or less openly discuss the role of contracting in shaping relations to the local context. Hence, Ruzza outlines how Italy emphasizes local contracting as a route 'to strengthen the stabilization process, enhance local ownership, and build capacities'. Similarly, Olsson suggests that local employment is part of a 'French touch' with roots in the colonial past. 'Afghanising' French engagement is considered to provide employment opportunities and diffuse tensions between foreign and local actors. This echoes the US 'Afghan first' approach espoused by prominent political and military officials. US employment of Afghans in part, is to ensure that they do not support or join the Taliban and, in part, to avoid resentment that might arise should third country nationals be utilized. In both the US and the EU contexts there is, however, an ambivalence about whether the Afghan first approach in contracting is really effective. Two detractions are discussed in both contexts.

First, while it may be important to build local capacities, the market may be a drain on the public forces as it undermines their status. Because of their higher pay, PMSCs are drawing personnel away from the Afghan National Army (ANA) and the Afghan National Police (ANP). As Canadian Major-General Ward, the Deputy Commander for Police Development and Training of the NATO Training Mission, explains: 'If they're all going across the street to earn more money (with) a competitor who can afford to pay more … it becomes a losing venture' (cited in Rennie 2010). Therefore, under Afghan government guidelines, PMSCs are now not to employ former ANA and ANP personnel unless they possess honourable discharge documentation. Additionally, the public Afghan forces are trying to keep up with salary levels. In late 2009, ANA and ANP personnel received pay raises. Incoming recruits now receive €184 monthly, a figure sometimes double the previous amount and yet PMSC personnel are still often paid more. However, attempting to retain the recruits in the public forces is an uphill struggle, especially since using private instructors is a way of signalling that the private sector military specialists have a status equal if not superior to that of the public forces. After all they are the *experts* responsible for training. Thus, the recruitment and training of the ANP and the ANA for which PMSCs are extensively used are also tasks that PMSC utilization can impede just as easily as it can advance. As Ruzza's discussion of these issues show, these issues are also of concern for the European presence in Afghanistan.

Second, even more strongly, Europeans and Americans have both highlighted the political importance of providing jobs and political ties through contracting but they have also (perhaps because they had little choice) been aware of the possible opposite effects. Vetting procedures are imperfect and local contracting can be directly counter-productive as it becomes part of financing local warlords. Companies may inadvertently hire opposition militants as illustrated by the scandal surrounding the 'Taliban' employees of ArmorGroup whose remains were discovered after a raid against a Taliban leader (SASC 2010). Similarly, US politicians have been vexed about logistics companies and their supporting PMSCs paying off insurgents in order to ensure safe passage for their convoys. Finally, and possibly most significantly, contracting may increase support for armed opposition by bolstering the status and influence of these groups. Hence, Ruzza underscores that the contracting of local employees is readily interpreted as giving jobs, status and opportunities to militiamen while negating the same to honest Afghans.

Security commercialization is, in other words, shifting the European military operations in Afghanistan; the priorities, the implementation and the imprint they leave. This is not how most European publics and policy makers think about their respective country's engagement in Afghanistan. Most would think that public officials were in charge whether it was to formulate an engagement geared to further security and development to bring progress to the population at large and especially to women (as in Norway, Sweden and Germany tend to) or whether it was to further geo-political ambitions and military alliance obligations (as in Denmark, Hungary and Poland). The chapters all confirm the yawning gap between the expert understanding of the amount of contracting involved in the operations and the public discussion on the issue. To the extent there is a policy, it appears *ad hoc*, driven by the occasional scandal and worries about the 'reputational costs' to the Ministry of Defense as Østensen puts if for the Norwegian case. This contrasts markedly with the US where contracting is more openly embraced and practiced and therefore also more critically, consciously and systematically debated.

The prospects of security commercialization in Europe

This leaves us with a paradox: European states and publics present themselves as more critical and suspicious than those in the United States of the growing security commercialization. Yet, ironically, not only are the European public discussions *uncritical* by comparison to the American ones, European approaches to the control and management of contracting are *lax and ad-hoc*. The chapters above give clear indications of why this is the case, including not least the tendency to obfuscate commercialization and to rely on hybrid contracting arrangements that keep the state formally involved. Military expert communities (public, private and hybrid) who think commercialization is warranted and necessary but who are aware that it is also contentious are not likely to change this. The many critical observers are unlikely to force them to do so since they focus their attention exclusively on US/UK developments while neglecting European developments. Precisely this attention deficit has been a condition *sine qua non* for making a substantial commercialization of military in Europe possible by minute technocratic, managerial and bureaucratic reforms of seeming irrelevance to the larger public. There are signs that this may be changing, of which this volume is one. It is high time for this to happen.

The developments in European militaries at the time of writing suggest that uncritical, lax and *ad hoc* approaches to commercialization are simply not good enough. The first reason is that the contractors who have been integral to the interventions now ending in Afghanistan and Iraq are bound to continue to be significant. They remain as the troops leave in a wide variety of capacities. But more significantly security commercialization has generated a path dependency that will shape the approach to military interventions in the future. Second, there are few signs that European military establishments will be less prone to commercialize in the future. On the contrary, the tendency is one where market solutions, public–private partnerships and dual-use technologies are understood as integral to the lean, professional and economically efficient militaries most European states are striving to develop, *pace* in-sourcing moves in Hungary. Finally, international trends including both the financial crisis and international defense collaborations – be it in the context of NATO, the UN or the European Union – amplify this trend by pressuring European states to increase their commercialization. Hence, it does not seem exaggerated to say that it is urgent for Europeans to confront the commercialization *in their own context* and not least to reflect on where they want to draw what limits for it and to discuss the form of regulation that is consequently necessary. This obviously is a vast task. This book's ambition has been limited to making it clear that the task is there in the hope that it will be dealt with.

References

Boot, Max. 2003. 'The New American Way of War'. *Foreign Affairs* 82 (4): 41–58.

Carreau, Bernard T. 2008. 'Outsourcing Civilian Capabilities and Capacity', in Hans Binnendijk and Patrick M. Cronin, eds., *From Civilian Surge: Key to Complex Operations*. Washington, DC: National Defense University, pp. 165–194.

CRS (United States, Congressional Research Service). 2007. 'The Federal Activities Inventory Reform Act and Circular A-76'. *CRS Report to Congress* RL31024. www.pol icyarchive.org/handle/10207/bitstreams/19376.pdf (accessed 20 December 2011).

CWC (United States, Commission on Wartime Contracting in Iraq and Afghanistan). 2011. 'Transforming Wartime Contracting: Controlling costs, reducing risks'. *Final Report to Congress*, www.wartimecontracting.gov/index.php/reports (accessed 7 October 2012).

——2009 'At What Cost? Contingency Contracting in Iraq and Afghanistan'. *Interim Report*, 29 June, www.wartimecontracting.gov/index.php/reports (accessed 7 October 2012).

Defense Industry Daily. 2007. 'NATO About to Lease Troop Helis for Afghanistan?' 6 November, www.defenseindustrydaily.com/nato-about-to-lease-troop-helis-for-afgha nistan-04157/ (accessed 1 November 2011).

——2011. 'Allies Absent in Afghanistan – Helicopters Hired'. 7 November, www.defen seindustrydaily.com/Allies-Absent-in-Afghanistan-Helicopters-Hired-05366/#fleet-rental-charter (accessed 1 November 2011).

Dickinson, Laura A. 2011. *Outsourcing War and Peace: How Privatizing Foreign Affairs Threatens Core Public Values and What We Can Do About It*. New Haven, CT: Yale University Press.

Dilanian, Ken. 2010. 'U.S. bans contractor from further aid programs'. *Los Angeles Times*, 8 December. www.latimes.com/news/nationworld/world/la-fg-pakistan-fraud-charges-20101209,0,5599307.story (accessed 1 November 2011).

Ettinger, Aaron. 2011. 'Neoliberalism and the rise of the private military industry'. *International Journal* 66 (3): 743–764.

Flaherty, Anne. 2009. 'Military hangs 'Help Wanted' sign in Afghanistan'. 22 March, www.google.com/hostednews/ap/article/ALeqM5ivTscD0Sy3hJdvyYgLFsJ_P-B_XwD973 2JS80 (accessed 1 November 2011).

GAO, United States, Government Accountability Office. 2010. *Continued Actions Needed by DOD to Improve and Institutionalize Contractor Support in Contingency Operation*, GAO-10-551T, www.gao.gov/products/GAO-10-551T (accessed 7 October 2012).

Hacker, Barton C. and Margaret Vining. 2006. *American Military Technology: The Life Story of a Technology*. Baltimore, MD: The Johns Hopkins University Press.

Korteweg, Rem. 2007. 'The Strategic Contractor'. *News Column*, Hague Centre for Strategic Studies, 19 September. www.hcss.nl/news/the-strategic-contractor/297/ (accessed 29 February 2012).

Krulak, Charles C. 1999. 'The Strategic Corporal: Leadership in the Three Block War'. *Marines Magazine*, January. www.au.af.mil/au/awc/awcgate/usmc/strategic_corporal. htm (accessed 1 November 2011).

Mahnken, Thomas G. 2003. 'The American Way of War in the Twenty-first Century', in Efraim Inbar, ed., *Democracies and Small Wars*. London: Frank Cass and Company Limited, pp. 73–84.

Markusen, Ann R. 2003. 'The Case Against Privatizing National Security'. *Governance: An International Journal of Policy, Administration, and Institutions* 16 (4): 471–501.

Martin, Jennifer S. 2007. 'Contracting for Wartime Actors: The Limits of the Contract Paradigm'. *New England Journal of International and Comparative Law*, 14 (Fall): 11–33.

Minow, Martha. 2003. 'Public and Private Partnerships: Accounting for the New Religion'. *Harvard Law Review* 116: 1229–70.

NATO, Media Operations Centre. 2009. 'Fact Sheet: NATO's Support to Counter-Nar-cotics Efforts in Afghanistan'. June, www.europarl.europa.eu/meetdocs/2009_2014/ documents/sede/dv/sede250110natonarcotics_/sede250110natonarcotics_en.pdf (accessed 7 October 2012).

Rasor, Dina and Robert Bauman. 2007. *Betraying Our Troops: The Destructive Results of Privatizing War*. New York: Palgrave.

Record, Jeffrey. 2002. 'Collapsed Countries, Casualty Dread, and the New American Way of War'. *Parameters* 32 (2): 4–23.

Rennie, Steve. 2010. 'Afghanistan to regulate private security'. *Toronto Sun*, 25 January. www.torontosun.com/news/canada/2010/01/25/12602481.html (accessed 1 November 2011).

Rockman, Bert A. 2005. 'The President, Executive, and Congress: The Same Old Story?', in Donald R. Kelley, ed., *Divided Power: The Presidency, Congress, and the Formation of American Foreign Policy*. Fayetteville: University of Arkansas Press, pp. 19–38.

SASC, Senate Armed Services Committee. 2010. *Inquiry Into the Role and Oversight of Private Security Contractors in Afghanistan together with Additional Views*. Washington, DC: US Senate, www.armed-services.senate.gov/Publications/SASC%20PSC%20Report%202010-07-10. pdf (accessed 7 October 2012).

Shanker, Thom. 2011. 'Warning Against Wars Like Iraq and Afghanistan'. *New York Times*, 25 February. www.nytimes.com/2011/02/26/world/26gates.html (accessed 1 November 2011).

Verkuil, Paul. 2007. *Outsourcing Sovereignty: Why Privatization of Government Functions Threatens Democracy and What We Can Do about It*. Cambridge: Cambridge University Press.

Weigley, Russell F. 1973. *The American Way of War: A History of United States Military Strategy and Policy*. New York: Macmillan Publishing Co., Inc.

Index